# INTO HELL I RODE

## AN AUTOBIOGRAPHY OF CHAOS, TURMOIL, RECOVERY AND TRIUMPH

## BY: DAVID G. ATWOOD, II

# DAVID G. ATWOOD, II

Contact the author at: **www.KnightedOutlaw.com**

Copyright 2011 By: David G. Atwood, II

License: Standard Copyright License

Publisher: Allyson Morgan Publishing

       12745 Avenues of the Americas

       New York, NY  10036

ISBN: 978-1-257-37994-1

This book is dedicated to my two dear friends:

# Jerry Wayne Beard

# &

# Lori Dawn Kuhnert

# DAVID G. ATWOOD, II

# ACKNOWLEDGEMENTS

This book has been a seven year endeavor. What started as a simple memoir, transmogrified into not only an autobiography of my life, but also as a biography of others. A great many people have been informative, cooperative and patient, and it was only with their insight and knowledge that this book was completed. It would be especially remiss of me if I didn't at least thank my papaw, Aaron Tolleson and my aunt, Pam Tolleson McLemore. Their help and encouragement has been a guiding force in the completion of this book. For the content and mistakes, I can only accept full responsibility, as they are mine to bear.

# DAVID G. ATWOOD, II

# PART

# ONE

# PROLOGUE

When the phone rings at my house at one in the morning, it's not an unusual thing. This morning, however, was the beginning of many such early calls. There are always the occasional friends who, for whatever reason, feel compelled to converse at early morning hours, or the occasional person who just needs a friend to talk to. My friends know that I am available twenty-four hours a day for them. But, this particular phone call was not a best friend; in fact, it was someone I barely knew. The voice on the other end was strained and nervous. Something told me things were not right.

"David, one of the sheriff's deputies has just shot and killed an unarmed high school student." As I rubbed the sleep from my eyes, the realization hit me that this is something that others and I had long feared would happen. As I grasped for more details the picture became more alarmingly clear.

The person on the other end of the phone was a sheriff's

deputy who had arrived on the scene minutes after the shooting. He quickly realized this was not a normal shooting by a scared and frightened colleague who was acting in self-defense. When I asked who the deputy was that did the shooting, in the back of my mind I knew it had to be Lionel Johnson. The voice on the phone only confirmed my worst fears.

Now, wide awake and notepad in hand, I began to form a clearer picture from the details that I had been told. It was not the first time I had received these "heads-up" tips from my cop friend. We had a mutual understanding that nothing he said would ever be directly attributed to him and that everything I wrote would be proof-read by him first before publication. Because he worked for a Sheriff who has been accused of many allegations of corruption and malfeasance, it would be detrimental to his career if it was ever found out that he was my "source" for many of my news stories.

I was operating an online news website dedicated to investigative research and reporting. Since my early childhood I have been fascinated by the principles and ideals of democracy upon which our country was founded. I believe it is a person's duty to fight injustice and prejudice and help protect people that are less able to fend for themselves. If you believe something is important, you have an obligation to fight for it. I figured the best place to start was my hometown of Vicksburg, Mississippi.

Most young people my age do not believe that their tiny voice can make a difference. It's hard to compete with the mass media. Most teenagers just don't care or are too busy to give a damn; they've been told they can't fight city hall. I, on the other hand, had seen too much injustice to just sit by and let it happen. Being only nineteen years old, I wondered if I could, or would, ever make a difference.

The state of Mississippi is a great place to grow up and raise a family. Our state has a bad reputation, but I always felt that there were enough of the "good guys" to overcome the negative. Not everywhere in our state is plagued with government corruption and racism. It's only the few places like Vicksburg that give the rest of the state a bad image. Many times

I ask myself "what am I able do to stop it?" Then, someone asked me to start a website to cover some of the news in Vicksburg and Warren County and use it to bring attention to some of our elected and appointed leaders who use their government offices for their personal gain.

To be honest, I wasn't the least bit interested. I had heard the horror stories of people before me who had tried to fight the corruption and had been literally and figuratively destroyed by the well-organized and financed, corrupted, political machines of Vicksburg and Warren County. I wasn't about to ruin myself and bring disgrace to my family name. But, what so often happens, life has other plans and events overtake the best-laid plans.

What became one of the best known and hated websites in Vicksburg was very appropriately named www.CorruptGov.com. Although it was unlike any other news reporting website, with time it became respected for its accuracy and in-depth coverage of the latest political and government scandals.

It so happened the same autumn of the shooting, I entered my name on the November election ballot. For several years I had considered running for an elective office in Warren County. I am one of those people who don't sit back and criticize. I am always looking for ways to improve on everything and the best way I thought I could improve the situation in Vicksburg and Warren County was by elective office- change from the inside, so to speak. Little did I know by running for public office and operating an investigative website, it would bring about my downfall in one of the most humiliating episodes of my life.

Of course, all of this was in the future and at the time nothing was on my mind more than trying to determine how a kid could end up dead, shot in the back of the head by a law enforcement officer who is sworn to uphold the law, not destroy it with hateful acts of vengeful violence.

By the time my cop friend and I had completed our conversation, I had a firm grasp of the circumstances surrounding the shooting. As time passed, and the investigation would later confirm, it was apparently clear that something had gone terribly wrong.

Sometime around eleven that night, Warren County Sheriff's deputy Lionel Johnson and another officer were dispatched to a noise complaint off of Halls Ferry Road, several miles outside the city limits. When they arrived a group of thirty or more teenagers were gathered in the yard listening to music and enjoying themselves after the local football team had won a game that weekend. Several of the team's players were among the group celebrating, including a young teenager whose grandmother owned the house where the party was taking place.

According to the witnesses, Lionel Johnson found the grandmother and advised her that she needed to break the party up and send the kids home. An argument ensued between the two, which resulted in Lionel Johnson rough-handling the older female. When the grandson stepped in, he was tackled and assaulted by Deputy Johnson. The details are still confusing about what occurred next, but what can't be denied is that Lionel Johnson fired his service pistol into the back of the teenager's head after he had placed the boy in handcuffs.

Lionel Johnson would later claim his weapon discharged accidentally only to change his story several days later to say he was acting in self-defense. Witnesses at the scene claim a much different scenario. No fewer than twenty people saw Officer Johnson and the teenager scuffle, with Johnson ultimately being successful in subduing the boy, only to fire his weapon in retaliation after the boy had been placed in handcuffs.

What really occurred that night might never be known. The two things that cannot be discounted is the fact that a young life was taken from this world and what followed that horrible night was a deliberate and malicious attempt by the Warren County Sheriff's Office to destroy evidence, obstruct justice, and hinder the investigation into the factual circumstances of that night's shooting.

Cover-ups are not new to government officials. Consider Watergate, Iran-Contra, Monica Lewinsky and the CIA Leak Scandal (i.e., Karl Rove & Scooter Libby). What is relatively new are the few dedicated journalists devoted to uncovering and stopping government abuse.

# DAVID G. ATWOOD, II

When told that Lionel Johnson had shot and killed someone, to be honest, I wasn't totally surprised. I have known Lionel Johnson for most of my life. As I have said before and still say, Lionel Johnson should have never been allowed to become a law enforcement officer. Talk to anyone who knew him as a child and teenager and they will tell you about his bullying, aggressive behavior, and egotism; it goes all the way back to pre-school. In law enforcement, these combinations are a deadly mix.

Many times I have heard Lionel Johnson bragging about how he broke a guy's arm with a nightstick or how much he enjoyed watching suspects cry in agony after being squirted with pepper spray. What really scared me was the day Lionel told a group of high school students how much he was looking forward to killing a suspect before he retired from police work.

The Sheriff of Warren County and I have always locked horns over my confrontational style of reporting his department's inability to uphold a decent standard of law and professionalism. This shooting was a wake-up call to a lot of people, but our Sheriff is a master of deception.

Martin Pace became a deputy when the department was still under the command of Sheriff Paul Barrett. Sheriff Barrett, elected in the 1960's, was the stereotypical southern sheriff. Sheriff Barrett ran afoul of the federal government in 1996 and was convicted in federal court of perjury, resigned from office in disgrace, and served several months in a federal prison in Pensacola, FL.

The thing, though, with government corruption is that it does not operate in a vacuum. When one person "bites the dust", there's another to step into his place. In Sheriff Barrett's place stepped Martin Pace.

Born and raised in Vicksburg, educated at the local private school, Porters Chapel Academy, you might be able to say he was just a "good-ole-boy". What would become a major influencing factor later in his life was his education at Porters Chapel Academy. Founded in the sixties at the height of the civil rights movement by a racist white supremacist organization, it was an alternate school for the children of white segregationists.

When it became politically incorrect to advocate segregation, the school board members changed the format to a "Christian" curriculum. This was a tactic commonly practiced throughout the south at the time. It, however, does not change the fact that so many of these "private" schools teach and promote intolerance of race and freedom of sexual orientation. I know because like Martin Pace, I was sent to Porters Chapel for a short period of time. Only now do I recognize the hate and prejudice taught at institutions such as those.

Shortly after taking office, Martin Pace wasted little time appointing his friends and cronies into high-level administrative positions within the sheriff's department, with little regard to ability or education. To say the least, chaos ensued and over time, it only became worse.

For several years, Martin Pace constructed a tightly woven community of thugs and criminals in order to secure his continued reign of power. Nowhere else in the state does a sheriff enjoy such immense, unsupervised power as Martin Pace. It should come as no surprise that the citizens have allowed this to happen.

Martin Pace has become so efficient at covering up his agency's underhanded dealings that it's very difficult to unravel the intricate underworld that he has created. The difference between the sheriff's department and the police department in Vicksburg, is the police department only tries to cover up scandal, unless scrutiny is a sure thing. The sheriff's department covers up at all cost. Their motto has become: "Admit nothing, deny everything, and make counter accusations".

I've often asked myself why the FBI or Department of Justice always refuses to investigate the complaints of police corruption in Warren County and Vicksburg. It seems as if they are almost allowed to operate their schemes without interference or oversight. Only later would I find out the true reasons for the federal government's uninvolvement, but by then I would be locked away in a high security federal prison and it would be too late.

Being a youthful, naïve teenager I could never comprehend the length that these people would go to protect their dishonesty, nor could I fathom the distant reach of the corruptor's influence. As with most teenagers my age, I had the feeling that I was ten feet tall and bullet-proof. I didn't believe that bad things could happen to me. I felt protected behind a powerful family name and the influence that name brought. Little did I know, it would be my own family who would cause my immediate downfall. When I began my quest to uncover and defeat corruption in my hometown, I had no idea that the path would eventually lead straight back to my own family.

The Atwood name has long been a fixture in Vicksburg. Since before the Civil War, the Atwood's have operated businesses and held government positions. We've been long respected as upstanding, God-fearing people. Even as a child, I could recognize the vast power and influence the Atwood's held, but unfortunately it was all a sham.

The financial anchor for the Atwood's is the family business, a Chevrolet automobile dealership. Founded in the 1950's by my grandfather, Emmett Atwood, it has provided the wealth and influence so widely sought after by other people. Perhaps no other family in Vicksburg has enjoyed such success and prosperity over the centuries as has my family.

Growing up, I was always instilled with a great amount of pride and respect for my family name. That's why, when I learned of the secret, deviant, underworld life of my family members, it became such a shock. Here was one of the most respected families in Vicksburg engaging in illegal and highly dangerous behavior right under the noses of everyone. Protected by the authorities, and in some cases actually encouraged, this criminal conduct has continued for decades. While the Atwood's are believed to be the "perfect" family, in actuality we've been haunted by scandals, adultery, illegitimate children, and drug and alcohol abuse. Only now has anyone been brave enough to step forward and confront these scandals, and I do so at great personal loss.

While considering writing this book and discussing the

content with different people I was asked over and over again why I would risk so much to expose the "dirtiness" surrounding my life and that of my family's. My only answer is atonement.

This is my story- a story of a young naïve teenager, raised in southern Mississippi, by a wealthy and prominent family- one who had so much to gain and in the course of only a few years, ended up serving a multi-year federal sentence in a high-security prison. What went wrong and why? This is the story.

# CHAPTER ONE

I was born on August 13<sup>th</sup>, 1983 to an affluent and wealthy southern family. My parents gave me the name, David Garland Atwood, II. At the time of my birth my father was a successful agricultural farmer in a small town in central Mississippi. My mother was a nurse who spent her time caring and administering to the elderly in the retirement home. I was the only child of my father and mother and was the first grandson in the Atwood family.

The life my parents gave me was orderly, structured, and safe. Our house was a nice, one story, three-bedroom brick home set off in the country amongst the fields and pastures of rural Mississippi. Although my father was a successful farmer, over time it became more difficult to provide a decent income by farming. When I was two years old, my father decided it was time to give up farming and move back to his original home in

Vicksburg, Mississippi. In Vicksburg, my grandfather, Emmett Atwood, owned a Chevrolet dealership and was able to provide my dad a job and paycheck.

My father was the last of his siblings to go to work at Atwood Chevrolet. His oldest brother, Ray, his sister, June, and the youngest brother, Alan, had all been working at the dealership for most of their lives. My grandfather was pleased that all of his children were now working in the family business. This business provided the Atwood family with the wealth, power, and influence that our family has been accustomed to for hundreds of years. Mention the Atwood name in Vicksburg and it immediately commands respect. The Atwood's have been a fixture in Vicksburg long before the Civil War and they share a history with the city that stretches back all the way to the 1850's.

The first Atwood in Mississippi was Turpin Green Atwood, an enormously wealthy merchant and cotton farmer, whose family was from Switzerland. Although little is known about my ancestor, history does tell us that he left his northern home in Rhode Island in the early part of the 18th century and moved to Georgia to begin cotton farming. According to the book, "Inventing the Cotton Gin", by Angela Lakwete, my ancestor then moved to Kosciusko, Mississippi and began manufacturing cotton gins for local farmers. Turpin Atwood soon became one of the largest gin manufacturers in the country. Harnessing the power of the local river, Turpin Atwood also ran flour and gristmills, owned dozens of slaves, and used part of his thousands of acres to farm cotton.

The town of Kosciusko, Mississippi was named after the Revolutionary hero, Thaddeus Kosciusko who served under George Washington in the Continental Army. The town and the surrounding area, which is in the geographical center of the state, is a vast collection of small cotton farms, hardwood timber, rolling hills, steep gullies, flatlands, marshes and swamps, and has a wide array of wildlife in which a new pioneer could use to clothe and feed his family.

When Turpin Atwood moved to Mississippi, little was known of his private life. There is little to suggest that he was anything but an upstanding, respected, and valued citizen and benefactor of Kosciusko. He and his wife, Elvira, produced a son in 1836, naming him David Chase Atwood. After Turpin Atwood passed away, his son, David, took over the family business.

When the American Civil War erupted in 1861, David Chase and his wife Josephine Genella were living in a new home in Vicksburg, Mississippi overlooking the Mississippi river. As with so many Southerners of the time, there was a huge surge of southern patriotism. After the firing on Fort Sumter in April 1861 and Lincoln's call for volunteers to invade the South and quell the rebellion, millions of Southerners rushed forward to defend their homeland. David Chase was no different. He recruited, armed, and organized over one hundred citizens of Vicksburg in defense of the newly formed Southern Confederacy. David Chase Atwood's unit of men was mustered into service around the first of May, 1861. The unit was christened, Company A, "Volunteer Southrons" and was assigned to the 21$^{st}$ Mississippi Regiment commanded by Colonel Benjamin Humphreys. David Chase was elected captain of the company; a rank which he would hold throughout the war.

The 21$^{st}$ Mississippi was a regiment composed of men from all over central Mississippi. When the regiment was formed on the courthouse square in Vicksburg, the men elected to be assigned to the newly forming Army of Northern Virginia, building itself across a little creek called Bull Run in Manassas, Virginia. Little did any of these men know, that by making this choice, the majority would never again see Mississippi.

Although the 21$^{st}$ arrived too late to participate in the first battle of Bull Run, they were attached to a brigade of other Mississippians under the command of General William Barksdale. David Chase and the 21$^{st}$ would meet the enemy for the first time during the Seven Day's Battle outside of Richmond, Virginia in June 1862. General Barksdale's brigade was ordered to attack and capture a small hill between the opposing armies. It was the 21$^{st}$ Mississippi that helped lead this attack on Malvern Hill and it is subsequently where David Chase received a severe leg wound and was nearly captured by federal troops.

David Chase probably recovered from his wound at Jackson Hospital in Richmond, where coincidence would have it, another ancestor of mine was recovering from a wound while escaping from a Union prison in Point Lookout, Maryland.

Confederate military records indicate that David Chase had sufficiently recovered so as to accompany his regiment and brigade with General Robert E. Lee and the Army of Northern Virginia on their march to Gettysburg.

While recuperating, David Chase's brigade had participated in two of the Southern Confederacy's' greatest victories, Fredericksburg and Chancellorsville. By the time he rejoined his unit, his men were seasoned veterans of the war, commanded by the now proven and very able commander, General Barksdale. It was for this reason that General Lee chose the Mississippi brigade to lead the advance on the second days' fighting at Gettysburg on July $2^{nd}$, 1863.

It was at this attack that General Barksdale and over seventy percent of the Mississippi Brigade would become casualties of the war. While leading his brigade through the Wheatfield and Peach Orchard of Gettysburg, General Barksdale was struck from his horse by a Union volley and had every senior commander in his brigade wounded or killed. Even with the high casualties, the Mississippi brigade succeeded in their attack and forced the Union troops from the field.

We know very little of what happened to my great-great grandfather that day. After the war and in his later life, he never spoke of his service in the army. I am sure he played a large part in comforting and rallying the men of his brigade who had survived. That day, the Mississippians of Barksdale's command achieved a stolid place in the history of that great battle. David Chase would remain with his Mississippi Regiment for the duration of the war and was present at Appomattox for the surrender of General Lee's army.

After returning home at the end of the war, he found his homeland in ruins. His house in Vicksburg had been practically destroyed during the siege. His plantation in Kosciusko was in ashes and tatters. The cotton gin plant, which had been the source of wealth for so long, was now wrecked and destroyed.

Throughout the South, many farmers were plagued with famine and disease; crops wouldn't grow and there were not nearly enough horses to plow and cows for milk. People died. For David Chase to survive and rebuild his life and farm is an amazing accomplishment. Many Southerners could not, and were forced to leave, moving to Texas, California, or elsewhere. But David Chase didn't. He stayed in Kosciusko. He replanted his crops, sold what land he could to pay for food, cut timber, and did whatever else he could to survive. It was very hard living in post-war Mississippi and having to endure an oppressive reconstruction made it worse. David Chase survived and prospered and it wasn't long after the war that his wife gave birth to their first child, which David Chase named after himself.

David Chase Atwood, Jr. was born on October 16th, 1878 in the farmhouse that still stands on the Atwood Plantation today. His father, the original David Chase, died sometime around the turn of the century. Both David Chase Atwood, Sr. and his wife Josephine Genella are buried in a Kosciusko cemetery. It wasn't until I began research for this book that I discovered David Chase, Sr. to be a 33rd degree Freemason and extremely devoted to politics and religion. Freemasonry, I would come to find out, is common throughout both sides of my family.

David, Jr.'s life revolved around outdoor activities, hunting, fishing, and shooting. From an early age Papa-At, as David Jr. was nicknamed in the family, had a love of the outdoors and wildlife. It came naturally for Papa-At to become a naturalist in his adult life. Because his father had been able to reclaim their lives and rebuild a shattered family after the Civil War, Papa-At and his brothers and sisters were able to live a comfortable life. Papa-At was able to build a new family home, construct a large lake on the property, increase the acreage of the farm, and provide his children with continued money and respect.

In 1916, Papa-At married Laura Dora England and on June 31st, 1917 their first child was born, a son, whom they named David Alan Atwood. In all, Papa-At and his wife would have eight children: six boys and two girls. They are, in order of birth, David Alan, Swanson, Geneva, Dock, Minna, Emmett, Bailey, and Bush. All of the children would go on to raise families and lead successful lives, my grandfather, Emmett, espccially.

Papa-At would live on Atwood Plantation until his death on December 18th, 1957. His wife, Laura, would live until December 23rd, 1980. Both provided love and security to their children. Their children were taught respect, discipline, and to value hard work- traits that would not always be adhered to in our family. They were taught admiration for our family history and ancestors and none ever forgot the service of their grandfather in the American Civil War.

Most of Papa-At's children would remain in the Kosciusko area. Some of them would serve in World War II. During the time after the war, my grandfather was unemployed and without direction. The only job he could find was as a traveling Bible salesman. His travels brought him to Gastonia, North Carolina, where one day he knocked on the door of a strictly devout Presbyterian and Freemason named Roscoe Garland Quinn.

As a traveling Bible salesman, he had many contacts with people and was sometimes invited to spend a night or two in the house of one of his customers. Roscoe Quinn was so impressed with the young Bible salesman he invited him to stay and meet his family. Roscoe's wife was a beautiful young lady named Francis Pearson who was born on Halloween 1908 and was the daughter of William Crawford Pearson and Fannie Bell Dunlap of Virginia.

Roscoe's great-grandfather was a Confederate soldier who served in the 51st North Carolina Regiment. His name was Thomas F. Quinn and was my other ancestor who was wounded and recuperating at Jackson Hospital in Richmond during the time Captain David Chase Atwood was there. Thomas Quinn's mother's name was Sarah Ferguson, a direct relative of the British Loyalist, Major Patrick Ferguson, who defended Kings Mountain against colonial militias in the Revolutionary War. Sarah Ferguson was married to James Quinn, Jr., whose father immigrated to the United States from England in the 1700's.

Roscoe Quinn and his wife both shared a long and rich family history that can be traced back many generations. Roscoe and Francis's marriage produced only one child, a daughter, (my grandmother), who was born on July 26th, 1930. Her name is Vivian Quinn and this is the young lady my grandfather, Emmett Atwood, decided to marry the first day he met her.

Soon after they married, Emmett took a job as a car salesman in Vicksburg and they moved from North Carolina. There my grandparents raised their family, which soon grew to three boys and one girl. Their names in order of birth are: Emmett Ray, Jr., Vivian June, David Garland, and Alan Quinn. My dad, David Garland, was born on May 27th, 1955.

After several years at the car dealership, my grandfather bought the company with money he was given by my grandmother's father, Roscoe Quinn. Emmett renamed the dealership, Atwood Chevrolet, Inc. and for the next fifty years this business provided and cared for the Atwood family as they grew from childhood, adolescence and into young adults. Every one of the children attended college, but only my Aunt June, would graduate. All three of the boys were much more into partying, drinking, drugs and getting into trouble.

My dad attended Mississippi State but failed to achieve passing grades and was kicked out. It was after being kicked out of college that my dad met my mother, Marjorie Joan Tolleson. My mother and her family were also from Kosciusko. Her parents were Aaron Arvel Tolleson and Melba June Casey.

My maternal grandfather, Aaron Tolleson, can trace his ancestry back to his great-great-grandfather, James Tolleson, a settler who came to the United States in the 1700's from Norway. James Tolleson's descendants settled throughout northern Alabama and central Mississippi.

My maternal grandmother, Melba June, traces her ancestry to the original Casey's and O'Sullivan's from Ireland that settled in the Mississippi area in the 1800's. Her father and mother were Herbert Casey and Maybelle Clara O'Sullivan. Herbert and Maybelle had seven children. They are: Helen

Maurice, John, Jimmy, Joe Dempsey, Melba June, Nannie Ruth, and Mary Anne.

All of my grandmother's brothers would fight in World War II or Korea. Her brother, Joe Dempsey, would earn the Purple Heart and Silver Star for his gallant action during the Inchon Landings in Korea, by his efforts at fending off a suicide charge by the Communist Reds. Joe Dempsey Casey became a local hero and would appear on the front page of the New York Times.

My grandfather's parents were Aaron Titus Tolleson and Ada Crystelle Crowe. Their marriage produced ten children: William Troy, Guy Pate, Hampton Lamar, Newton Hugh, Nannie Inez, Jeanell, Winfred Alton, Thelma Lee, Aaron Arvel, and Virginia Wynette. Most of my grandfather's brothers would serve in World War II and all would return home safely to marry and raise families of their own.

When my maternal grandparents married in 1951, both worked in education. Aaron was principal at the local high school and June worked in the Office of the Superintendent for Attala County. A year and a half after their marriage their first child, Randy Aaron was born, followed by Pamela Diane, and then finally my mother, on April 5$^{th}$, 1963.

My grandparents were raised to be devoutly religious people and that is how they raised their children. Although my mom and aunt would choose different paths for their lives, my Uncle Randy and his three boys would all remain very active in the Baptist church.

When my dad and mom met in the early eighties, no one knows for sure whether it was love at first sight. What everyone does agree on is that at nineteen years old, my mother was too young to be starting a family. At the time of their marriage, my dad had purchased and was farming several hundred acres of land in Camden, Mississippi and began cotton farming. On August 13$^{th}$, 1983, their first and only child was born, a son, (me), whom they named David Garland Atwood, II.

# CHAPTER TWO

There are times when I have vivid recollections from my childhood. Probably my earliest memory would be riding on the tractor with my dad when I was about two years old. Much of my early few years of life were on the farm in Camden and I remember very little. I do, for some reason, recall the day that Dad, Mom, and I moved from our little farmhouse in the country to Vicksburg and into the house of my grandmother, Vivian Atwood. The year was 1986 and farming had become so unprofitable that it was becoming more of a burden for my dad to care for his family. So the decision was made to move his wife and son to Vicksburg and take a job working for his father at the family dealership.

Prior to this move, my grandfather and grandmother Atwood had built a twelve thousand square foot mansion in one of the richest neighborhoods in Vicksburg. However, it was during the building of their mansion in 1978 that my grandmother, Vivian, became suspicious of some possible infidelity in her marriage.

After secretly hiring a private investigator to tail her husband, several shocking secrets were revealed. First and foremost, her suspicions were confirmed. Her husband, my grandfather, Emmett Atwood, was having extramarital affairs with numerous women.

Fast-forward to 1999. I was sixteen years old and as a hobby had started participating in Civil War reenactments. I was at one of these events in Northern Mississippi when I was introduced to an older lady by the name of Mary Lou Jones, a resident of Kosciusko, and wife of a physician. When introducing myself she recognized my last name and asked if I was related to any of the Atwood's in Kosciusko or Vicksburg. I was and told her so. She became slightly excited and explained to me that her best friend in college was my grandmother.

Knowing my grandmother went to college in North Carolina and that there probably wasn't any way they could know each other, I became more inquisitive. Mrs. Jones explained to me that her best friend in college was a lady named Pam Cheek, and that during their college days she'd been seeing a car salesman from Vicksburg named Emmett Atwood. Mrs. Jones just assumed their relationship was serious enough to justify a marriage and wrongly concluded that Pam Cheek had married my grandfather. After hearing this story and having known of some past infidelities of my grandfather, I called my grandmother and asked her if she had ever heard of a woman named Pam Cheek.

Well, of course she had. This was one of the ladies that her private investigator had caught my grandfather having an affair with. Apparently, Emmett Atwood was quite the lady's man. There were several women that he not only was having affairs with, but was also paying their college tuition, and room and board at several different colleges throughout Mississippi. What was most damaging and the most hurtful to my grandmother was the private investigator's discovery that Emmett had an affair with one of his African-American employees and had fathered an illegitimate child from her.

# DAVID G. ATWOOD, II

This has been one of the most guarded secrets of the Atwood family. Only in later years would I discover through my own investigations that Emmett had given large sums of money to everyone involved who was aware of his illegitimate child with the African-American woman. Not only were there rumors he had paid off the local judge to seal the court records, (which is illegal to do), but had also paid the African-American mother thousands of dollars to dismiss her paternity suit and to take the illegitimate baby and move to another state. This was the real cause of his and my grandmother's divorce in 1979.

Most people would not consider fathering an illegitimate child with an African-American woman to be a taboo, but a person has to understand the time in which this took place and you also have to account for the fact that my family has a long history of connections to racist organizations like the Ku Klux Klan, White Citizens Council, and Sons of Confederate Veterans. Apparently, my grandfather's political convictions and racial biases don't matter in the bedroom. As I will explain in later chapters, these connections would come back to haunt not just me, but other members of my family.

At the end of my grandparents' divorce in 1979, my grandmother was tremendously relieved to be out from under the pressure and distrust that existed in her marriage. Because of the infidelities and the wish to keep them private and out of the courtroom and out of the minds and mouths of his friends and social acquaintances, he ensured my grandmother, now his ex-wife, was well taken care of. She got the brand new mansion, a hefty alimony, a new car from the dealership every eight thousand miles, and enough other extras to insure a happy and carefree standard of living for the rest of her life.

By the time my dad, mom, and I moved from the farm to my grandmother's house in 1986, several things had changed since her divorce. The two main things were that she was now working as a first-grade teacher in the Vicksburg-Warren County Public School System and her daughter, my aunt, had moved into the basement of the mansion.

After graduating high school and earning her

undergraduate and master's degrees from Mississippi State University, June Atwood, my aunt, moved back home to Vicksburg and took a job at the family dealership working for my grandfather.

My aunt, whom I would later have legal problems with, and who would be a main contributor to my incarceration in Federal prison, didn't begin her life as the rude, malevolent, cold-hearted bitch that so many know her as today. During her childhood and early twenties she was a bright, lovely lady. It was in the eighties, when my aunt began struggling with many problems. It was a time that she finally began accepting her feelings of being different, a "different" that most people will never know the feeling.

Her moods began to change, she started having violent fits, and before long she was suffering from chronic depression. She began obsessing about herself and those around her. She became obsessive-compulsive, mean-spirited and rude. The relationship with her father and brothers quickly deteriorated. By 1984 her depression had become so severe that she felt as though suicide was her only escape.

After supposedly swallowing hundreds of sleeping pills and washing them down with vodka, she lapsed into a coma and would have died had she not been rescued. For several days she laid in a coma on the verge of death. Miraculously, she pulled through. Although she would never be the same afterwards, she did seek years of psychiatric counseling, which probably also included months of in-patient hospitalization. As much as was possible, the family tried to tuck her out-of-sight and keep her from public view. This scheme resulted in her being moved into the basement of my grandmother's new house.

More than twenty years later, she still seeks professional help. In the opinion of her family and those who see her every day, her condition has only digressed.

The mansion that Dad, Mom, and I moved into in 1986 was a three-story, five bedroom, nine bath, brick monstrosity of a home. My aunt lived on the bottom basement floor; Dad, Mom, and I lived in the two bedrooms on the second floor, and my grandmother lived in the master bedroom on the third floor.

By this time, I was nearing three years old and had begun to talk and pronounce my first words. From that point on my father became "Daddy", my mother "Momma", my grandmother Atwood was "Meme", my grandfather Atwood was "Pops" and my maternal-grandparents became "Papaw and Mamaw".

In 1986 Pops had remarried a beautiful socialite from Texas named Camille Webb, who was the heir to one of the wealthy oil magnates in Vernon. They had built a nice house and were living happily together. Whether Camille knew of Pop's sordid past, no one knows. I am sure she knows now, though, or will when she reads this book.

In September 1988, I was five years old and it was time for me to start school. My parents enrolled me at the local school, Jett Elementary. I don't remember my kindergarten teacher's name, but I do remember how much I enjoyed coloring, singing songs, playing on the swings at recess and then taking those afternoon naps. That was the best part of the day.

One day at recess there was a car that caught fire in front of the school. I watched in amazement as the firefighters in their gear turned out to fight the fire. I knew then that I wanted to be a firefighter someday. Maybe it was then, or maybe it was later, but something happened in my life that ingrained a sense of honor and commitment into my mind that would direct me on a path to be in a position to always help people.

For three years we had lived with my Aunt June and Meme. At the end of my kindergarten year my parents decided to move into an apartment complex outside of town and change me to a new school. Partly, the reason for this change in residence was the fact that my Aunt June's mental illness was causing lots of friction with Dad and Mom.

There would be days when she was perfectly normal and then, without warning, she would break down into fits of hysteria and become violent and abusive. Meme could deal with this behavior, but Dad and Mom could not. Aunt June would go weeks without coming out of her bedroom in the basement- work would pile up on her desk at the office. Quiet whispers and snickering would be exchanged between co-workers. If my aunt had been employed at a real business, not run by her father, her outbursts and behavior would have gotten her fired.

As it was, Pops tried to do everything he could to care for his only daughter. There's only so much he or anyone else could do. It's only natural for us to have compassion for people who suffer from mental illnesses, but there's also a realization that you can only go so far to try to help them. I think everyone went as far as they could to try to help my aunt, but she just never wanted or would allow anyone to help her.

My dad became angry and frustrated. This wasn't his sister that he grew up with; this wasn't the same person who would take him horseback riding when they were kids; this wasn't the beautiful blue-eyed sister he remembered. But the decision was made: my dad didn't like being dependent on anyone anyway. He wanted his own house, own backyard, and his own privacy. Until he could find or build a house, though, we had to live in the apartments.

My dad was working at the family business, Atwood Chevrolet, as the parts manager and he made good money. His younger brother, Alan was the sales manager; his sister, when she was there and in her right mind, was the administrative assistant; and their oldest brother left the family business and started his own car dealership, a disaster that ended in failure and bankruptcy. Once again Pops was called to the rescue to bail one of his children out of financial ruin and starvation. This would be a scenario played over and over again.

In the summer of 1989 we officially made the move from Meme's mansion to our little 750square foot apartment. I was enrolled at Culkin Elementary School and started first grade that summer. My new teacher was Mrs. Duncan. A strict disciplinarian (paddling was still allowed then), Mrs. Duncan tolerated very little play and demanded constant dedication to our studies. No more afternoon naps, no more coloring books. Pop quizzes and homework were the new order of the day.

I think most six-year-olds would have a hard time adjusting to this new routine, especially with a teacher like Mrs.

Duncan. But I remember having very little trouble. I might not have admitted it at the time, but looking back, school was sometimes even fun. I remember getting in trouble only one time in first-grade and that was when I was caught stopping up the school bathroom toilets with construction paper and then overflowing them. I'm sure the punishment could have been worse.

The principal at the school was Mr. Grogan and it was rumored he had an electric paddle and would use it freely on any young boy or girl who was sent to his office. Thankfully, that day, I wasn't paddled with an electric piece of wood. I was, however, forced to call my dad at work and tell him what I had done. I probably would have preferred the paddle.

This brings up an excellent point and sometimes a sore subject between my dad and mom. Because my dad had been raised by a father who believed in strict physical punishment for his kids' youthful transgressions, my dad believed the same. My mother, however, had been raised by parents who were less inclined to use the belt or hand as a means of punishment. This would later cause many fights between my parents when my mother would believe my dad's punishment to be too strict and my dad would believe my mom's punishment was not tough enough. I was caught in the middle, mostly on the side of my mom though. I mean what kid DOES want a spanking?

No one would argue that either of my parents weren't strong-willed. This didn't make good marriage material. I cannot fault one or the other for their eventual divorce. Things were done that they are both guilty of; however, my dad has a horrible temper and often flies into bouts of rage when things don't go his way or when he is frustrated by a problem. Obviously, the marriage to his wife and the day-to-day business of raising a child often frustrated him.

I was probably about four or five years old when I first witnessed my dad strike my mom. I was scared to death. I had never seen my dad so angry. He had a look in his eyes like he wanted to kill her. I hid in my bedroom closet, covering my ears. I wanted the yelling and screaming to go away.

My mother tried to explain to me that my dad was only having some problems and it would never happen again. But a five-year-old doesn't understand grown-up problems. I don't remember what their fight was about but I do remember the violence. That image has stayed with me forever.

It was the beginning of a series of fights between my parents that only got worse over time. My dad soon turned to the whiskey bottle for distraction, but it only caused more problems. Unfortunately, my dad was only fulfilling a history of alcoholism that has plagued the Atwood family for decades and continues to be a source of misery and pain. But as a seven-year-old boy, I didn't understand any of this.

I was in second grade and my teacher was Mrs. Justice-same school and same classmates as the year before. I especially remember a lot about this year because it was the same year that the United States invaded Kuwait and drove out Saddam Hussein's army. Mrs. Justice had a son that was in the army and was serving in Saudi Arabia at the time. Our class wrote him greeting cards and also took up donations for other members of our country's military.

Second grade was also the year I learned to write in cursive and to add and subtract. Looking back I am amazed how early my class started work on such a complicated curriculum. Children today sometimes don't start that stuff until third or fourth grade. It wasn't that I or my other classmates were overly smart, we weren't in an advanced class; things are just different today than when I was in school.

By second grade, the family life at home was quickly deteriorating. My parents were fighting more, my father becoming more physically and verbally abusive, my mother cried a lot. It was hard to live in that situation. It was during this time that my father started becoming abusive to me. Maybe he didn't like the way I did something, maybe I said the wrong thing, sometimes he said I didn't act "man" enough, or I might accidentally drop something and send him into a rage. I had always gotten spankings with a belt, but my dad never hit me with his fist or kicked me, but that was changing.

You see in the movies where a kid goes to school with bruises or scratches and the ever-vigilant teacher automatically recognizes child abuse. That doesn't happen in the real world because I went to school all banged-up and no one ever took the time to notice. Again, maybe it was the times, maybe back then people didn't care as much whether a parent was being abusive to their children or not. I couldn't continue to live in fear of being beat-up, kicked, stomped, slapped around, or worse.

One thing I will never blame my mom for is getting a divorce from my dad. The summer that I finished second grade the conditions living in our house were so bad we had to leave. My dad always kept guns in the house and would never think twice about threatening my mom or me with our deaths. The day that really clinched their marriage's fate was when my dad went into such a rage that he really did try to kill my mother with a butcher knife. That was it- we were out of there.

After filing the official papers for divorce it took several months for it to go through the court system. Had my mom actually tried to fight my dad for alimony or half of the assets she would have most decidedly lost. The judge who presided over divorce cases at the time was Richard Braddock, an old friend of the Atwood family, someone who in my opinion had been on the Atwood payroll for a long time (remember my grandfather's little infidelities?).

My mother only wanted a divorce and custody of me. It was questionable whether she would get child-support, but by some miracle my dad agreed to pay a small sum of money a month, although it would be harder to actually collect it. When my parents got a divorce my dad washed his hands of my mom and me. He just pretended neither she nor I existed. If it weren't for my Meme, I would have lost all contact with the Atwood family after the divorce. I am sure my father wished I hadn't even been born- a suspicion he would later confirm to me.

Staying in Vicksburg was not an option for my mother and me. Besides me, she had no other family there. All of her family, including her mother and father were in Kosciusko. But instead of moving back there, where there were practically no employment opportunities for a single mother, we moved to Pearl, Mississippi. My mom's sister, Pam, lived there and we were able to find a decent single bedroom apartment close to her house.

Pearl is a suburban neighborhood outside of the state capitol. My mom was able to find a job working for Ford Motor Credit making decent money, enough to get us by. I never went hungry or without nice clothing. My mother sacrificed so that I could have a standard of living that we were accustomed to in Vicksburg. My mother is a noble woman and although we didn't always get along, I came first in everything in her life.

For the third time in my life I had to start at a new school and make new friends. My third grade teacher at Pearl Elementary was a lady named Mrs. Campbell. Maybe it was me, maybe it had something to do with the divorce and the problems I was having adjusting to my new life, but she and I were locking horns constantly. She was the first teacher that I did not get along with, the first person other than my parents to discipline me with a paddle and she didn't waste any time throwing me out of her classroom. For the first time in my brief childhood, I didn't make friends with the people in my third-grade class as easily as I had at my other schools.

I don't remember having "issues" to deal with concerning the divorce of my parents. I know it was a lonely time, not just for my mother but for me as well. Although we couldn't do it every night, I always looked forward to going over to my Aunt Pam's house to eat dinner and play on her motorcycle. It was one of these times on her motorcycle that it got a little carried away with me and ran into her storage shed, damaging the door and wall.

As with any kid my age, I think we tend to hide and forget about some of the bad things that happen in our lives. For me, I've had to rely on my mom and other relative's interpretations of those first few years of my life. So much has happened in my life and happened so quickly, without writing it all down or depending on someone else, you forget.

It was in early 1992, my mom and I had been on our own

for almost a year. We had a good routine. Her job was going well, my school was getting better, I was making more friends and my grades were improving under Mrs. Campbell's tutelage. I think my mom was having a harder time adjusting to the single life, as I had to adjust without a father. She was able to save her money and we took our first trip to Disney World together.

Never has my mother been afraid to travel by herself. For as long as either of us can remember we've always been taking trips together or doing things on our own. We are both independent people. The Disney World trip might have been pushing it, though. Here is my mother, twenty-eight years old, along with her eight-year-old son, by themselves, in a strange new place.

Although we did make it to Disney World and Wet & Wild Waterpark, we got ourselves lost plenty of times, but we had fun and spent a lot of quality time together.

This far into her being single, my mother began dating again. I can imagine it was difficult after being with my father for so many years, but she soon found someone who for a time would be everything she ever dreamed of in a husband.

In the meantime, my love life as a third-grader wasn't coming along too well. That spring, our elementary school had a mini-prom celebration. I was named third-grade Prom King and a gorgeous little girl named Kelly Adams was named Prom Queen. I had seen her before. She wasn't in my class but was in another third-grade class and I knew she was someone I would like to "talk" to. I was just too shy to go up and speak to her. Being named Prom King and her Prom Queen gave me an excellent chance to talk to her. She was my first crush, although, of course, nothing ever came of it. I still remember turning beet red and the skin on the back of my neck burning every time I saw and talked to her.

As with every school there's always a bully or two and always some poor kid gets picked on- it's a part of growing up. I think everyone, at some stage in their life gets picked on by a bully or someone bigger than them. My school was no different.

I vaguely remember another student several years older

than me at Pearl Elementary. His name was Luke Woodham and he was the over-weight kid that everyone picked on. I have never been a bully; in fact I've tried to stop it whenever I saw it. While at Pearl I was picked on. I had big ears and was called "dumbo", but Luke was called worse. Several years later after I had left Pearl and moved back to Vicksburg, Luke brought a gun to school and shot and killed several of the students and teachers. This was the first of many high-profile school shootings to take place across the country. Had I remained at Pearl and gone to high school there, could I have been one of the victims of that school shooting that day?

Thankfully, third-grade would be my one and only year at that school. By the end of the school year I had decided on a different course for my educational training...boarding school.

# CHAPTER THREE

Not having a father figure during this critical stage in my life was a difficult adjustment. There were a few times that I went to spend a weekend with my dad, but much of that visit would be spent with my Meme while my dad was off drinking alcohol and frequenting the strip clubs. When we were actually around each other there was not much bonding. No emotion and no outward display of affection.

Can I blame my dad for this? I don't know. His father was the same way. My dad's two brothers are not loving and affectionate to their children either. My dad's oldest brother has two daughters and a son. He spends little time with them, although I have heard that lately he is beginning to become better in his old age. Their youngest brother, Alan, has three boys. The three of them are practically raised by their mother.

I've often wondered if lack of affection was somehow

hereditary in my family. My Meme didn't get much love from her ex-husband. My dad, uncles, and aunt didn't get it either. Could my Pops have done a better job? Sure, he could have! Is there anything I or anyone else can do about it? No!!! But a nine-year-old doesn't understand these things. I just wanted to know why my dad didn't love me.

If there was any one person who has always been there for me and has tried to fill in where my own father left off, it was my mom's father, my papaw. What I couldn't get from my dad, my papaw made up for. He took me hunting, taught me to fish and to work with wood and build things; everything my dad couldn't or wouldn't teach me, my papaw did.

He let me raise chickens at his house- which turned out to be a huge mistake because those chickens lived for twelve years and he had to take care of them. He and I did so much together and I loved going to spend my weekends and summers at his house. The first fifteen summers of my life were spent at his house in Kosciusko.

During Christmas breaks, my mother and I always spent our time at his and my Mamaw's house. Not only would my mom's sister and brother and their families be there, but my Mamaw was the best cook in the world and we would always have tons of food and lots of good stories to tell. My papaw, cousins, and I would go deer, squirrel, and rabbit hunting, camping and fishing. It was always the most fun I ever had.

My papaw filled the gap left void by the absence of my own father. Living in the South, hunting and fishing is a big thing. My papaw bought me my first .22 caliber rifle, taught me how to use it and practice gun safety. We went hunting every chance we could. It was he who taught me the respect and understanding that I have for firearms and the power they can yield.

Although my papaw is a staunch democrat, it wasn't until later in my life that I would share his political convictions. Make no mistake about it, my papaw is a man's man. He was a high school principal for twenty years. He is a devout Christian with an enormous amount of compassion and love. Although he and I would later disagree over the influence religion was playing in my own life, his faith in me and my ambitions never faltered.

My Mamaw, on the other hand, has always been worrisome and over-protective. It's no big secret that she rules the household. What she says, always goes. I notice this same behavior in my own mother as she grows older and make fun of her about it on a regular basis. While my Mamaw can, and is an excellent cook and can make the best jellies and jam in Mississippi, she is a constant nag and will worry a man to death. Aren't all women like that, though? Nevertheless, she's a wonderful Christian woman who deserves tremendous respect for raising three great kids. All of her kids have married respectable spouses and become wonderful people.

Her son, Randy would marry Denise Dees and they would raise three boys, all of whom have become successful in their lives. My uncle Randy would graduate from Ole Miss with a degree in pharmacy and would become one of the most respected pharmacists in Columbus, Mississippi. Her second child, Pamela, would marry Harry McLemore and raise a little girl. Her third daughter, my mother, would raise me, and then have two more children from her second marriage- which brings me to an excellent point...my stepfather.

Not long after her divorce from my dad, my mom began to date again. There were several young men she met from work, several she knew from high school and college, but nothing ever blossomed into a relationship, until she met an attorney from Vicksburg named Jerry Campbell. Jerry was a graduate of Ole Miss law school, and was roommates and fraternity brothers with the Mississippi Governor, Haley Barbour.

My first impression of Jerry was that he seemed to be a real decent guy, but I didn't exactly like the fact that someone was using up my mother's time. It's hard for someone that was my age to understand these things. I didn't, and I am sure I put some strain on my mother's relationship with Jerry in the beginning. Jerry, as it would turn out, was a patient and kind man. He treated my mother well and would always try to include me in most everything they did.

While my papaw took the place of my real father, Jerry was around me a lot more often and tried his best to be a positive role model. Jerry wasn't into the things that I was, though. He didn't hunt, he didn't have four wheelers, and he didn't like outdoors type stuff. He *did* like basketball and baseball, something that I was interested in. I had played baseball in little league and would play in high school and I was fairly good. Jerry took me to some of my games and helped me practice. Fathering was new to him, but he tried. I was a pain in the ass sometimes but he was a nice guy and took care of me.

When he proposed to my mother in my third grade year, I didn't have a problem with it. I knew Jerry was wealthy and I was happy that my mom had found someone who could take care of her.

That summer, my dad paid for me to go to a summer camp at a boarding school in French Camp, Mississippi. They had a summer program that lasted two weeks where kids my age went to swim, ride horses, canoe and do other fun things that kids normally do at summer camp. My mother didn't have a problem with me going and my dad thought I would enjoy it.

Every summer, since kindergarten I had attended a one-week summer camp in Kosciusko called Central Hills Baptist Retreat. It was a place for boys my age to go and spend time participating in outdoor activities, spiritual worship, and bible study. I liked it there. I always had a lot of fun when I went, but French Camp was really different. There were never any prayer sessions and forced bible lessons or propagandized religious indoctrinations. It was mostly just fun.

After summer camp was over, I remember discussing the possibility of going to school at French Camp full time. Jerry and my mother were getting married soon, and although I genuinely enjoyed being around Jerry, I do not think I was actually very happy that he and my mother were getting married.

When the issue was brought up with my dad, he was at first hesitant to let me go, but he soon acquiesced when Jerry offered to help cover some of the cost of tuition. My mother was favorable to the idea but hesitant to trust my wellbeing to a group of strangers. It took a lot of convincing, but finally my mother decided to consider it and we talked it over throughout the summer.

Another factor in my considerations about going to boarding school was the fact that part of me was just not happy living at home with my mother and Jerry. After they were married, my mother soon became pregnant with her first child. Having a baby around didn't please me in the least. My brother had been born on January 16th, 1993. They named my new brother, Aaron Fisher Campbell. Soon after having Fisher, my mother became pregnant with another child and gave birth to my little sister, Mary Hannah Campbell on March 15th, 1994.

Perhaps there was a tinge of jealousy, but I had always wanted my mother to myself. Now with two newborns, my mother's attention would be divided. It was this final factor that motivated me to go to French Camp for my fourth grade year.

French Camp is a Christian boarding school located about ninety miles north of Jackson, Mississippi and is situated on the historic Natchez Trace Parkway. It was originally founded in 1885 as a girl's school but eventually became coeducational. My great-aunt, Geneva Atwood England attended there in her early childhood and it is a respected learning institution by numerous religious organizations.

As my first day approached, I expected an atmosphere of structure, discipline, and Christian learning. I hoped that I could make friends with new kinds of people and enjoy some of the recreational opportunities that I would not normally be able to living with my mom and Jerry.

In the autumn of my fourth grade year of school, I moved into the Moriah dorm at the south end of the nine-hundred-acre community. My dorm parents were Bruce and Karen Hotchkins. I shared a room with a boy from Grenada, Mississippi. We attended school everyday until late afternoon, after which, we were free to do what we wanted.

French Camp had swimming pools, baseball fields, horseback riding, canoeing, and numerous other things that would keep a boy busy. Most of my days were spent riding horses and playing baseball. Later in the year I was accepted into the choir and was soon traveling around the state singing.

Time passed fairly quickly my first few months at French Camp, but by Christmas I was ready to return home for a visit with my family. Meme had recently bought a large piece of property in south Warren County and started building a new house.

In what was surely a spectacular piece of cunning on behalf of Meme, she managed to get my Pops to purchase her mansion from her. This in essence, required Pops to pay for the house twice- the first time shortly before their divorce. Meme used the money to buy my dad and Aunt June their own pieces of property and herself some land also with the intention of everyone building their own houses. Since everyone's land was connected, we would all be living beside one another.

That Christmas break was the first time I was able to see the property for myself and the thought of being able to roam around hundreds of acres of land thrilled me to pieces. I was even more excited when my dad told me that he would soon start the construction on his new house.

After returning to French Camp, my life proceeded as normally as could be expected. I was allowed to come home and visit with my family every month or two and I began to cherish the time I was able to be back with them. Papaw and Mamaw only lived a short drive away from French Camp and they would try to drive up and visit as much as possible. When my mother couldn't come get me, Papaw would and I stayed with him many times during my two-year stay at boarding school.

The summer between my fourth and fifth grade years I spent with my dad. The construction was proceeding with his new house but Meme's house had already been completed and I was able to stay with her at night and roam over the property during the day. There was also a lake where I could fish for bass and a small creek that I could play in. Several times that summer I saw signs of lots of deer. Both my dad and I were looking forward to hunting the following season.

When I returned to French Camp for my fifth grade year,

I expected much the same as I had the previous year. I was a year older and a grade higher in school. My friends there were still the same and my dorm parents hadn't changed either. What had changed was the demeanor of my dorm parent, Mr. Hotchkins.

Troublemakers were always dealt with swiftly and effectively by Mr. Hotchkins- usually with a paddle or belt. So far, I had avoided doing anything that would result in me getting whipped. But at the start of my second year, Mr. Hotchkins became abusive and threatening to not only me, but other children as well.

The first time he paddled me was for a minor infraction-having my radio turned on past lights-out. The second time was for arriving late to class one morning. The third, fourth, fifth, and more blended into one long semester of constant abuse.

I tried telling my mother about it. I tried talking to my dad. Unfortunately, my mom was starting to have problems with her pregnancy and with having to care for my baby brother, it left little time to hear, much less do anything, about my constant complaining. My dad could have also cared less. When he managed to pause long enough from his drinking and skirt chasing to answer the phone, I was told to toughen up and deal with it like a man. My dad has always thought that I wasn't masculine enough to be his son. Perhaps from an early age he suspected me of being gay. Regardless, my dad has always advocated anything that's rough, tough, and mean. It's remarkable I ever made it to adulthood.

I went from being a happy, outgoing kid, to a reserved and frightened child. There were several kids who Mr. Hotchkins was especially brutal to. I happened to be one of them. Most of the children didn't have parents to call and cry to. Only rarely was I even allowed to make calls, but when I did, I mostly cried and begged my mother to come get me. Looking back, I don't know if she believed me or just thought I was over-exaggerating the claims of abuse. Regardless, by Christmas time, I was practically frantic to come home on my holiday break.

During the short time I was at home for Christmas, I literally begged, cried, and pleaded with my mother not to send me back to French Camp. I had even gone so far as to take Polaroid pictures of the bruises left on my body by Mr. Hotchkins. My mother was concerned enough to call and complain to Mr. Hotchkins, but not enough to pull me out. She was determined to make me finish the spring semester. My dad and I discussed the possibility of my coming to live with him, but he wanted me to finish out the semester also before he would consider letting me come to live with him.

After going back in January, I had one goal on my mind and that was to make it through as best as I could until school was out for the summer. Having to endure more abuse from Mr. Hotchkins was almost more than I could take, so fortunately, I found ways to avoid the dorm as much as possible and keep my mind occupied with other things.

By the time summer finally arrived I was a nervous wreck. I had spent the entire spring writing letters to my dad and calling him as much as I could, begging to be allowed to come home and live with him. To his credit, I think he realized how much I had changed and was determined to try something different. His house was finished and he was living alone. I guess he thought it wouldn't be such a bad thing if I did move in with him.

My mother had given birth to my little sister earlier that spring after an extremely difficult pregnancy that had required delivering the baby three months early. After being born so early, Hannah almost didn't live through her neonatal care. She was too small and weighed too little. Her lungs and heart had not properly formed and the doctors called Mother and Jerry into the nursery several times to say their last goodbyes to their daughter who wasn't supposed to live many more hours, but each time Hannah pulled through and is now a healthy and beautiful young lady.

Unfortunately, my brother had also at this time, become very sick with a severe bone infection and was at serious risk for several weeks before being saved by a brilliant gay doctor at Baptist Hospital named Bill Causey. Dr. Causey and I would later become good friends and eventually be incarcerated together in federal prison. But that's a story for a later chapter.

Having to deal with all this was an extremely stressing time for my mother and Jerry. I don't think there was ever a more stressful point in their marriage than at this time. Jerry was staying in the hospital at night with Fisher, while my grandparents stayed with him during the day.

Mother was partially bedridden and when Hannah came home from the hospital, she had to constantly take care of her. The last thing they needed was me stepping into the picture and adding further to their troubles. This is when the final decision was made for me to leave French Camp after finishing fifth grade and move out onto the property with my dad.

On my last day at boarding school, I gave away most of my belongings, packed the rest, said goodbye to my friends and got into the car to leave. I never looked back and I never regretted leaving. French Camp was something I initially enjoyed, but in my second year, Mr. Hotchkins had made my life so rough that I was ready to do anything to get away from there. When leaving, I had everything to look forward to and was for the first time in several years, truly happy about where I was going and what I was doing. My dad had even started to clean himself up and stop drinking.

# CHAPTER FOUR

     I consider my sixth-grade year one of the best years of my life.  I was eleven years old by then and for the past two years had been through hell.  I was on the rebound and had a lot to look forward to.

     During the summer after coming home from French Camp, I moved all of my personal belongings to my dad's house.  My dad was making good money at the dealership and was able to buy me a horse and a new four-wheeler. There was also an old Toyota truck that my dad let me use to drive around our property.  I could carry my little .22 rifle with me everywhere I went and most of that summer was spent exploring every nook and cranny of our property.  I could spend all day riding my horse and still never cover all of the land.  It was just too big.  A lot of nights I spent camping out alone.

     My dad knew I was independent. I had learned a lot about the outdoors at boarding school and with my Papaw.

Nevertheless, my Meme was worried to death about me and made my dad buy me a puppy.

Ginger was the name I gave my dog. A mix between a Labrador and a pit-bull, she was the perfect companion. I raised her from a puppy and she became my new best friend. No more would I have to be alone during those long romps in the woods. I even taught her to retrieve and do a few tricks. Every little boy remembers his first puppy. I was no different, I also remembered mine.

When the summer was over I started school at South Park Elementary, our local community school. My grandmother had taught first-grade there for many years but by the time I started sixth grade, she had retired. I had two teachers, Mrs. Brown, an overly large African-American lady who reminded me of "Mammie" from "Gone with the Wind". My other teacher was Mrs. Lana Little, a lovely blonde haired lady who had at one time entertained the thought of marrying my father. Instead, she would have to settle for being my math and science teacher.

I quickly made friends. Justin Lovins, Josh Lawrence, and Michael Winningham were my best friends and we did everything together. My dad owned a ski-boat so we spent a lot of time on the river. They all had four-wheelers, so a lot of time was spent riding through the woods. We all spent time camping on the weekends. I quickly became the person that everyone wanted to be friends with.

It wasn't long after I began my sixth grade year that I had my first run-in with the law. My best friend, Justin Lovins and I, lived only a few miles from one another and it was very easy for us to ride our four-wheelers back and forth to each other's house. There was also a small neighborhood nearby that offered us a chance to ride our four-wheelers through. One weekend we had the bright idea to ram people's garbage cans with the front of our four-wheelers.

We would haul butt down the road and when we found someone's house that had the garbage cans by the road we'd use the front of our bumpers to knock them over. It was a lot of fun until I ran over a garbage can that was full of wooden blocks and other scrap pieces of lumber. I hit it going about twenty miles an hour and was launched off the front of my four-wheeler and into the pavement in front of me.

My friend Justin was too scared to stop and check on me so he took off and headed back home. I picked myself off the ground and instantly realized I was in pretty bad shape. I didn't have time to be concerned with myself though, that garbage can was still lodged under my four-wheeler. I had to use every ounce of strength to pull it out from under the chassis, while the blood ran down my forehead and arm.

How I did it, I am not sure. But after getting the garbage can out from under my four-wheeler, I hauled ass out of there and back to my house. My injuries were worse than I initially thought.

I had a big gash on my head where it made contact with the concrete, both of my elbows were skinned up, my ankle had swollen three times its normal size and what was worst of all, the four-wheeler bumper was bent and it's headlight broken. I wasn't sure what would upset my dad more, me being hurt or the four-wheeler being damaged.

To make matters worse, Justin was nowhere in sight. I could not believe he could just leave me laying there. When I made it back home, my dad was already looking for me. Apparently, Justin had seen my crash and thought I was seriously hurt and had rushed to his house and called my dad to tell him what had happened. I mean, what are friends for, huh?

Unfortunately, Justin wasn't the only one who snitched me out. Someone in the neighborhood had seen us knocking over garbage cans and had seen me wreck. They called the Sheriff. At the time, the Sheriff was more worried about whether I was alright, rather than the garbage cans. So, when my dad took me to the hospital the Sheriff showed up.

My dad thought it a good idea that Sheriff Paul Barrett talk to me in the strongest language possible for an eleven-year-old boy to understand that running over people's garbage cans is not acceptable. Of course, I was scared to death.

To make matters worse, my dad thought it would be a

good idea to take Justin and me down to the county jail and let the sheriff give us a tour so that we would know where the bad people went when they did bad things. So, several weeks after my little four-wheeler accident we were taken around the jail and shown what a horrible place it was.

This wasn't the only time that I got myself caught up in something where I ended up getting hurt. Several months after the garbage can incident, Justin and I were camping out beside an old storage shed located on my property. There was a big fifty-five gallon steel drum that had trash in it, but other than that we thought it would make a good place to build a fire in. Oh, what a big mistake that was.

Unbeknownst to us, there were several old, unused propane bottles in the bottom of the barrel. After trying several times to get the trash to burn I poured a couple cups of diesel oil into the barrel and put a match to it. It began to burn then.

After several minutes however, right as I was adding more wood and trash to the fire the propane bottles exploded. The blast blew me back several yards. My shirt and pants caught fire. This time, Justin didn't freak and run; instead he stayed and helped me put the flames out. I couldn't see and my face felt like it was still burning. Justin said all my eyebrows and hair had been singe off. I knew I was in very bad shape.

Justin put me on the four-wheeler and rushed me back to my house. My dad was at work and the only person close by was my grandmother. When she saw how bad I was, she knew immediately that I had to get to the hospital as soon as possible.

Our house was about twenty minutes from the nearest hospital and it would take almost an hour for the ambulance to make it out to our house, pick me up and then take me back to the hospital. Instead, Meme called 9-1-1 and told them what happened and to have the nearest deputy sheriff meet us on the road and escort us to the hospital.

Meme loaded me in her car and off we went. Of course, I couldn't see anything- the blast had severely damaged my eyes- but I could definitely feel that we were moving fast in her car. I used to joke with Meme about her slow "old-lady" driving, but this day she would have made any race car driver proud. Somewhere between our house and town we met the deputy and he escorted us the rest of the way to the hospital where my dad was already waiting.

There are only a few things that I remember after that. I was in severe pain and the doctors were worried whether I would ever regain the use of my eyes, my eyelids were nearly burned shut. I had lost all my eyebrows and eyelashes and was missing a good portion of the hair on top of my head. I remember being given pain medication but everything after that was a blur.

I woke up two days later still in the intensive care unit of the hospital, hooked up to IV's with bandages on my face. I wasn't in much pain other than the times I tried moving my mouth. However, when the nurse came to my room with the intent of scrubbing my face with a gauze pad, I had to draw the line.

That lasted all of about two seconds before the pain was most unbearable. I know the nurse was just trying to do the best job that she could, but I pitched the biggest fit anyone ever saw. The only way I was going to let that nurse do her job is if I did it for her. So, for the next hour I very gingerly proceeded to scrub the burnt skin from my face. I think finally the nurse just gave up and left me alone. Thankfully, I was released from the hospital a day later. When I came home, the recovery had to continue and I spent several days in bed before I began to regain the use of my eyesight. I had received second-degree burns over most of my face and thankfully, the doctors said my eyes were partially closed when the blast went off and it was only a miracle that my sight was not damaged.

This accident occurred on a weekend and I spent the following week in the hospital and bed recovering. I probably should have spent more time recuperating, but I was very anxious to get back to school and the Monday of the following week I started back. Of course, all of my friends had been aware of what had happened and had called and sent "get-well" cards. Most of my family helped out in some way as well. I had never been one to seek sympathy, so it was a little frustrating when I first went back to school because everyone wanted to help me. I think though, that this only helped speed my recovery by making me more dependent upon myself.

About three weeks after the accident I returned to my family doctor for a check-up. Thankfully there would be no permanent scaring or other damage. My eyesight had returned to normal and my hair was beginning to grow back. All-in-all, I took this whole incident as a learning experience. Even today, I always try to pass on my knowledge of fire safety to my friends, because any carelessness with fire can result in a lot worse consequences. This is something my family would learn in later years when my little sister, Hannah, and several of her friends were severely hurt with third-degree burns.

After I had recovered from this accident, I quickly returned to my devotion of hobbies and sports. During this time of my life, my Aunt June was in one of the better stages of her ongoing mental illness recovery. Meme, Aunt June and I were both heavily into riding and showing horses in different competition events. One of those events being team penning, a sport where three riders try to sort certain cows from a herd, isolate them and then pen them into a small enclosed arena, while being timed by a stop watch.

This was a hobby that we all were becoming very good at doing. My dad had bought me my first horse several months before my accident as a reward for making the all "A" honor roll at school. Since then, every Friday night, Aunt June, Meme and I would travel around to different parts of the state to attend these team-penning events. We became very good at what we did and were winning a lot of money and trophies.

Unfortunately, about a year after we began to win championships, my aunt dropped off into another depression and isolated herself from everyone. She would lock herself in her bedroom and not come out for days. There's a joke inside the family about this. When Meme was building her house out on the property, she specifically had the architect design a small kitchen with stove and refrigerator right beside Aunt June's bedroom so that when she fell into her depressions and fits of hysteria and locked herself in her room, she would have something to eat and a way to prepare her meals without having to come out and be seen.

Another joke inside the family is that when my aunt was a little girl she was running a high fever and Meme had to put her in a tub of ice water to bring down her temperature. Apparently, Meme didn't add enough ice and the subsequent fever is what caused my aunt to act the way she does today.

An eleven-year-old boy doesn't understand these things though. All I knew was that Aunt June was "sick" and couldn't come out of her bedroom and could not take us to any more team pennings because she "didn't feel good". I feel sorry for her today, even after all the horrible things she has done to Meme and me.

I still feel sympathy for her because I know that deep down, inside her mind, behind all the illness and sickness, there is a wonderful person. Several times my Pops and Meme both have tried to get her in-patient care, which all of her doctors have said would result in a tremendous improvement in her condition, but Aunt June won't do it. She would rather live with her afflictions for the rest of her life, than spend a few months in an in-patient treatment facility, under constant observation, in order for the doctors to recognize, identify and treat her many conditions. It is a sad, sad thing and I have hoped that one day my Aunt June would get the treatment that she needs, because when she is in her right mind she is really a loving, thoughtful and caring person.

Now, like I said earlier, sixth-grade was the best year of my life. Of course, I was only eleven years old, but this was when I first discovered girls and the girl I had my eye on was the prettiest girl in my class, Amber English. (I always set my standards high!)

When a boy is eleven years old he doesn't understand such complex things as homosexuality. I didn't even know much about the "birds and the bees". The only knowledge of the female anatomy I had stopped on the last page of the Hustler magazine I found in my dad's dresser drawer. I have known since being aware of my presence on this Earth that I had "feelings" for my male friends that other boys my age didn't. But, I didn't know or understand what these feelings meant and I certainly wasn't going to act on them. As far as I knew, homosexuality didn't exist; no one ever told me that two men or two women could fall in love with one another.

And in sixth-grade I still couldn't make much sense of it. My friends were becoming interested in girls, so I followed right along. I had become friends with Amber at the first of the school year but was too shy to ever ask her out. A sixth-grader's life is so complicated about male-female relationships, it's very hard to build up the nerve to ask one another for a date. But, I finally built up the courage and she said yes. I was finally going on my first date.

Amber and I became boyfriend and girlfriend in March of 1995. The extent of our relationship was a movie on Friday night or perhaps a few hours on Saturday at the skating rink in Vicksburg. At school we really weren't allowed to talk to one another. Girls and boys sat in different parts of the cafeteria during lunch and we were both a little embarrassed to be caught passing notes back and forth in class. When I was hurt in the explosion, I was so scared about her seeing me in that shape that my dad was forbidden from letting her come see me; instead she sent me a nice little teddy bear that I still have to this day.

After sixth-grade was over, Amber and I broke up. We couldn't really see each other much because we were both dependant on our parent's transportation and they were always busy. It was probably for the best because both of us would be going to different schools for junior high. I was going to the local Catholic school, St. Aloysius and she was going to Vicksburg Junior High. But, before I move on to the next chapter, I must cover in detail one of the most important and significant events in my dad's and my lives, as well as the families.

In December 1994, during my sixth-grade Christmas break, a young attractive twenty-year-old woman accepted a part-time job at Atwood Chevrolet working the switchboard and answering phones. Dad, who was thirty-nine years old at the time, immediately noticed her. This young lady was named Elizabeth Greenlee and had an uncannily resemblance to the actress Sarah Michelle Gellar, who played "Buffy the Vampire Slayer" on television. Because of this, Miss. Greenlee was known to her friends and family as "Buffy", a nickname that has stuck with her. Buffy, although resembling the actress, had bright red hair and pretty green eyes. There was no doubt she was attractive to an older, divorced man like my dad.

The problem was, no matter how attractive she was, by no means was she "marriage" material. Buffy was the most obnoxious, self-centered, uncouth, uneducated, piece of white trash filth to ever crawl out of the trailer park ghetto, and when she caught the eye of my dad she extended the deadly tentacles of lust and latched onto him and wouldn't let go.

Dad had just been divorced, he had several women he was seeing on the side, and he was not about to get married again and wasted no time telling her so. He was just looking for a piece of ass and that was his only intentions when he asked Buffy out on a date.

Of course, I remember from day one, Buffy was nice as pumpkin pie to me. She was willing to do anything and everything with my dad and me. She went hunting with us that winter, she took my friends and me to the movies, and at first I really thought she was a nice person. Neither my dad nor I knew of her secret deviant intentions and past behavior. From the very beginning Buffy told my dad and everyone else that she had a lot of "female problems" and that it was impossible for her to get pregnant. In fact, she went so far as to claim that before she met my dad, she and her last boyfriend had tried repeatedly to get pregnant but it just couldn't happen.

For all of Buffy's faults I have to give her one thing, the woman was cunning. She knew that if she could entrap my dad into getting her pregnant there would be a good chance he would marry her or at the very least she could extort tons of money from him to cover up a bastard child.

By February 1995 Buffy was pregnant and my dad was

going insane.  Our family has a lot of secrets and when my dad, his brothers or his sister do something, Pops will do anything necessary to cover it up.  Having a bastard child in the Atwood family was not and is not acceptable.

Two options were discussed- paying Buffy a large sum of money to keep quiet and disappear, or let my dad marry her very quickly before people realized she was pregnant.  My dad chose the latter.  Very quickly and very quietly, a justice of the peace was summoned to perform the marriage rites.  My dad had wanted a Baptist preacher but because Buffy was antireligious, she wouldn't allow it.  So, in a small private ceremony, void of friends and family, my dad was married to Buffy.  No honeymoon, no decorating the car with shaving cream and empty soup cans, just an official, quick ceremony with no emotion and unfortunately, no pre-nuptial agreement.

I was too young to understand what was going on, and as such, was left out of the conversations.  However, I was able to pick up on some of the incoherent ramblings from my Aunt June and piece together most of the facts.  I didn't really care at the time though because Buffy was always nice to me and I was looking forward to having another baby sister.

Almost literally overnight, Buffy turned on me. She became abusive, yelling and screaming, pushy and offensive in her language to me, but always outside the presence of my dad.  When I tried to talk to my dad about it, she always denied it happened and he began to believe her.  This was the start of a pattern of behavior from Buffy that would continue for the next three years.

By the time sixth grade was over and summer arrived, I'd made the all "A" honor roll.  Buffy was four months pregnant, and I was going have to decide what junior high I was going attend for my seventh and eighth grade years.  South Park was only a kindergarten through sixth-grade school.  There were two junior high schools in the school district: Warren Central and Vicksburg Junior High, both public and both with bad reputations for drugs and violence.  If at all possible, my family wanted to keep me away from there.

# INTO HELL I RODE

Going to a private school was still an option. Vicksburg had two of them, Porters Chapel Academy and St. Aloysius Catholic School. I knew that Porters Chapel had a horrible reputation as an institution of learning and an even worse sports department, but on the other hand, St. Aloysius wasn't a good choice either. I wasn't Catholic first off, second it was known as a "prep" school where the "who's who" of Vicksburg would send their snobby kids and thirdly I seriously doubted whether I would fit in. Unbeknownst to me, without my consultation, and against my better judgment, my father decided for me- St. Aloysius it was.

# CHAPTER FIVE

During the summer between sixth and seventh grade, I spent most of my time attending summer camps. My Papaw and Mamaw in Kosciusko had sent me to a summer camp all of my life called Central Hills Baptist Retreat and I loved it. I was definitely going back that year. There were so many fun things to do. It was a lot like French Camp but lacked the abusive discipline. Central Hills was geared more towards sports and becoming closer to God and Jesus Christ.

It was a week long summer camp, during which time you with a group of boys camped out in tents, made hobby crafts, perfected your skills on the rifle and archery range, rode horses, and played all kinds of different sports- all the while learning about becoming closer to the Lord. At the time, I was almost twelve years old and had not developed the negative feelings toward religion that I have today. To me, summer camp was just another way to spend part of my summer having fun, regardless of the religion being taught.

At the end of the week, there would be a final prayer service where anyone was encouraged to become saved and baptized. Many of my friends, myself included, decided to be saved. It wasn't a real conscious choice; it just seemed like the right thing to do. Of course, my grandparents were very happy and I myself was pleased to see them happy.

There were two other weeklong summer camps that I went to on my break from school. Warner-Tully, which was a boys and girls camp south of Vicksburg, revolved around outdoor sports. We were able to do a lot of canoeing and exploring through the woods. The camp director was a rattlesnake cowboy who promised us a good show if someone was able to find one of the deadly critters.

Living out in the country like I did, you run across snakes fairly often. They're nothing to be scared of, but you must respect the ones that have a poisonous bite. There have been many times that I've caught non-poisonous snakes to keep as pets. Every time, though, I've run across a poisonous one, it usually ended up dead.

While at Warner-Tully, I was looking for one so our camp director could catch it and play around with it. On the next to the last day, I found one. No one else at the camp had been able to locate one. Everyone had looked everywhere, leaving no stone unturned, but no luck. I found mine curled up behind the cabin.

After the director arrived, he caught the rattlesnake, which was a good four feet long (big for rattlesnakes) and showed us its fangs and distinctive patterns on its back. He taught us how to recognize non-poisonous from poisonous by comparing the size of their heads. Poisonous snakes have a triangular head while non-poisonous do not. He took a small stick and placed it under the snake's fangs and showed us how to get venom from the snake. It was all quite interesting and a learning experience.

Our camp counselors also took us on long nature hikes. We learned about compass navigation, edible and non-edible plants, survival skills (I was particularly good at this), how to build fires, and how to hunt and snare wild animals for food. By the time the week was over, I'd learned a lot and was anxious for the next summer so I could come back and do it all over again.

The third and last camp I went to for the summer was Tara Wildlife. Tara Wildlife would later play a bigger part in my life than just a fun summer camp, but that story comes in later chapters. It was about an hour north of Vicksburg. Its summer program revolved around hunting and marksmanship. They taught you gun safety, then took you out to the range and let you shoot high-powered rifles and muzzle-loaders. They would then take you to the skeet range to shoot shotguns.

I don't mean to brag, but I was the best rifle shot, even beating out the instructors. This would be a talent that I would carry with me for a long time and would eventually carry over into handguns. At Tara we also took nature walks, or in this case, nature rides on four-wheelers. Tara had the only bald-eagle colony in Mississippi and it just so happened that it was time for the babies to hatch when we were there. Looking through a pair of binoculars we counted five eagles in all. That's something not everyone in his or her lifetime will be able to see.

We also took boat rides through the cypress swamps looking for alligators. We found a few but they weren't very big. One night we went spotlighting for deer and frog gigging. We were taught how to use a climbing stand for hunting, how to build a duck blind, and how to track wild animals. It was a really fun time and by the time it was over, summer was almost done and I would be starting my new school.

Because St. Aloysius had a dress code of only allowing boys to wear khaki pants and collared polo shirts, I had to update my wardrobe. I was used to wearing jeans and t-shirts to school and an occasional warm-up suit. The public schools had much more to worry with than the way someone was dressed. When they did try to experiment with a dress code, it ended in a disaster. St. Aloysius was a whole other story- pressed pants and shirts were the order of the day with two-piece suits worn on days that the school had Catholic Mass. Of course, I was not Catholic and didn't participate in mass, but that still wasn't an excuse not to dress up. St. Al, as everyone calls it, was unlike any school I had ever attended. I was warned beforehand that it would be different, but I honestly had no idea.

As I said in an earlier chapter, sixth grade and the summer that followed was the best year of my life. After finishing the school year with all A's on my report card, I had started the summer feeling magnificent. My vacations to summer camp had gone great, everyone in the family was getting along very well, Buffy was expecting a baby girl in the fall, and I was looking forward to starting junior high school.

I'd heard stories about St. Al being a stuck-up prep school. None of my friends were very thrilled that I was going. But, I always tried to put a good face on things and make the best of a bad situation. There were several reasons why I went to St Al. First and foremost, and the most important, there were not any African-American students there.

Second, it was the best academic school in the area. As I've said, my dad and most of his family are horrible, racist people and although I'd gone to public school most of my elementary years, my dad was afraid for my safety at the junior high and high schools because of the violence that occurs there. I was too young to argue against this "father-knows-best" mentality. It didn't matter to me who my classmates were- I've always got along with and respected people of other races and cultures, but I didn't have a say in it. My dad wanted me to go to an all-white school, so that is where I went.

I remember my first day and how odd I felt. I had gone to new schools before but never with this "class" of people. My parents were wealthy, we had money, and I had come from an "old-money" family, but we weren't stuck-up snobs by any means. Most of these children at this school were and it was highly irritating.

St. Al is a relatively small school with only about three hundred students in the seventh through twelfth grades. There were only forty in my class. Everybody knew everybody. For some reason I just didn't think I was going to fit in too well here and I didn't.

My first day of school, I received my class schedule. I had history, pre-algebra, science, English, study hall, library, and a very odd class I had never heard of- theology. I knew it had something to do with religion but because I had never gone to a Christian school before, I had never been exposed to religion in the classroom. It was a little odd to say the least, but the teacher seemed to be a really nice lady named Mrs. Cris Patin. Over the next two years she and I would become close friends and I would depend on her heavily for advice and counseling.

I have always loved history. It's been my favorite subject, but I knew from day one that my history teacher was going to be a big bore. Coach Rogillio, whom we called Coach Ro, was a retired military man who was now teaching history at St. Al. To say the least, he was the most boring, unexciting, boorish teacher I've ever had in my life. It's no wonder children hate history so much, with teachers like Coach Ro, everything would be a bore.

I had other teachers too, but none stuck out like Mrs. Patin and Coach Ro. I had played little league baseball and almost decided to try-out for St. Al's team. The baseball coach definitely tried to recruit me, but I just wasn't sure. After thinking about it, I decided not to play- I had way too many other things to do at the time.

My science teacher was Coach Graves and although science wasn't a favorite subject of mine, I liked the class because Coach Graves was pretty easy going and always had some funny jokes to tell- some maybe a little too raunchy for twelve-year-olds, but we liked them anyway. Several years after I had left St. Al, Coach Graves made some sexual jokes towards a junior high student that were just a little too suggestive and was terminated. When I was in school he could have gotten away with things like that, but not in today's world.

The first several months went by very quickly. Before I knew it, Halloween was here. Buffy was expecting to give birth any day and when Meme picked me up from school on Halloween I knew something was up. Everyone was hoping that the baby would be born on October thirty-first. Meme's mother, my great-grandmother, Francis Quinn's birthday was on the thirty-first and it would be great if one of the great-grandchildren could be born on her birthday.

I spent all afternoon and part of the night with the rest of the family at the hospital. Seven minutes after midnight on November 1, 1995, Buffy gave birth to a little girl. We'd missed the deadline by seven minutes and everyone was disappointed.

I took the next day off from school and escorted Buffy and her new baby home from the hospital. My dad had a three-bedroom house and I had to give up my bedroom and move to a smaller room so the baby could have room for all the stuff that babies have to have. I didn't argue though. Several weeks before the baby was born, I quietly, and by myself, moved all of my belongings and furniture into the smaller bedroom. This would be the start of the many such concessions that I would have to give into to keep Buffy happy and my dad's life bitch-free. For the most part though, at this time, Buffy and I were still sort of getting along.

After the baby was born, a lot of things changed and changed quickly. School wasn't going as good as it could have been either. Because I wasn't happy there, my grades began to sink. In return, my dad grounded me. No more four-wheeler, no more horseback riding, no more nothing. This kept me stuck in the house with Buffy every day after school, which, in turn, caused my dad to get bitched at when he got home from work, and it all just made matters a lot worse for everyone as the circle of chaos went round and round.

Things wouldn't get really bad until the following year when I was in the eighth grade, but after Buffy's baby was born things got a lot worse. That Christmas my dad bought me a pellet pistol the he had promised to get me for a long time. I had rifles and shotguns but never a pistol. Buffy raised all kinds of hell about it and it utterly ruined Christmas morning. Buffy had no compassion for anyone but herself and would not think twice about ruining anyone's holiday or anniversary.

The New Year came and went and it was soon spring break. My dad had planned a vacation for us to go to Gatlinburg, Tennessee. I had been there before and had always had a wonderful time and I was really looking forward to going.  Meme was even going to come along with us and after we'd spent a few days in Gatlinburg, we were going to drive over to Gastonia, North Carolina where my great-grandparents lived.

The first part of the vacation went very well.  I was always a good kid to ride on long road trips and never got on anyone's nerves.  But two days after we got there, Buffy and I got into the biggest fight ever.

On the second night we were in Gatlinburg, we all went over to the go-cart racetrack and rented carts to race.  During the race, I swerved in front of Buffy's cart and the left rear fender of my cart caught the front of hers and spun her around, and of course she wasn't hurt.  There were other people spinning their carts out too, but Buffy went ballistic on me. She was screaming and pushing me, calling me names and just acting a total fool in front of dozens of people.  It was totally embarrassing to Meme and my Dad.

No one had ever talked to me the way she had, in private or public.  My dad wasn't taking up for me and Meme didn't know what to say.  I had had enough, I told Buffy that it was an accident and she didn't have to be such a "fucking bitch".  That started another shit storm and for the rest of the vacation she and I did not speak.

Even when we went over to my great-grandparents' house in Gastonia, we still spoke less than ten words to one another. This would be the first time my great-grandparents had met Buffy and seen their new great-grandchild.  They were not impressed. Immediately they thought Buffy was a conniving, gold-digging whore, and they told my dad and Meme just that, in not all too different terms.  If only my dad had listened to everyone back then, he wouldn't have been in that troubling position in the first place.

We finally made it back home and I restarted school.  My grades had improved somewhat but I still wasn't making many friends.  I just didn't fit in with most of those people there, so most of my time was spent by myself or on the library's computer.  The internet was something new and it quickly became one of my favorite pasttimes.

I was so happy when the school year finally ended. It had been a tough year and a lot of things had happened. I had absolutely no plans for the summer. I wanted nothing more than to just sit around my house and do as little as possible, but of course, that lasted all of about two weeks.

Buffy didn't have a job. She wouldn't work. Her excuse was that she needed to stay home and take care of the baby and although she had plenty of time on her hands, she refused to take me anywhere. But she would leave the baby and me with a babysitter while she went and did her own thing. If I wanted to go to the mall or the movie with some friends, she wouldn't take me. She complained that it was too much trouble for her to load the baby in the car and take me to town. So for the first two weeks of my summer vacation, I had to sit at home and watch "Days of our Lives" with Buffy.

It only took a short time before the fights increased and life was completely miserable. I looked for an escape. The summer before, I'd had plenty of summer camps to go to but now I felt I was getting a little too old for that stuff, plus Buffy had told my dad that she thought it was a waste of money for me to go to a summer camp. So, of course, instead of having to listen to Buffy bitch and pout, my dad just said no to summer camp.

Instead of sitting around my house fighting with Buffy, I decided to go spend some time with my Papaw and Mamaw in Kosciusko. I always loved going to their house and it now gave me an excellent excuse to get away from Buffy.

The attention and care that I didn't get at my own house I received at Papaw and Mamaws'. Mamaw cooked all kinds of good food- my favorite being chicken and dumplings. Papaw and I could go fishing everyday if we wanted, I could sleep late and stay up all night. I could have my friends and cousins over to spend the night and I never had to listen to anyone bitching at me. Yes, going to my grandparents' house was the best thing I could do for my summer break. Both sides of my family were from Kosciusko and there were plenty of cousins my age that I could have fun with.

I spent my time hanging out with Pete and Will Atwood, then there was Matthew and David McCool. They are all the grandchildren of my Pop's brother. I had a few friends too; by far, my best friend was Jordan Sims. His dad was a general with the Mississippi Air National Guard where he flew and piloted KC-135 tankers. Jordan only lived about a mile from my Papaw's house, so it was easy to ride four-wheelers and dirt bikes back and forth to each other's home.

Pete, Will, Matthew, and David all lived on several hundred acres of land that had also been in the Atwood family for a long time and they were close enough for Jordan and me to ride our four-wheelers to their houses.

The whole summer was consumed with camping out, fishing, and playing paintball war. Paintball is a sort of war game where the players have guns that shoot out small paint balls with compressed $CO_2$ gas. All my cousins had one and they played all the time. I had some money saved up so I went to Wal-Mart and bought me one too. Although it hurts like hell when one hits you, we had a blast playing.

None of us were old enough to legally drive yet, but that didn't stop us from taking one of their farm trucks and driving around on the town. I'm sure if the cops would have caught us or if Will's parents would have found out, that would have been an end to our summer, but no one discovered us and we continued to have fun.

I had been at Papaw's house for a few weeks when I was introduced to a very nice, good-looking girl named Morgan Bishop. She was a sweet girl and I immediately liked her. Her dad was a Baptist preacher and she came from a very nice family. This was a girl I really thought I'd like to date. Besides Amber English, whom I had dated in sixth grade, Morgan was the only other girl I had an interest in. So, for the next six weeks Morgan and I went out as much as we could. I still hung out with the guys during the week, but on weekends I was usually at Morgan's house. I was having so much fun that time just zoomed by and before I knew it, summer was over and I would have to be going back to Vicksburg.

It was hard saying goodbye to everyone because it had been a great summer. I knew I would be coming back up to spend the weekend with Papaw and Mamaw but I knew that all the fun we had been having was over. I promised to stay in touch with Morgan as much as I could and try to visit as much as possible but it was difficult leaving one another. We really liked each other.

A couple of days before my thirteenth birthday on August thirteenth, my Papaw carried me back to my house in Vicksburg. Had I known that Buffy wasn't going to allow me to have a birthday party, I definitely would have had one with all my friends and cousins in Kosciusko. But, my dad had always given me a big party on my birthdays and I was going to try to honor that tradition.

Like I said before, Buffy was a very cruel person. I think that everyone's birthday is special, especially their $13^{th}$, $16^{th}$, $18^{th}$ and $21^{st}$. I wanted to celebrate becoming a teenager, but when I brought up the subject of having a birthday party, Buffy shot it down. I didn't understand the reasoning behind her logic, but she said I couldn't have a birthday party because *SHE* didn't get to have a birthday party when *SHE* turned thirteen.

I was devastated. How could she have convinced my dad of this bullshit? I had always had a birthday party and gifts. Hell, we even gave Buffy a party when she turned twenty-one. I couldn't figure out how she had convinced him of this. But, as I would later find out, she would make my dad's life such a living hell when she wanted something, that instead of listening to her bitch, he would just give in to her. And so he did. If it had not been for my mother, I wouldn't have had a birthday. This was not the way I wanted to start my eighth grade year.

I didn't want to go back to St. Al after the horrible year I'd just had, but the only other alternative to public schools was Porters Chapel and it didn't have a good reputation. No, I didn't have a choice in the matter; I was going back to St. Al.

I really thought this year might be better, and it was. I had made a few friends and was beginning to get accepted into the different "social" groups. But my home life was turning into a major hell-on-earth.

For the most part I had the same teachers, but I had a new history teacher. Coach Ro was still a teacher of mine except this year he was teaching physical science, another big bore. History would definitely be a little livelier, if that's the word you can use. Coach Jimmy Salmon taught eighth grade history and he was quite eccentric, to say the least. He loved to terrorize his students with a long piece of metal pipe he kept behind his desk. Any indiscretions would cause him to bang that metal pipe on his desk or yours, bringing immediate order to the class.

We were quite afraid of him at first until we all realized he was just a big tenderhearted, nice guy. He would never say an ugly thing to anyone in his life. He quickly became one of my favorite teachers.

I still had Mrs. Patin for theology, and surprisingly enough, my best grades came from her class. I had never studied the Catholic religion but I learned a lot in her class and was one of her best students.

I still spent most of my time in the library on the computer. I had never had a computer at home and everything about one totally intrigued me. I learned everything I could. I asked my dad one time to buy a computer for me and he seriously considered it until Buffy found out and shot that idea down, too. That didn't stop me, though from learning how to type and how computers operated. By the end of eighth grade, I knew more than anyone in that school about computers and the internet. Everyone began coming to me when they needed to know how to do something or research a term paper.

Eighth grade was starting off a lot better than the previous year but things at home were getting worse. Every weekend possible I was going to stay with my mom or my Mamaw and Papaw. Buffy still wasn't working but she refused to pick me up from school, cook any food, or do the laundry.

My dad had to take off work at three o'clock every day, pick me up at school and take me back to the dealership where I had to wait until he got off work at five-thirty before we could go home. All the while Buffy was sitting at home, watching her soap operas and talk shows. Dad and I would have to pick some fast food up on the way home just so we wouldn't starve to death. If we wanted milk or eggs, we had to go to the grocery store and get it ourselves. Buffy refused to do anything and the fights that resulted were destroying my life.

There were so many fights that there's no way I could ever remember them all. The worse fight ended with my dad pulling his pistol and trying to shoot himself in front of Buffy and me. We grabbed his arm at the last second and the bullet went into a wall and through their bedroom where it finally lodged in the bricks. I was so scared and shook-up, I ran from the house all the way down to Meme's, crying uncontrollably, where I told her what had just happened.

Meme knew things were bad. She knew Buffy and my dad fought all the time and that I was caught up in the middle. She knew my dad was drinking alcohol more and more and she had tried talking to him but it did no good- nothing ever did. It had been a long time since my dad had hit me with his fist, not since my mom and he were married had he raised a hand to me but now with these horrible fights and his alcoholism, he became more violent. He never struck Buffy but it got so bad he never thought twice about striking me.

Things were so bad I really thought about running away. I didn't know where I would go but anywhere had to be better than what I was going through. Christmas came and went and things only got worse. My only escape was when I was at school or when I went to my papaw's house in Kosciusko. For the most part I was quiet about what went on at home, but I did tell Papaw and Mamaw and my mother a few things. Some of the stories were so outrageous I don't really think they believed them. But yet again, if I hadn't been living the nightmare every day, I probably wouldn't believe some of the things that were going on in my home either. It was that bad and there was nothing I could do but grin and bear it.

On the weekends that I couldn't get away to my grandparents, I tried to start going to church with my dad's brother and his family. My Uncle Ray had a son my age, Chase, and he and his mom and dad knew what I was going through. They had witnessed Buffy's temper. They knew how she treated my dad and they were very kind to offer to let me spend my Sunday's with them. They came and picked me up Sunday morning, we went to church and then we ate Sunday dinner and I would spend the afternoon with them. It was the little things like this that got me through. I had no one to talk to about these things, so every second I was away from my house was a blessing.

I didn't really feel comfortable talking to my mom. We were still very close and we got along a lot better than Buffy and I, but I realized she and Jerry had their own family and I wasn't exactly sure where I fit into this picture. I didn't feel quite as comfortable when I would stay with them. I know Jerry tried to treat me fairly and he is a good person, but I just didn't fit in well. The only person I really felt like I could talk to was Meme. She lived out there and she saw what horrible things Buffy was doing to the family. She sympathized with what I was going through.

Buffy had, by this time, ruined my dad's relationship with the rest of his family. From day one, Buffy and Aunt June hated each other. The relationship with his sister was the first to go. Then Buffy made up a story about my dad's younger brother, Alan, sexually harassing her. Daddy believed her and Alan and him no longer talked. Then, the relationship ended with my dad's brother because my Uncle Ray was picking me up on Sunday's, taking me to church with his family, and doing other things with me that she nor my dad would do. Buffy was completely isolating my dad from every other person in his life, including me.

My family life was a time bomb waiting to explode. I could only occupy my mind with other things for so long. Things at school were a lot better than they had been the year before. I was playing baseball and involved in several school organizations and once again, I was on the honor roll. But all of this was just a cover to hide the horrible life I was living at home.

Mrs. Patin and I had become close friends and I trusted

her completely.   Although, at first I was reserved telling her about my home life, I soon realized that she was an excellent listener and a very sympathetic person; I unloaded a lot of my troubles on her.  I also tried talking to the school counselor, Mrs. Pierce.  Her husband was Doctor Paul Pierce, the Atwood's family physician and although she offered some excellent advice, nothing came close to the relationship that Mrs. Patin and I shared.  There have been very few people that I could trust totally and Mrs. Patin was one of them.

As the school year end was rapidly approaching, I shared my anxieties about leaving St. Al with Mrs. Patin because she knew I wasn't totally happy there.  I had left South Park my sixth grade year the happiest person in the world only to come to St. Al and start all over again.  I wanted to go back to the public schools where all my friends were, but I knew my father would never allow it.

One weekend in April 1997, several weeks before school was out, I was at my house and I don't remember what I was doing, but I happened to overhear Buffy talking to someone on the phone. Buffy must have thought I wasn't in the house because she was having a very loud conversation with someone in regards to me.   She wasn't trying to hide what she was saying. What I heard shocked me!

Buffy was discussing with someone ways she could get me kicked out of the house and sent away. Whoever she was talking to was in complete agreement with Buffy's plan and even offered several ideas that Buffy might use. One of those ideas was to get Buffy to tell my dad that I had been sexually harassing her. Another was for Buffy to tell my dad that I had threatened her and the baby.

As I sat behind my bedroom door and listened to her and her phone companion talk about how to get rid of me, I became absolutely furious. I had foreseen something like this happening a year or so before when Buffy had really started being mean to me, and making my life a living hell, but I never thought Buffy would actually go to such lengths as making up lies and turning my own father against me.

Later that night I laid in bed thinking of some way that I could circumvent Buffy's plan and warn my dad about it. The more I thought about it, and the more I replayed the events over in my mind, the less I believed that my dad would *believe* me. He always had taken up for Buffy in our fights. He had always taken Buffy's word over mine. And without undeniable proof, he would not believe me when I told him what I had overheard.

The only thing I could think of that might help me was to go to Radio Shack and get a phone recording device and tape all of Buffy's phone conversations. That way, even if she tried to deny it to my dad, she wouldn't be able to and she'd be caught in her own lies.

After purchasing and setting up the recording device, I didn't have to wait long to get some really incriminating evidence. Within the first couple of days, I had enough of Buffy's phone conversations recorded to easily convince my dad of her devious intentions. At one point, on one of the conversations, Buffy made the comment that she wished she could find someone to kill me. When I heard that, I knew immediately that it was time to do something. Since I only had about a week left of the school year, I was determined to get away from my dad's house and Buffy just as soon as it was over.

On the last day of school I had arranged for my dad to meet my Papaw in Canton, Mississippi to drop me off so I could go back to Kosciusko with my papaw. I had made an extra copy of the recordings to take with me, but had left the original in my tape player at home. My plan was to get to my Papaw's house and then call my dad, tell him about the tape, and get him to listen to it. What my plan was going to accomplish, I do not know. Somewhere deep inside me, I had hoped that it would cause my dad to leave Buffy and divorce her.

As soon as I got to Kosciusko I was able to let my Papaw and Mamaw listen to the recording. To say they were shocked would be an understatement- they were downright appalled. I told them that I had left an extra copy of the tape in my stereo system so that my dad would be able to hear it, but they also, were skeptical about whether my dad would do anything about it or not. Regardless of what my dad thought or what he might do, Papaw and Mamaw were determined not to allow me to go back to my dad's house as long as Buffy was living there.

We finally decided to call my dad and tell him about the tape and how he could listen to it. Papaw felt that this was a situation better left for the adults to handle, so he made the call to my dad. Papaw patiently explained why he had called, how I had recorded Buffy's conversations, and where my dad could listen to it.

About two hours later my dad called back but it wasn't with the news I'd hoped. He had listened to the recording but didn't think that anything should be done about it. He explained to my Papaw and me that it was just Buffy acting hysterical during one of her mood swings and that she didn't mean anything by it. More distressing was the fact that my dad wanted me to come back home immediately. Fortunately, Papaw and Mamaw were not budging from their stance that I would never go back to that house as long as Buffy lived there.

After some harsh words back and forth, Papaw finally settled the matter by threatening to take the recordings to the sheriff's office and also to child protective services. While my dad might have felt like he could control the judges and sheriff of Warren County, he didn't want the trouble of having to defend a half-crazed wife. For the time being, I was allowed to stay at papaw's house until other arrangements could be made.

Papaw, Mamaw, and I discussed over the next couple weeks what my options would be. At one point we felt it would be best for me to live with them in Kosciusko, but finally Meme and Aunt June stepped forward and offered to let me live with them back in Vicksburg. Even though I would be going back to the same piece of property where my dad and Buffy lived, we felt it was a better arrangement than me living in Kosciusko.

After another couple of weeks of working out the details, it was settled that at the end of the summer, I would leave Papaw's house and move into the house with Meme and Aunt June.

# CHAPTER SIX

So far, this had been a really screwed up summer. I was stressed, my grandparents were stressed, every day was another crisis of some sorts and I was not happy. I tried to take my mind off things as much as possible and spent a lot of time hanging out with my cousins and other friends there in Kosciusko. Papaw had an old three-wheeler that I would ride back and forth to everyone's house. Kosciusko is such a small place, everywhere can be reached by either walking or riding on an ATV.

All my cousins were around my age and we had a lot in common and had a really good time. They all knew what I was going through with my dad and stepmother; they had heard the tape recordings and they knew I needed something to do to keep my mind off all the bullshit. None of us could drive yet, so most of our activities revolved around either my grandparent's house or their's. Some of us even went to a summer camp for a week down on the Mississippi Gulf Coast. Again like the last summers, time was moving by very quickly.

In addition to hanging out with my cousins all the time, I became friends with a guy whom I will call Daniel. Daniel was from Kosciusko; he was born and raised there. He knew all of my family and I knew most of his. Daniel was slightly older than me and was just a good ole country boy, hard-working and a little rough around the edges but extremely good-looking, with a muscular, toned body. Since the first day I met him I'd had a puppy-love crush on him.

I was a few weeks shy of my fourteenth birthday and I was still very confused about my sexuality. I knew I had unexplainable crushes on guys, but some part of me just couldn't begin to accept it. It was one of those things I dreamed about, but would never think of acting on. But that all changed when I met Daniel. For the first time in my life I had a huge crush on another guy and it was freaking me out.

From the first day we met, Daniel and I became inseparable that summer. We did everything together. I didn't know whether he shared the same feelings for me or not and I didn't care. I was just happy being able to hang out with him every day. He would pick on me a lot and make cute little sexual remarks towards me. I didn't know if he was serious or not, but many times I hoped he was.

One weekend towards the end of the summer his parents left to go out of town and Daniel invited me over to spend the weekend with him. To say the least, I was a little excited. During the past few weeks I had really convinced myself that all the sexual remarks had meaning and that Daniel really wanted to fool around. Maybe "fool around" are the wrong words to use, but I had a good feeling that Daniel wanted to do more than just be friends.

If he did, then this weekend was the perfect opportunity to try something. I was petrified with fright, but I knew if Daniel was serious then this would definitely be something I wanted to experience. As it turns out, I was right.

The first night I stayed with Daniel alone we started

wrestling over the remote control and before I knew what happened we were locked in an embrace, lips joined together and one tongue massaging the other. It was the greatest feeling in my life. In as little as two seconds, I felt as if fourteen years of stress and burden had been lifted from my shoulders. While I was awkward and nervous with girls, this seemed to be the most natural and easiest thing in the world. For once in my life, I was wrapped in total and complete ecstasy.

The rest of the details of that night are Daniel's and mine, never to be shared. But, what blossomed that night was the beginning of a long and cherished friendship that would last for over a decade... but going back to that weekend in August of 1997, I was the happiest person in the world.

I had finally found someone my age that was also gay. I felt relieved I wasn't the only boy in the world going through that agonizing experience, feeling shunned and excluded from "normal" society- feeling like you're at the bottom of a hundred foot well, screaming up to the top. After going through the fight of my life with my dad and Buffy, it was great that there was someone I could finally trust with every little secret of my life and not feel ashamed.

Daniel and I were both virgins. We felt the same pressure and anxiety about being gay. For a long time I felt that I was the only person in the world going through what I was going through, but now Daniel gave me hope that I wasn't the only one and that it wasn't just me that was screwed up.

My only regret was that we didn't become "closer" sooner. With only two weeks left in the summer before I had to go back to Vicksburg, things were strained. We literally spent those last two weeks, down to the minute and seconds with each other. We made big plans for him to come down to my new house and visit as often as possible. He was soon going to be getting his license and would be able to drive down on his own- finally independent of parents for transportation. Those last two weeks went by way too fast, faster than any two weeks in my life.

On my last day in Kosciusko I went around to all my cousins and friends to say goodbye. It had been a bittersweet summer, marred by the fiasco with my Dad and Buffy, but overcome by my new friendship. Friends-with-benefits is what we called it. You couldn't really call it "dating", that didn't sound macho. Best-friends with lots of extra benefits is what I like to call it. Regardless, I was in love and even though I knew we would see each other a lot, it wasn't the same as seeing each other every day.

Daniel and I continued to see each other on a regular basis. After I was locked away in federal prison, Daniel made sure to write letters and I called him at least every two or three weeks. We still have a strong friendship. But, when our summer together was over and he got a job and events in my life unfolded, time became precious and we slowly began seeing less and less of each other. The puppy love that had been so strong that summer eventually subsided into respect and admiration for one another. We still care very much for one another and had I been able to stay in Kosciusko, things might have been different. I came away from the whole experience with a new outlook on life. I didn't hate myself anymore for being who I was. I felt strong, independent and ready to meet my new life awaiting me in Vicksburg.

# CHAPTER SEVEN

I left Kosciusko the day after my fourteenth birthday; it had definitely been an interesting summer. Looking back now, with the gift of hindsight, it seems that I always had my best times while in Kosciusko. Now with the summer over, I was looking at starting a new school, yet again and living in a new place, making new friends, and starting all over again.

I moved into Meme's extra bedroom just down the hall from Aunt June. If you ask her today, Aunt June will swear that she never wanted me to move in with her and Meme, but at that time she was nothing but sympathetic and kind to me. She knew what I had been going through living under the same roof with Buffy. Those first few months Aunt June did everything she could to ensure I was comfortably settled and had everything I needed.

There were still some other matters to be taken care of.

# INTO HELL I RODE

Although Buffy had thrown the majority of my personal items out into her yard where Meme and Aunt June had to go collect them, there were still several things that needed to be gotten from my old house. After Meme talked to Dad about it, everyone thought that the best thing for me to do would be to go down there one day, when no one was home, and collect everything that belonged to me. So that is what I did. Meme and I went down there shortly after I arrived back in Vicksburg. We had several garbage bags that we were going to use to collect the rest of my clothes and personal belongings, but while we were there I decided to make a pass through my dad and Buffy's bedroom to see if any of my stuff was in there.

There was an unspoken rule in my dad's house that I never went into their bedroom while I was living there, but I no longer lived there and I needed to make sure nothing of mine was in it. As I was going through my dad's closet, I found a dry cleaner's hang-up bag; it had been folded up and placed in the bottom of a Tupperware box with loads of clothes piled on top. When I opened it, I was shocked at what I found. It was a white Ku Klux Klan robe, complete with hood and tear drop patch- a symbol that the owner had participated in a lynching.

The discovery hit me like a bolt of lightning. I lost my breath and had to gasp for air. I knew my dad honestly hated gays, whether it's his only son or not, and I knew my dad was a racist pig. He has used racial slur remarks his entire life. I just never thought he could actually be a member of the KKK. Surely this robe had to belong to someone else, or either a plausible explanation existed for its existence.

Thankfully, Meme wasn't looking over my shoulder when I found the thing. She was in another room folding up some of my clothes. Had she been there she probably would have made me put it back where I found it. After what I had been through that summer, I wasn't about to put the KKK robe back in the box and forget about it. No sir, as of right then, that robe was going to be put in a safe place, out of reach from everyone but me.

I quickly hid it in one of my bags and went on about my business, but I wanted to get out of that house as quickly as possible. Meme and I didn't waste any more time looking for my stuff. We had enough as it was and I was getting nervous thinking my dad would show up and know that I had gone through his closet and found his KKK robe. My dad was a violent man. There was no telling what he would do when he found out it was missing and I didn't want to be around when he did.

Several days later, I began to pepper Meme with questions about my dad's past. I was determined to learn if what I suspected was true. Meme gave no indication that she knew anything about my family's connection to the Ku Klux Klan, but it wasn't likely that they would have told her anything about it, had they been. I don't think that's one of the things you tell your wife or mother; then again I could be wrong.

It took over a year for Dad to realize his KKK robe was gone. By that time I had not been anywhere near his house. In fact, the day Meme and I were there to collect my clothes was the last day I stepped foot in that house. I never got blamed for taking it and dad never came out and said exactly what he was missing, but I knew what he meant when he told everyone he had lost a "certain item of clothing that means a lot to me". It would take nearly six years more for me to discover the true sordid history of my family's underworld dealings, and by that time I wanted nothing more to do with any of them.

A lot of things happened in my last month of summer. August was a very important time of year. It is not a time that I will easily forget. There's only so much a person can endure in such a short amount of time. Everyone's heard the phrase, "when it rains, it pours", well that's true. If I thought August was a bad month, more horror was still to come. It was just the end of summer and I hadn't even started school yet- ninth grade would prove to be a test unto itself.

Meme and I had to make a choice as to what school I was going to attend. St. Al was out of the question; I did not want to go back there. I wanted to be around normal people, not stuck up egotistical pricks. We seriously considered me going to Warren Central High School, the public school for the Warren County children.  It was a pretty decent school, but just way too big-nearly five thousand students.

A better choice was Porter's Chapel Academy.  Porters Chapel was a small, private school for white students.  I knew several people who went there.  It wasn't exactly the "Andover of the South" but it would do.  By this time, I was used to starting new schools and although I was a little nervous, it made things easier knowing several of the popular people there and I quickly fit right in.

At the time Porters Chapel's principal was a man named Fred Fuller.  From the first day I met him I knew he and I would have conflicts.  It was just one of those things I could foretell.  Within the first week I learned that no one liked him- teachers included.

History has always been my favorite subject and I looked with anxiety to meeting my new history teacher.  History was the last class of the day and when I walked into the classroom I was relieved to see posters and paintings depicting famous Generals and battles from the Civil War.  Shirley Rush was the teacher, and I knew instantly that she and I were going to become great friends.  I liked anyone who had an appreciation for history, especially southern history dealing with the Civil War.

After class I stayed behind and talked with Mrs. Rush for thirty minutes.  It must have driven Meme crazy waiting for me in the parking lot not knowing what had happened to me on the first day of my new school.  But the friendship that resulted from that thirty-minute conversation would last for a long, long time.

Mrs. Rush was a very elegant lady- smart, friendly and a devout Christian.  She had taught at Porter's Chapel, or PCA as we called it, since the early seventies.  Her husband worked for the U.S. Army Corps of Engineers as an electrical engineer.  Come to find out, they only lived a few miles from me.  Since her childhood, Mrs. Rush had loved everything to do with the history.  She knew her history forward and backwards, and I could sit entranced for hours listening to her lecture about great military leaders and big battles of the Civil War.

The past summer I had gone with my uncle from

Kosciusko, Jimmy Atwood, to a Civil War reenactment in Louisville, Mississippi. Uncle Jimmy owned two original civil war cannons and he travels around the country doing reenactments. The weekend I spent with him at the reenactment was so much fun I knew I wanted to start doing them full-time.

Mrs. Rush knew some people in Vicksburg who did the Civil War reenactments and she introduced them to me. That introduction would start a hobby for me that would last for a very long time. Mrs. Rush also interested me in an organization called the Sons of Confederate Veterans, a historical group whose purpose is to preserve southern history. I became a member of the Sons of Confederate Veterans (SCV) in September 1997 and would remain a member until October 2002, a point at which I realized that most members of that group were not there to preserve southern history, but rather to distort it into racist and prejudiced agendas.

By the middle of September 1997, I was settled into my classes and was becoming very popular. I decided at that time to run for Vice-President of the ninth grade student council. This would be my first taste of politics. I didn't do any fancy speeches or hang posters all over the school. I simply went and talked to every member of my class and asked them for their vote and when they voted, I won! I considered it a joy and a privilege to represent the freshman class. My duties for the year entailed doing absolutely nothing. Responsibility didn't come with the job- that didn't come until eleventh and twelfth grade- but for the time being, I was content with the title.

Now things were going pretty well. I was happy living with Meme and my half-crazy aunt. We got along well and probably for the first time in my life I didn't dread coming home from school every day. Meme carried and picked me up from school, she fixed my breakfast and supper and I ate lunch at school. I always had clean clothes and I didn't have to worry about getting bitched out when I did something wrong.

It was quite a change from the days of living with my dad and Buffy. In return for these wonderful things Meme did for me, I always cut the grass, weeded and trimmed the flower beds and hedges every week and kept the property looking clean and orderly. I kept my room clean, did my homework and studied hard in school. Finally, I had some stability in my life, but then that changed again when my great-grandmother in North Carolina had a stroke and the world, as I knew it, stopped.

The year before, in September 2006, my great-grandfather, Roscoe Quinn passed away from a massive heart attack. My Meme's father had lived to be eighty-eight years old. Since then, my great-grandmother, whom I called "Grandmamma", had lived by herself, taking care of her own needs, free of any outside help. She had been in picture-perfect health. She was eighty-nine years old, never suffered from a major illness and had never had major surgery. No doubt she was lonely and depressed after the loss of her husband but no one expected her health to deteriorate so quickly.

At the end of September, I was sitting in my room watching television when Meme knocked on my door and walked in, her face was ashen white. I knew something bad had happened. Before she could get the words out, she collapsed in my arms, her eyes full of tears. Between my own panic at not knowing what happened and her pitiful cries, I was able to find out what was wrong.

Grandmama had been found by her sister, Grace, earlier that morning, confused, upset and with slurred speech. Grandmama had been rushed to the hospital where the medical team diagnosed her condition as a stroke.

Meme and I quickly pulled ourselves together and sat down on the couch to decide what we were going to do. We knew that Meme had to get to North Carolina as soon as possible. After spending several more minutes reassuring Meme that it might not be as bad as we thought, I sent her to her phone to start trying to get plane tickets for her and Aunt June to fly out the next morning. I used my phone to get the number to the hospital and started calling to see if I could get in touch with someone who could give me some more news on my Grandmama's condition.

I was able to reach the hospital and they put me through

to Grandmama's intensive care unit. The nurses were all friendly and assured me that my great-grandmother was ok, although she had had a minor stroke. They even let me talk to her. By her voice on the phone I could definitely tell she wasn't herself, but what was important to me was that she recognized my voice and responded to all my questions. I promised her that Meme was on the way up there as soon as she could get a flight, and then I handed the phone to Meme and let them talk.

Meme and Aunt June left the next morning on the earliest flight to Gastonia, NC and I went to stay with Pops and his wife, Camille. I kept in touch with Meme every day. At first, the stroke didn't look to be as bad as we assumed, but then Grandmama suffered numerous mini-strokes, which made her condition worse. After two weeks in the hospital, they sent Grandmama home.

Aunt June flew back to Vicksburg while Meme stayed in North Carolina. It was decided that they would have to eventually bring Grandmama back to our house. Meme and Grandmama stayed in North Carolina for another few weeks and by the time they made it down to Vicksburg, I had moved out of my bedroom and into the sun room of the house.

Aunt June had driven up to North Carolina and picked Meme and Grandmama up and brought both of them back to Vicksburg. This would be the first time seeing my great-grandmother after her stroke and I was a little scared and nervous.

Meme, Aunt June and Grandmama arrived home late at night, but I was there at the door waiting. Grandmama looked the same to me and it was great that she recognized who I was, but the stroke had caused her a lot of damage and it was very sad seeing her in that condition. Never again would she be able to depend on herself; from now on she was dependent on Meme, Aunt June and me for all her needs. It was going to be a tough job- caring for a loved one after this sort of thing always is.

This was the start of a very troubling time. Not only did Meme have to raise her fourteen-year-old grandson, but she also had to care for her eighty-nine year old mother. At first things weren't so bad. Grandmama could eat by herself, use the bathroom without any assistance and was generally pretty much like she was before her stroke. Every now and then she would forget where she was or who she was talking to. We didn't know it at the time, but Grandmama was in the early stages of Alzheimer's disease. The stroke only aggravated an already existing condition.

# CHAPTER EIGHT

Things were changing fast. As I mentioned earlier, I had become interested in Civil War reenactments. I met a few guys who participated in them and they invited me to attend one on the Mississippi Gulf Coast at Confederate President, Jefferson Davis's home, Beauvoir, which is French for "Beautiful View". To say the least it was a very beautiful place. Anyone who has ever been to Beauvoir will know what I am talking about. The house is right on the beach and the grounds have lavish rose gardens and other botanical plants. There's a lagoon that runs through the middle of the property and it's filled with ducks and geese. It was a wonderful place to have a reenactment.

Because Meme was busy taking care of Grandmama, my mother offered to take me down there and drop me off with the guys who had invited me there in the first place. I had a little money in my pocket and planned to buy a civil war uniform and some other gear that I would need to participate in the battles. Mrs. Rush had let me borrow one of her reproduction civil war rifles to shoot.

For anyone who doesn't know what a civil war reenactment is or has never seen one, they are quite interesting. The whole purpose of one is to preserve the memory of civil war battles and give today's modern society a glimpse at how wars were fought and how men lived during those times. I'm not quite sure why this is appealing to some people. I guess men just never grow out of that toy-soldier phase. But however you look at them, I think they are fun and a learning experience.

This being my first reenactment, I didn't do much. I laid behind an earthen wall and shot blank black-powder rounds at oncoming enemy soldiers. That was fun, but what I liked best about the whole event was the ball dance they had Saturday night. I had never been exposed to hardly any type of dancing except those few that I went to when I was at St. Al. I could hardly call that dancing though; a girl and boy trying to grind their hips together in-sync with the rhythm of the music. It definitely wasn't anything close to what I was witnessing at the reenactment at Beauvoir.

I learned to do the grand march, patty-cake polka, Virginia reel, Carolina promenade, and the military two-step. I was a natural and loved it. I quickly learned all the dances and was begging for more when the night ended. The music was great, too. The band was the 12th Louisiana and they were really good. I really thought I would like this civil war reenactment stuff.

It had been a great weekend. It was the first time since Grandmama had come to live with us that I had left for more than one night. We were adjusting pretty well considering the circumstances. Aunt June expressed her displeasure, but she always had something to complain about.

Things quickly deteriorated, though, at the end of November. Aunt June was becoming more agitated at having to live in a house with three other people; she had always been a loner- content to spend her time alone, in her room, away from everyone else. Now with Grandmama and me living there, her world, and ours for that matter, had changed.

Our house was plenty big; it wasn't like we had to make pallets on the floor for people to sleep. Meme did everything she could to make sure everyone was comfortable. Meme is a very strong woman; she had a lot to deal with. Grandmama required constant attention and care. If you ask me, I think Aunt June became jealous because for the first time in her life, she was coming in second.

Meme had always taken care of Aunt June all these years. Aunt June had become dependent on Meme for everything- food, clean clothes, medicine, alcohol, and everything else. For once, she had to fend for herself and she didn't like it. Pretty soon, Meme and Aunt June were arguing. Then I'd get involved and then everyone would be mad. It wasn't very fun times.

I tried to help out as much as I could. Every day when I came home from school I spent several hours with Grandmama so Meme could take a break and do what she needed to do. Aunt June never helped do anything and a lot of times only made things harder on Meme and me.

My dad and his brothers never stopped by to visit with their grandmother and they never offered to help in any way. They said that they didn't want to remember their grandmother in that way. Meme and I were stuck. Meme felt the rejection by her own kids. In a way the rejection surprised her, but in a way it didn't. Her children had always been so self-involved in their own lives that nothing came before their interests and money. It was a pitiful thing.

By the end of November, Aunt June had decided to move out of the house and into an apartment complex several miles down the road. I wasn't part of her decision to do this- no one even involved me in this conversation. I came home from school one day and Aunt June had a moving crew at the house moving all of her furniture and personal effects out. I was sort of surprised. I didn't think things were too bad, but then again I had not been privy to the private conversations shared between Meme and Aunt June. They came to a mutual understanding that things would probably be better if the house wasn't so crowded. So as it was, Aunt June moved out of Meme's house in November 1997, ending nearly fifteen years of dependency on her mother for housing and care.

Recently, I have asked Meme whether she felt relief at finally getting Aunt June to move out of her house. Unequivocally, her answer was YES!!!

Aunt June and I always had gotten along, though there were times that we grated each other's nerves, but as a whole we got along fairly well. But, that also was changing. After moving out of Meme's house, our relationship suffered. Aunt June continuously isolated herself from the rest of the family. She refused to come to family gatherings or come over to dinner when invited by Meme and me. It was very unfortunate because if there was any time that Meme and I needed family, it was then.

Christmas of 1997 was a strange time. Every year the whole family got together Christmas morning at Meme's house and opened gifts, but not this year. Only Uncle Alan and his wife and three kids came over. My dad and Buffy were nowhere to be seen- they didn't celebrate Christmas very much anyway. Aunt June was in one of her depressed states and refused to leave her new apartment and Meme's other son, Ray, didn't bring his family by either. Instead, Meme, Grandmama and I spent our holiday together and for the first time in a long time, we were all very happy together. It didn't matter about all the things that had happened in the past year. It was Christmas and we were supposed to be happy.

After the holidays were over, a very peculiar thing occurred- our phone was entirely too quiet. Family didn't call anymore; no one stopped by the house. Their excuse was that they couldn't handle seeing Grandmama in that condition, and that that's not the way they wanted to remember her. But, in reality, Grandmama was the same person she had always been. Meme and I took care of her everyday and although she was sick, she was the same great person I remember from my childhood. Nothing had changed. My family was just too big of assholes to take a few minutes out of their day to stop and call their mother to check on how everyone was doing. Do I blame them? Hell yeah, I blame them! Is there, or was there anything I could do about it? Nope…so why bother?

The year 1998 rang in with a new promise of hope. So many things had changed since the year before. I was hoping this year would turn out better.

A few months before, I had joined a reenactment unit and had attended several events with them. The name of the unit was the 1st Arkansas Mounted Cavalry, led by Johnny Hutto. There were several members that I should mention. The first, of course, was the Captain, Johnny Hutto, his wife Sharon, and the executive officer, Sam Reyna. Johnny and Sharon Hutto were both veterinarians from Little Rock, AR. Sam Reyna was a high school principal from Helena, AR. Another member of our group that I became good friends with was Larry Dixon from Olive Branch, MS.

With these guys, I began traveling all over the south going to civil war reenactments. Most of the time, I had to borrow equipment from someone to use. I hadn't quite bought everything I would need. Sharon and Johnny loaned me one of their horses numerous times. Reenacting was definitely going to be a hobby that I was going to like and stick with.

After the New Year, Meme and I started talking about buying me my own horse to use in the reenactments. Up until that time, when I had wanted to go horseback riding, I would use one of Aunt June's horses that we kept out at the house, but there was no way she was going to let me use one of her horses in a civil war reenactment. Hell, you couldn't even shoot around one of her horses without getting it spooked. It was time I got my own horse.

I searched the local newspaper looking at the classifieds hoping to find the right horse. Eventually I did, and several weeks after the first of the year I had a new horse to start taking to the reenactments. First though, I had to train it to be used to the gunfire.

The first horse that I could truly call my own was an eight-year-old quarter horse gelding whom I called Cody.

Thankfully he was a pretty laid back animal. He didn't spook easy, which was a good thing because I would be doing a lot of gun shooting around him. It would be another couple of months before I could get him to a reenactment, but in the meantime I spent many hours riding around our property.

Meanwhile, things at school were becoming interesting. I had had my first gay experience the previous summer. I didn't regret it, nor did I feel like it would be something that I wouldn't want to do in the future. I was still a little confused about it all though. A part of me still wanted to get married and have children one day. I still wanted to date women, but I just wasn't sexually attracted to them.

There were a few girls at Porters Chapel that I had an eye on. For a while I flirted around with a cute blonde named K. K. Willis, although the relationship never went anywhere. Another girl, Kala White, and I hung out often but there just never was any physical attraction there. I felt more pressured than anything to have a girlfriend, so for a while I pretended.

Mrs. Rush and I were still doing things together, although after talking and listening to her regular sermons on being a devout Christian and turning away from the lustful sins of desire, I thought it best not to share any of my private thoughts with her. I seriously doubted my right-wing conservative history teacher would accept it any more than my dad or anyone else in my family for that matter. I missed talking to Daniel and I desperately wanted someone who I could reach out and talk with about these things. As I would later learn, it's very, very hard to find anyone to talk to about growing up gay in Mississippi.

For the time being I was contented with talking about the civil war and going on artifact digs with Mrs. Rush. Her history and geography classes were quickly becoming my favorite subjects. Although I didn't always make the highest grade in her class, I was by far the best student.

In March of 1998 two of my good friends from Porters Chapel, Jackie Evans and Sheryl Walker, were involved in a horrible rollover car crash. Sheryl lost her arm at the shoulder and Jackie suffered severe spinal injuries. Both girls' lives would be forever and completely changed.

Back in October I'd taken Jackie to homecoming as my date. Sheryl and Jackie both were two very sweet, kind and compassionate people. That accident couldn't have happened to any better people. If ever there was a warning about not drinking and driving, this would have been it.

It's been several years since I have seen either of the girls, but from what I hear, since the accident, neither girl has been able to cope well and both have resorted to more alcohol and drugs. I made a promise to myself that when I started driving, I would never drink and drive, nor would I ever ride in a vehicle with someone who had. It would be a personal mandate that I would adhere to for the rest of my life.

The last few months of my ninth-grade year were marked with another tragedy, although not as severe as Jackie's and Sheryl's car accident, but yet, not without its own serious consequences.

Earlier in the chapter I wrote shortly on Porters Chapel's principal, Fred Fuller. Mr. Fuller and I, as I said earlier, never really saw eye-to-eye from the beginning. A lot of people resented his rude, brash style of management, none more so than I. To put it plainly, Fred Fuller was an obnoxious asshole that had no more business being a principal of a school than he had flying to the moon. He was rude, crass and for lack of a better word, just a downright dickhead. No one liked him. He and I had locked horns earlier in the year over a form of punishment he chose to inflict on students serving after-school detention.

The school had two large dumpsters where all of the trash was thrown, including leftover food items and grease from the cafeteria. Mr. Fuller made the students serving punishment go down behind the dumpsters and pick up trash and other biological waste that had fallen out of the dumpsters. Not only was this an already nasty and potentially dangerous punishment, Mr. Fuller refused to give any of the student's protective eye, face or hand wear. For someone who was just beginning to realize the benefits of passive resistance as a method to fight tyrants, this just was not going to do.

I don't remember what I did, but I did something wrong, probably just a minor infraction of the rules, in order to get after-school detention. My plan was to refuse Mr. Fuller's order to pick up biological waste and see how far he was willing to push something he knew he had no authority to enforce. This would be my first test of strength against such tyranny. I had the backing of the entire student body and for the most part, the silent encouragement of the faculty. There would be a show-down after school.

I didn't pick up trash that day or the next; in fact I was suspended for one whole day, a sweet price to pay to make a very important point. I had the last laugh though. I appealed my suspension to the school board and had it overturned. The school board agreed with me that Mr. Fuller went beyond his authority. Not only that, after filing a complaint with the Mississippi Department of Environmental Quality (DEQ), Mr. Fuller was given sixty days to have the waste area around the dumpsters professionally cleaned without any assistance from the student body. To say the least, I had won my first victory against the "system" and I had earned immense respect from my fellow classmates. I was the man-of-the-hour.

It was no secret at Porters Chapel that Mr. Fuller and Mrs. Rush didn't get along. Mrs. Rush had been teaching at PCA for over twenty years; Fred Fuller, less than one. Mrs. Rush was into history and the civil war. Fred Fuller was born in the north, and a transplanted Yankee who understood next to nothing about these things. A confrontation was in the making.

It finally came about over a poster in Mrs. Rush's classroom that depicted three Confederate Generals: Robert E. Lee, Thomas "Stonewall" Jackson, and Jeb Stuart. Mr. Fuller claimed the poster was racist. Mrs. Rush insisted it was just a part of history, after all, she also had posters of northern Generals as well, like Grant and Sherman- definitely not heroes to anyone living in the south, but part of history nonetheless. But, that wasn't the point; Fred Fuller was just looking for an excuse to terminate Mrs. Rush's employment. The poster and Mrs. Rush's refusal to remove it was the excuse.

Mr. Fuller did this less than two months before the end of the school year. I was the first to know. Mrs. Rush and I had become very close. She had been my all-time favorite teacher. She was very popular at PCA and if Fred Fuller thought for one moment that the students of PCA were just going to stand by and let him do this to one of the best teachers there, he was out of his mind.

Acting in my capacity as vice-president of the ninth grade student council, I immediately convened the entire class and shared my thoughts with them on what could be done. Whatever it was that we were going to do, we would have to act soon. Time was running out.

Every single boy student was in agreement that it was wrong for Mrs. Rush to be fired. Not only had Mr. Fuller told Mrs. Rush that she couldn't hang up a confederate poster in her room, he had also tried to enforce a rule that no one could wear any t-shirts that displayed the confederate flag.

Lately the confederate flag has gotten a bad reputation for things that it might or might not stand for. That is a matter of personal opinion, but what shouldn't be part of the argument is trying to tell one person or another, what they can and cannot wear. After all, this is still America and we have a protected right to freedom of expression, none more so than in the south, especially in Mississippi when it comes to all things dealing with the former southern confederacy. There was just no possible way Fred Fuller was ever going to be able to enforce that kind of dress code on the country backwoods southern boys and girls who went to school at PCA.

Deer hunting, mud-trucks, and confederate flags are a part of life down here and by trying to pass such a rule, he did nothing but alienate the entire student body. Although I agreed in principle with Mr. Fuller on what the confederate emblem stood for, I believed that a person, more importantly, had the right to wear what they saw fit. By the end of the year everyone was sick of Fred Fuller and was willing to do anything to get rid of him. Firing Mrs. Rush was the last straw in many people's books.

After speaking with many of the students in the grades

above me, I realized that having a petition drive was the most effective method of preserving Mrs. Rush's employment. In less than a week, we had every single student's signature, minus a couple of students whose parents were personal friends of Fred Fuller's. Out of three hundred fifty-two high school students, three hundred forty-eight signed our petition requesting that Mrs. Rush be reinstated and that Fred Fuller be terminated from his position as principal at PCA. It was a remarkable success.

Never in the history of PCA had this happened. We were confident of our ultimate success. Several days later I personally delivered copies of our petition to the school board members. They promised to take the petition under consideration and inform us within thirty days of their decision. Everyone was excited by the possible outcome. I was certain that Mrs. Rush would be reinstated and Fred Fuller would be the one to be fired.

About a week before the school board was set to make a decision, Mrs. Rush called me on the phone to tell me that she had been offered a job as a college professor at the local community college. She wasn't sure whether she was going to accept the position or not. I was devastated at this prospect. After all the hard work we had done to try and save her employment at PCA and now she was considering going to teach at another school. One part of me could sympathize, the other was being selfish.

After all, Mrs. Rush had spent a good part of her life dedicated to PCA. It hurt that after all the time and effort she put into the school that it could so easily turn its back on her. I could understand, but we'd just have to sit and wait and see what the school board was going to do. Mrs. Rush promised not to make a decision until after the school board had ruled on the petition.

The school board did make a decision, although it was only half of what we wanted. They could not agree whether to renew Mrs. Rush's contract, but they all agreed unanimously that Fred Fuller should no longer remain as the principal at PCA, and so, two weeks before school restarted, Fred Fuller was fired.

It wasn't exactly what we were looking for. I, along with the entire student body, had hoped Mrs. Rush would come back to the school to finish out her career teaching there, but sometimes things don't work out that way. It's funny how things seem to have a way of working out. It ended up being better for Mrs. Rush taking the job at Hinds Community College. It gave her an opportunity not only to improve her own educational background, but to instruct on a deeper, more intellectual level.

Ninth-grade had been another killer year. So much had happened yet I had so little to show for it. I had cut my teeth in the political arena. I had proven to myself and to others that I could be an effective leader. In two months, I organized the entire student body of the school and effectively lead those students toward a common goal. We didn't get exactly what we wanted, but we got more than what we would have gotten had we sat on our asses and done nothing.

Things had changed though. For one, I was getting older. I was beginning to think long-term. What did I want to do with my life? Where did I want to go to college? What should I study? These questions were very heavy on my mind as I started the summer. In a little more than a few weeks, I would be old enough to get my driver's license, which brought on a whole new set of rules and responsibilities.

Ninth grade had taught me to always question the purpose of certain rules. What goal did that rule intend? What were its limitations? Who benefits from that rule? Who is harmed by that rule and should it even exist at all? These are all very important things that I had begun to think about.

My stepdad was a lawyer; I was intrigued at the power he wielded. Jerry was a very smart person who cared deeply about his clients. Being a lawyer was something I seriously thought about. I loved to argue and fight for the injustices I perceived. I don't think I ever made a conscious decision to become a lawyer; I think I just realized that if I ever was to get anyone to listen to me, I'd have to become a lawyer.

Unfortunately, later in my life I would become much more involved in the legal system than I had ever wanted. After my incarceration in federal prison, I lost all respect for the law. I was wrongly convicted for a charge I didn't commit. I saw how lawyers manipulated and twisted laws for their personal benefit. Judges legislated their personal agendas from the bench, and God have mercy on the poor soul who happens to be the one made an example of. The law today is corrupt and unfair. I didn't know then what I know today. I was naïve and gullible. A mistake I would make over and over again in my life, but one I was quickly learning from.

# CHAPTER NINE

I had never had a summer job before. Most of my summers had been filled with playtime and sleeping late in the mornings. This would be the first summer that I would hold a full-time job. The Vicksburg National Military Park hires several high school students every year to act as tour guides, volunteers, and participate in live-fire demonstrations of civil war artillery and small arms.

Much like the reenactments, we dressed in hot, heavy wool uniforms and several times a day we would demonstrate the loading and firing of a real civil war cannon and other small-arm rifles. It wasn't exactly hard work, but again it wasn't necessarily comfortable either. Summers in Mississippi can reach temperatures of over a hundred degrees and this was definitely one of those summers.

I had wanted to go back and spend the summer with my

grandparents in Kosciusko, but two things changed my mind from doing so. First was the fact that I couldn't leave Meme and Grandmama alone for very long. Meme depended on my help more than she depended on anyone else and I had to be close at all times.

Second, one of the main reasons I had wanted to go to Kosciusko in the first place was so that I could spend time with Daniel. He and I had seen each other several times during the past year, but we were really looking forward to spending another amazing summer together.

Instead and unfortunately, he was going to spend his summer in Colorado with his dad working on a horse and cattle ranch. Daniel would be gone all summer so there was no point in me going to Kosciusko and spending all my time up there. I was going to spend a couple days each month visiting Papaw and Mamaw, but now that I was working full-time, as my cousins were, it was harder and harder to find time to do all the fun things we had done the summers before. Growing pains is what you might call them- getting older brings on more responsibility.

I did have one big trip planned. On July 3, 4 and 5, 1998, the city of Gettysburg, PA was hosting the largest civil war reenactment ever to be held in the world in commemoration of the 135th anniversary of the battle of Gettysburg. Over thirty thousand reenactors from around the world were planning on going. It was not something I was going to miss. Several people from my reenactment group were going up there. There would be no problem hitching a ride with them. This would be the furthest from home I had ever been.

The anticipation was so exciting. Never had this many reenactors come together to recreate a battle from antiquity. Everything would be full-scale, meaning that there would be the same number of reenactors participating in the battles, as had been actual numbers of troops engaged in the real conflict. This was definitely going to be a once-in-a-lifetime thing and I wasn't about to miss it.

We were to be gone for a whole week. It would be one of the most satisfying experiences of my life. Not only would I participate in the largest recreation of a civil war battle, I would be participating in recreating the most important one. Anyone who knows anything about history knows that the battle of Gettysburg was the "high-water" mark of the Confederacy. The three-day battle claimed more than fifty thousand lives, the single most costly battle in the entire war. Regiments, brigades and whole divisions were virtually destroyed and decimated.

Confederate general, George Pickett, led his fifteen thousand man division in a huge bayonet charge on the third day in an attempt to shatter the center of the Union line, only to have eighty percent of his division killed or wounded. It was a horribly tragic day. My great-great grandfather had been at Gettysburg. He had made a charge the second day of the battle that cost his brigade their commander and over half of their men.

As I stood on the very spot that my great-great grandfather's regiment had been placed on that epic day, I looked out across the vast fields of wheat and grass and gazed at the peach orchard in the corner of the field which signified the furthest point the 21st Mississippi had been able to penetrate before being beaten back by enemy fire. I pondered a moment what it must have been like that day.

I slowly made my way through the tall grass towards the peach orchard and as I reflected, I realized that the men who made this charge and the ones opposing them, believed in more than just the politics of their respective governments; they believed in something deeper than themselves. No matter how much we study the politics of the American Civil War, we will never be able to grasp what exactly was the cause that made millions of men volunteer to fight.

After coming back from the reenactment at Gettysburg, things started moving very quickly. I would soon be turning fifteen years old, the legal age to drive in Mississippi at the time. School would be starting back soon also. I planned on running for sophomore student council president that year. I was looking forward to meeting the new principal, whoever that might be.

I hoped that the school board members would have the common sense this time not to pick a total idiot. Mrs. Rush had been my favorite teacher and I was looking with skepticism at who might replace her. No one, in my opinion, would ever be able to replace her teaching skills, wonderful personality and in-depth knowledge of history. Things would definitely be different without her.

On August 13th my mom came and picked me up and we went to the driver's license station and got my thirty-day permit. Using my permit, I could drive a vehicle as long as there was another licensed driver in the car over the age of twenty-one. I was so excited- this being the first step toward getting a real license.

Meme and I had talked about getting a vehicle. We knew it would have to be a truck. We just hadn't decided on what to get yet. All of my friends drove trucks and I would definitely need one if I was going to start traveling to reenactments and carrying my horses by myself. Meme and I finally decided to put it off until after I got my real license.

A couple of days after I got my permit, I started back to school. The first thing I did was introduce myself to the new principal. My first impression of the guy was mediocre. Carmichael was the guy's last name and he was young and looked totally helpless. His wife had also gotten a job at the school teaching science classes. Both of them had taught school before, but Mr. Carmichael had never been a principal. He was going to get an education.

Apparently, Mr. Carmichael had heard about everything that happened the year before with Fred Fuller. He was well aware of the petition drive I had organized, my complaint to the Department of Environmental Quality and the fight over the garbage waste cleanup, the efforts to save Mrs. Rush's employment and the ultimate success of my efforts at having Fred Fuller fired. I don't think Mr. Carmichael really knew how to handle me.

On the one hand, he didn't want to piss me off; on the second, he didn't want me thinking I could just run all over him. I was more worried about whether he would try to pressure his personal views on the student body. After a long conversation he assured me he had no plans to try and dictate what the students could and could not wear.

As it turns out, Mr. Carmichael was more liberal in his views than I initially gave him credit for. He wasn't a strict hard ass; he had a fairly decent sense of humor, and he wasn't afraid to get down on our level sometimes at the pep rallies and football games. He really seemed to be an alright guy, but he only lasted two years at PCA before he was fired and replaced. PCA would go through five or six different principals in less than ten years, would almost go bankrupt, and would almost have several federal discrimination lawsuits filed against it for trying to deny admission to black students.

Like I said in the beginning of this book, Porters Chapel Academy was a racist, white supremacist school. It was founded during the civil rights movement for the sole purpose of providing an education to white students who didn't want to go to school with African-Americans. It still has that racist mentality today.

In my ninth-grade, when Fred Fuller was still the principal, he allowed an African-American student to enroll in the high school. That black student lasted less than two weeks before he was run off. His name was Anthony and while he was at PCA he was ridiculed, made fun of, and called "nigger" on a regular basis. The teachers did nothing to stop it and some even encouraged it.

I was one of the only people who would stop and speak to him on a daily basis, even when hardly anyone else would. I was berated for doing it, but when I believe strongly in something, nothing can change my mind. I remember the hate and prejudice my own father preached when I was a child. It always made me cringe in disgust. I had promised myself a long time ago that I would never be like my father and when no one else would stand up for Anthony, I did.

Nothing I could say or do could stop the hate that permeated from that school and eventually Anthony couldn't handle it anymore either. Even though he was a smart, extremely gifted individual who came from a good home with wealthy parents, the white kids wouldn't give him a chance and so he was forced to leave.

As I said earlier, the sheriff of Warren County and Vicksburg, Martin Pace, went to school all his life and graduated from PCA. To hear him today talk about what a great school it was and how much he misses going there, always reminds me of the school's racist past and what those students did to Anthony back in ninth-grade. The thoughts make me sick.

Several more African-American students tried to enroll at PCA but were literally turned away at the door. I think several either threatened to file or actually did file discrimination lawsuits against the school. As a result PCA admitted one or two "token" black students in an attempt to satisfy a federal judge. By no means has the ideological hate that's been part of PCA for so long changed. It's still there and will always be there.

Most of my friends at PCA knew I was very liberal in my thinking, especially on issues like civil rights, but on other political issues I had some republican views. Most of the Atwood family is republican, so I grew up surrounded by it and didn't know any better.

For example, at the time I believed in conservative Christian values. I didn't believe in abortion. I thought we should have a large and strong military. I believed in the death penalty, and thought negatively about social programs. Maybe liberal is the wrong word to use, but I definitely did not believe in government interference in the private lives of its citizens. After I was arrested on false terrorism charges by the FBI, I had to totally rethink my views on politics.

At the start of my tenth-grade year, the Monica Lewinsky scandal was gripping the nation. I remember everything being practically frozen with indecision about a seemingly simple thing. Although at the time I wasn't a very big fan of President Clinton, I remember thinking, "My God, what is the big deal about?" Who cares whether the man likes to flirt around with other women besides his wife? It's not like almost every republican congressman and senator aren't getting some private sex on the side, that they wouldn't want the world to know about, and those that aren't getting any is because they're either too damn ugly to attract women or can't get their dicks up if they could. Sex is a part of everyday life and everyone is doing it, or at least everyone wants to be doing it. Get over it and move on.

Tenth-grade was the year that I really began to consider a career in politics. I definitely had the passion for it. I had the oratory skills, and I believed strongly for those things that I thought were right and wrong. When I ran for president of the sophomore student council, I was confident it would be the start of a long political career. When it came time to vote there was no doubt that I would win- no one ran against me. The entire student body of the sophomore class, all forty of them, wanted me in as president. They knew I was willing to be the "lightening rod" for the things that needed to be accomplished. As it turned out, my tenth-grade year would turn out to be rather uneventful and would pass fairly quickly.

Thirty-days after my fifteenth birthday, I went back to the driver's license station and got my real license. I think this is one of the most important events in a teenager's life- finally having the freedom of driving a vehicle. It was important to me, but I didn't exactly have anything to drive, just yet.

The next day Meme picked me up from school and we went to Atwood Chevrolet. As we pulled into the parking lot, I asked Meme why we were there. It wasn't exactly normal going to Atwood Chevrolet after I got out of school. I was kind of expecting Meme and me to do some shopping for a truck but never did I expect her to tell me to get out of the car and go pick out any truck that I wanted. I had to catch my breath for a minute and then ask again if I had heard her right. Yes, I had. We were here to get me any truck I wanted.

I got out of the car and walked up and down the rows of Chevrolet trucks that were on display in the parking lot. I looked at the ones with leather, CD players, four-wheel-drive, and so on. I finally chose a 1998 Chevrolet Z71 4x4. It was maroon in color and had a CD and cassette player, cloth seats and a few other little extras. It wasn't the nicest truck on the lot but it also wasn't the worst. Everyone at the time was driving either a white or green Z71 pick-up truck, but I wanted one that was different.

When Meme had told my dad that she was going to buy me a new truck he went ballistic. He didn't believe I should be driving anything until I got older. It didn't matter to him that I was a burden on Meme and Grandmama by having to be hauled around all the time. Grandmama had been with us now for almost a year and her Alzheimer's disease had only become worse. It took a lot of work for Meme and me to get her up and ready every day. Plus Grandmama didn't like taking long rides in the car and Meme couldn't leave her there by herself.

Meme needed me to have something to drive so it could free her up from having to worry with taking me to school every day and all the other important things that went along with raising a teenager. But, no one understood that, especially my dad. They didn't realize what Meme and I went through trying to take care of Grandmamma- it was a twenty-four hour a day job. They never came by the house, visited, or offered Meme any help; as far as they were concerned we didn't exist anymore.

That's why Meme didn't worry too much about getting me a new truck. She felt it wasn't any of her kids' business what she did with her money. They didn't call or visit her anymore and so they didn't have any right to poke their noses in her business. If she wanted to buy a Rolls Royce for her grandson, then, by God, she was going to do it whether they cared or not. Meme is her own woman and no one has ever been able to tell her what to do. It's where I get most of my independent spirit.

I can't stress the point enough what an uproar in the family it caused when Meme bought me this truck. Ray, June, Dad and Alan all went ape-shit over it. They swore up and down I had manipulated Meme into buying me a brand new, twenty-five thousand dollar truck. None of them believed for one second that it could have been because Meme wanted me to have something nice and new to drive and that she needed something that was going to be dependable and something that she wouldn't be embarrassed riding in with me.

Several weeks before we bought my new truck, Meme had tried talking to my Uncle Alan and Dad about getting me something to drive, a truck preferably. They had shown her a couple of broken down pieces-of-shit vehicles with well over a hundred thousand miles on them. Meme knew I was going to be doing a lot of traveling and she knew that she was going to be riding around with me a lot, too. Ever since she was a teenager she'd always had brand new vehicles. Meme wasn't going to settle for anything less and it was totally her decision.

Regardless, I was blamed for everything. This was only just the beginning of the large rift that was separating the relationships with that side of my family. Over time it only became larger and worse.

Not long after I got my truck I started going to reenactments by myself- well not really by myself if you count my horse as company. I had bought a horse about two years before; he was a quarter-horse, and I named him Cody. He wasn't anything special but he was very gentle and wasn't spooked by gunfire. He'd make a perfect cavalry horse to ride in the reenactments. Now that I had a truck, I had the independence to start going to any and all of the reenactments that I wanted to, and believe me, I hit them all.

In the fall of 1998 my unit and I participated in civil war reenactments all across the south. We went to Hope, Arkansas, home of President Bill Clinton; we went to Tupelo, Mississippi; West Point, Mississippi; Atlanta, Georgia and we did one reenactment at my family's ancestral home in Kosciusko, Mississippi. All of them were a lot of fun and I had a great time doing them.

Back home, things were going pretty good as well. Tenth-grade was turning out to be an okay year. There were lots of football games, pep rallies and after-game-parties. It was the first exposure I had to alcohol. I tried it, but couldn't stomach the taste and swore off liquor for a long time.

There were several girls that were interested in dating and I went out with them, but nothing ever came of it but friendships. I had to deflect questions sometimes from my buddies about why I didn't have sex with this girl or wouldn't go out with that girl. I just chose to tell everyone I was very picky and didn't like any of them. Still, the questions were there and it bothered me.

Sometime during the month of November I went to a rodeo outside of Vicksburg with some friends of mine. We were hanging out and having a good time and I struck up a conversation with a cute girl named Liz Clark. Liz was eighteen and went to the local public school, Warren Central. I was still fifteen years old but I wasn't shy about talking to an older girl. I didn't think about sex with girls all the time, so it made it easier for me to talk to them.

Liz was an easy girl to talk to, kind, generous, and very polite. I wasn't attracted to her sexually but I definitely liked her. Come to find out, Liz had just broken up with her boyfriend, Stephen George, and was out trying to keep her mind off the break-up. They'd been together since they were both thirteen years old and after being together so long, a break-up was difficult. I think Liz confided in me because she could sense that I wasn't just talking to her trying to get in her pants; I was genuinely concerned. She and I became close friends after that night.

For a while we hung together all the time. When you would see one of us you'd see the other. We were with each other every day after school and most people just assumed we were dating, and of course, I didn't let them think any different. Liz Clark was an attractive girl with a great personality and lots of guys had their eyes on her. She would have been a great catch for any lucky guy, but as luck would have it, for the time being, she was with me.

I never let on to her that I was gay or wasn't sexually attracted to her. It wasn't exactly something I was comfortable telling people yet. But when I did come out of the closet, Liz was one of the first to know. Liz never had a guy talk to her that didn't want to get in her pants.

From day one, I had told Liz that she needed to do what made her happy. She still felt stressed about her break-up with Stephen George. If she wanted him back, I told her she needed to take him back. I think this threw her for a loop. She couldn't figure out why another guy that had feelings for her would ever tell her to get back with her old boyfriend. It was surreal to her, but I had nothing but Liz's best interest at heart. She was a best friend and although I had feelings for her, they weren't the feelings that cause a man to be sexually attracted to a woman. Liz was just a super-great person and anyone who knew her would have instantly liked her.

From what I knew, Stephen treated her well. I just think they spent way too much time together and never gave each other room to breathe. I told Liz this and I thought that if they got back together with an understanding that each of them should have some time to themselves, things might work out better. Liz took my advice and several months after she and I met, she and Stephen got back together. Liz and Stephen both would have much larger roles to play in my life down the road, but that comes later in the book.

In December of 1998, Grandmama had been living with us for one year and two months and I had been driving for a little less than four months. Everything owned by my great-grandmother was still at her house in Gastonia, North Carolina. It was past time that someone go up there and get some of it.

Meme had determined to eventually sell Grandmama's house, but first we had to get everything out of there. She'd already given Grandmama's car to her first cousin, Parks Quinn, but there was still furniture, beds, televisions, kitchen appliances, clothes, and tons of other personal items that had belonged to my great-grandfather and great-grandmother.

Meme had talked about getting that stuff out of there for a long time. She'd approached my dad about going up there in a U-Haul and getting the stuff, but he claimed he was too busy and my uncles said the same thing. They weren't going to lift a finger to help anyone. Finally I just said that I would do it. Hell, I'd been traveling to other states and pulling a horse trailer by myself since I started driving. If I could do that, then I could certainly drive the twelve hours to North Carolina and bring back some of my Grandmama's stuff.

A week before Christmas I left on a Friday afternoon, planning on driving all night, straight through, getting there about daylight the next day. This would be the longest trip I had ever driven by myself. But, as with most things in life, I wasn't scared to do anything alone. The drive itself was not that bad; it's fairly easy. I had ridden with my family up there many times. I got sleepy a couple times toward early morning but made it there shortly after six Saturday morning.

I immediately went and climbed in the guest bedroom bed and fell asleep. Everything in the house had remained untouched for over a year. Meme's cousin, Parks, had periodically checked on things to make sure everything was ok, but nothing had been changed on the inside since the day, the year before, that Meme, Grandmama and Aunt June had left coming back to Mississippi. To say the least, things felt a little creepy. It was the same house that my great-grandfather had passed away in over two years before. When I had been there on vacation and for the holidays, everything had always been festive and exciting. Now, it was all quiet, dark and cold.

Parks was planning on coming by about noon to go with me to rent a U-Haul trailer and then was going to help start loading all the stuff up that I was taking back to Vicksburg. I had about six hours to get some sleep. My plan was to get everything packed up Saturday afternoon and then leave out early Sunday morning.

Meme had given me a list of things to get from the house, including some more of Grandmama's clothes and personal items, all the dishes and good china and silverware, some framed pictures, the master bedroom suit, mattresses and last but not least, the piano.

It not only took all of Saturday afternoon, it took a good part into the night for us to get everything loaded and situated inside the U-Haul. And Lord, the piano was the worst. That was the heaviest thing I ever moved in my life. Parks was almost seventy-five years old and I was just a scrawny little fifteen-year-old, but somehow we managed to get all this stuff loaded into the small U-Haul. I was worn out by the time we finished. All I wanted to do was go crawl back in bed and get some more sleep, but instead I stayed up another few hours and talked with Parks about how everything was going in Vicksburg with Grandmama and Meme.

By the time I crawled in bed at eleven o'clock that night, I was not looking forward to the long drive back home, but I made it without any trouble. I probably drove a little too fast on the interstate with the trailer behind me, but I was ready to get home and soon made it there in record time- ten hours.

That night when I got home I unhooked the trailer, went inside, did my homework and went to bed. I had to go to school the next morning. Meme had some guys from the dealership come out to the house on Monday and help unload everything while I was gone to classes. I was so thankful I didn't have to struggle with the heavy piano.

Although Grandmama had good and bad days with her memory, she did remember a lot of her personal items and furniture and it made her happy to finally have them again.

# CHAPTER TEN

Christmas came and went fairly quickly. I spent Christmas Eve with Meme and Grandmama and then got up early and drove to Kosciusko where my mom and the rest of the family were. Since I was a kid I had always tried to spend Christmas Day with Papaw and Mamaw in Kosciusko. Now that I was able to drive, I could spend half my holiday with Meme and Grandmama and the other half with my mom's side of the family. We always had a lot of good food and plenty of presents. This year my Papaw and Mamaw bought me a twelve-gauge shotgun, which was always an important gift for any boy growing up in the south who is a hunter.

After the holidays were over, time started moving very quickly. There wasn't much going on at school; my grades had slipped slightly lower than the year before but still high enough to be proud of. I was sure to try to attend every sporting event to support my school's athletic teams. I was still going to civil war reenactments at least once a month, although they'd slowed down in the wintertime. Grandmama's health had begun to deteriorate and she required the constant care of Meme and me.

Sooner or later, we were going to have to hire a nurse to come during the day to help take care of her. Grandmama wasn't able to leave the house anymore and Meme wasn't able to do anything either, so a lot of times I would volunteer to stay with Grandmama a few hours while Meme went to town and ran errands and took care of other business.

More often than not, I would be the one who took care of everything. Meme entrusted all of her personal affairs into my hands and every day after school I usually spent a few hours taking care of the things that she couldn't. For a while, Meme and Grandmama were totally dependent on me, and I was surely not going to let them down.

Around the first of February I became interested in joining my local volunteer fire department. Being a firefighter had always intrigued me and by becoming a volunteer firefighter I would not only be able to do something that I enjoyed, but it would also give me the opportunity to serve my community-something else that meant a lot to me too. The Fisher Ferry Volunteer Fire Department had about twenty members. Some of them I already knew, but after joining I made a lot of new friends.

I especially became close with a couple named Kenny and Wendy Staggs. They had been members of the fire department for a long time and were willing to take me under their wing and show me the ropes. Kenny's full-time job was as a 911 dispatcher but he would soon be promoted to assistant coordinator over 911 and then made coordinator over the Warren County addressing office. Wendy was a stay-at-home wife.

Over the years Kenny and Wendy and I have developed a very strong relationship like that of almost family. While I was locked away in prison they were sure to look after Meme and make sure she was taken care of and didn't need anything. They are two very good people whom I love very much and soon after we met in 1999, Kenny and I became inseparable friends. When I finally decided to announce that I was gay, Kenny was the first to know and he and Wendy have been totally supportive.

Soon after joining the fire department, I made another trip to Gastonia, North Carolina and picked up more of Grandmama's furniture. This time I took a friend along with my gooseneck horse trailer that had plenty of room. This trip we were able to get almost everything out of the house, minus a few odd and end pieces that would have to wait until another trip.

In April of 1999 I broached the subject of buying a boat and jet-ski to Meme. She didn't seem to have a problem with it. My dad had always had a boat and lots of my friend's parents owned watercraft. Meme said we could go shopping and if they weren't too expensive she would consider buying them.

It didn't take long for me to find what I was looking for. I eventually settled on a Polaris three-seater jet-ski and a sixteen-foot Bayliner ski-boat. I would finally have something fun to do every summer other than ride around in my truck all day. My dad had taught me how to drive a boat and jet-ski several summers earlier and I had taken a boater's safety course from the Mississippi Department of Wildlife- something I would recommend for anyone using a watercraft. The knowledge you gain from a class like that is invaluable.

Shortly after getting my boat and jet-ski, I met a game warden named Mike Ouzts, who would later also turn out to be an invaluable friend and mentor to me.

I was down at the boat ramp on the riverfront, putting my boat into the water when an older, gray-haired game warden walked up and started talking to me. My first impression was that I had done something wrong. A cop just coming up and starting conversation with me was odd, but Mike Ouzts was really just a nice guy. I had known of Mike before I met him and I'd always heard good things and was finally pleased to meet him. We sat at the riverfront and talked for about an hour. He gave me his card and invited me to come riding with him sometime in his game warden truck. I was interested in law enforcement and would jump at any chance I could.

Mike Ouzts' career in law enforcement had begun when he was nineteen years old.  He had run for constable and had actually won, becoming the youngest elected official in the entire United States at the time.  Even the Governor of the State sent his congratulations to Mike on election night.  No one expected Mike to win that election, but he did and he won by a large majority, proving that anyone can do anything if they have the determination.

After serving a four-year term as constable, Mike became a Warren County deputy sheriff.  He served in that role for nearly fifteen years, resigning only after the sheriff, Paul Barrett, was convicted of federal charges and forced from office.  Mike then became a game warden, working for the Mississippi Department of Wildlife, Fisheries and Parks.  After doing that for four years, he took a job as the Chief of Police for the Vicksburg-Warren County Public School Police Department.  He finally retired after twenty-five years of public service.  He now lives in a small town in Louisiana and works as a part-time deputy for the parish where he resides.

Mike has had a long and industrious career in law enforcement.  He has seen many things and been through a lot.  One of the worse things in his life was to go through the ordeal of seeing his boss, Sheriff Paul Barrett, be convicted in federal court, serve prison time and resign from office.  Sheriff Barrett and Mike were very close.  Sheriff Barrett had supported Mike's run for constable years earlier.

Mike learned quickly and became one of the best law enforcement officers in the state of Mississippi, winning the 1998 Officer of the Year Award, beating several thousand other contestants throughout the state.  I've said over and over again that the entire country needs more law enforcement officers like Mike Ouzts.

After Sheriff Barrett was forced to resign from office, Mike could very well have become sheriff.  He definitely had the political backing and support, but the job was a bigger headache than Mike wanted.  He probably also could have stayed on as a deputy but as soon as he saw that one of the detectives, Martin

Pace, was going to become sheriff, he got out of there as quickly as possible.

While Mike was fair toward everyone and believed in not only protecting the community but also serving it, Martin Pace was only attracted to the position because of the power it wielded. Martin Pace cared nothing about the welfare of the citizens of Vicksburg and Warren County, only about increasing his own power and influence (and as I would later find out, his pocket book also), but I didn't know about any of this at the time. All I cared about at the time was my own little world and what revolved around it.

After Mike and I met that day we quickly formed a close friendship. Mike and Kenny were also good friends and we did a lot of stuff together. Mike also introduced me to two of his best friends; one of them was Dane Davenport, an eighteen-year veteran of the Mississippi Highway Patrol. Dane and I also would become close friends. Mike introduced me to another friend who was a Jackson Police Officer, Ron McClelland. He and I would become friends for a while also. After meeting Ron, we soon stumbled into discovering that each other was gay. He was nearly thirty years old and I was only fifteen. He wanted some type of relationship, but I didn't. When he didn't get what he wanted, he practically stopped talking to me.

Through my friendship with Mike, I was able to make other important contacts throughout the law enforcement community, hoping that one day, the contacts would pay off and I would be able to obtain a job with one of these agencies. I didn't have such a low opinion of police then, as I do today. At the time I believed all cops were fair and honest, but oh what an education I was going to get!

Soon after meeting Mike, he introduced me to one of the current constables in Warren County, Glen McKay. Glen is what I call one of the "good guys". He also ran for constable at a young age and won. He never worried himself with trying to become a deputy sheriff. He saw what was going on behind the scenes before anyone else did and wanted no part of it. I've spent hours and hours talking to Glen McKay and I soon began to piece together things he told me with the things that Mike and Dane told me and also with other things I was able to put together myself. It hit me that no one in the law enforcement community really liked, or respected, Sheriff Martin Pace.

There had been a few deputies to remain in the sheriff's department after Paul Barrett left, but for the most part everyone resigned or found jobs elsewhere when Martin Pace became sheriff.

After most of the deputies left the Sheriff's Department, Martin Pace brought in several of his good friends who were not going to question his methods of authority and put them in high-level administrative positions. One of the first problems he ran across was what to do with Paul Barrett's number-two man in the department.

Otha Jones had been with the Warren County Sheriff's Department since the early seventies. He was the first African-American ever in the history of Warren County to hold the number two spot in the sheriff's department. Paul Barrett did this at a time when African-Americans were not very popular in the south, especially in law enforcement.

As soon as he became sheriff, Martin Pace attempted to fire Otha Jones. The outrage from the community was astronomical. You see, Martin Pace needed his own crony in the number-two spot. The last thing he needed was someone he didn't trust overseeing the day-to-day operations of the sheriff's department. So, instead of firing Otha Jones and risk losing his newly acquired power, Martin Pace placed Otha in charge of the jail; basically a demotion from what Otha Jones had been doing overseeing patrol operations.

Then, there was the fight over the call numbers. When someone becomes a deputy they are assigned a call number that they use to identify themselves to the 911 dispatcher when using the radio. The sheriff is assigned the call number "WC1". For almost twenty years, Otha Jones's call number had been "WC2". They go all the way from "WC1" to "WC70", the lowest on the totem pole of deputy sheriff's.

When Martin tried to change Otha Jones's number from

"WC2" to some insignificant number on the bottom of the list, again he suffered outrage from the community. Martin Pace wanted his best buddy, Jeff Riggs, as the number-two man in the department, but some people were determined to fight that as long as possible.

Again, rather than risk losing the next election, Martin created the call number "Unit 2" for his crony, Jeff Riggs. Now there was a "WC2" and a "Unit 2" and it confused the hell out of everyone. No one knew who was in charge. Martin Pace and his cronies were slowly freezing out Otha Jones and everyone else who didn't play by their rules and keep their mouths shut about the illegal and corrupt activities going on inside the department.

By talking to Mike, Dane and Glen, I learned more than I ever wanted to know about the secret workings of the sheriff, his minions, and the department. It was then, in the summer of 1999, I determined that I would do something to change the way things were being done in Warren County. I made the decision then that as soon as I could, I would run for constable, win, serve a few years and then run for sheriff. I would beat Martin Pace and change Warren County, putting the citizens' welfare and safety before personal wealth and gain.

I didn't try to hide my ambitions from anyone either. I let it be known that I was interested in running for constable. I had spent a lot of time with Glen McKay. I learned what a constable did and how they worked. It would definitely be something that I would have liked to do. I'd just have to wait until I was old enough, and that would be several more years.

At the first of the summer, Meme and I had discussed the possibility of me finishing my last two years of high school being home schooled. It was an odd discussion to say the least. She wasn't exactly supportive of it, but my cousins in Kosciusko, Will and Keri Atwood, had been home schooled their entire lives and as a result, would be graduating several years earlier than they would have had they gone to public or private schools. They were just as smart, if not smarter, than kids who had grown up in the public education system.

The way things were going, had I remained at PCA, I

wouldn't have graduated until May of 2001. I wanted to hurry up and graduate so I could start college a year early and get on with my life. I had taken the ACT test two years earlier and had made a composite score of 21- high enough to get me into any college in the area that I wanted to go. It wasn't exactly like two more years at PCA was going to help me anymore than a year of home schooling would. The home schooling program that I was looking at taking was a fast-paced advancement course that would allow me to fit two years of schoolwork into one year.

Another incentive for doing it was that it would free up a lot more of my time so that I could help take care of Grandmama during the day while Meme was able to take care of other business. By this time, Grandmama required constant care and couldn't be left alone for more than a few minutes. We had a nurse that came during the day to help with her care, but it was an extreme burden as anyone who has ever had a relative suffering from Alzheimer's will know. To see a loved one suffer in such a way is terribly heart-breaking and the stress was taking a toll on Meme.

Meme and I spent a long time talking about our future and what I wanted to do with my life. We discussed me possibly going into the military reserves, college, and other future career plans and whether or not to finish my last two years being home schooled. I was surprised when my mom actually came out in support of me finishing my last two years of high school doing home schooling. She knew that if I worked hard I could get everything done in a year and begin college early, something I'd always talked about doing.

After considering everything, Meme finally decided to let me enroll in the home schooling program with a promise that if I didn't finish in one year I would reenroll at PCA and finish my senior year there. I had no intention of letting anyone down. My goal was to enroll in college in August of 2000 and I was going to meet that goal.

Everything seemed to be going pretty well until Grandmama's health really took a plunge at the end of May and she had to be hospitalized. She passed away in June, 1999.

Meme's and my attention immediately turned to taking care of Grandmama's final wishes and burial.

For the first time in over a year, our family would all be under the same roof, not something that I thought would go over very well. The Atwood family can barely get along when they are apart, much less when they're cramped together. Everyone flew to North Carolina for the funeral. Grandmama would be laid to rest beside her husband who had passed away in September 1996. Meme took care of most of the funeral arrangements- she couldn't expect help from anyone else.

Throughout the entire funeral I remained beside Meme holding her hand and comforting her. My dad, uncles and aunt only seemed to be going through the motions- totally emotionless. They acted like they weren't at the funeral of a dearly loved one. Hell, most of them hadn't even seen their grandmother at all in the past year. All they cared about was getting back to Vicksburg. None of them had the foggiest idea what Meme and I had been through these past two years. Slowly before our eyes, Meme's mother, my great-grandmother, deteriorated from a strong vibrant woman to a sickly, mumbling, old lady and no one had the slightest clue how much it had affected Meme and me.

To them, this funeral was nothing more than an irritation, just something to have to get all dressed up for. Meme realized this and so did I. There was other family at the funeral also; Grandmama's side of the family also all came. Her nieces and nephews and their families all attended and the majority of Meme's and my time was spent with them. There was definitely a rift in the family and the funeral only exacerbated it. Meme and I had tried to take special care to insure that the funeral was carried out exactly as Grandmama had wanted it. My dad, uncles and aunt tried to do things their own way. It was a strained tense time.

The day after the funeral, everyone flew back home to Vicksburg except my dad and I. I was volunteered for the job of helping to clear out the rest of the furniture from Grandmama's house. My dad had no idea that I had made two trips already.

This would be the first time we had talked in almost two years. I wasn't happy about it, but realized that Meme needed me to do this.

Dad and I rented a large U-Haul truck and spent the day loading everything into it. We spoke as little as possible and when we did it was usually him trying to tell me that I was doing something wrong. I shot back that I had done this twice before and made it home in one piece and that I must have been doing something right. I was not looking forward to spending twelve hours in this U-Haul truck with him on that long drive back to Mississippi.

We left the night after the funeral, planning to drive straight through, but neither of us had gotten much sleep the night before. After only a few hours we were both tired and had we not spent the rest of the way fighting and yelling back and forth, I am sure someone would have fallen asleep. My dad always had a complaint about something. His favorite saying was that he regretted not sending me to a military boarding school from the start of my childhood. I never had enough respect for my elders. I could never do anything right. I was a failure and an embarrassment to the family. I wasn't man enough. The complaints never ended.

It was pretty much the same stuff that I had heard all of my life- big deal. Then he brought up a rumor he had heard. Someone had told him I was gay. Stuck in a U-Haul truck with a raging, abusive father who had more contempt for gays than he did the African-Americans he claimed to have hated so much in his rants and raves about the Ku Klux Klan, I was petrified with fright.

Regardless of whether it was true or not, I had to listen for an hour straight, about the horrible dangers of the homosexual "agenda" and how they influenced and corrupted young teenage boys like myself. My dad was convinced that some old gay dude had waved a "fairy pixie wand" over me and magically turned me gay overnight.

Never could he comprehend that I had been this way my entire life. I listened about how God deals out the ultimate punishment for gays and that unless I wanted to burn in the fiery depths of hell for all of eternity I had better swear off "ass-fucking and dick-sucking" forever. I sat in my seat and cringed at that last thought. If he only knew what I had done with Daniel, but this was one argument I wasn't planning on winning, so I remained quiet. I just sat there and took the verbal abuse wishing the damn trip would be over as soon as possible.

Somewhere, about two hours before we reached home, I fell asleep. I dreamed that my dad and his night-riding Ku Klux Klan buddies had caught Daniel and me in bed together and were about to hang us from an oak tree. It was a sickening dream and it jarred me awake. Thankfully, we were home.

# CHAPTER ELEVEN

Life for Meme and me was considerably different after Grandmama passed away. Things were lonely and void. For the past two years, every day of our lives had been focused on the constant care of Grandmama. Now there was nothing to do anymore. Meme started playing a card game called canasta with a group of ladies from her church. They played on Monday and Thursday nights. That still left a lot of time for doing nothing.

Meme tried busying herself by taking care of the final arrangements of Grandmama's estate. In all, there was over one million dollars in property, stocks, bonds, annuities, and insurance. My great-grandparents had their hands in all kinds of stuff and it took Meme forever to try and sort it all out. The biggest relief was finally getting Grandmama's house sold. It wasn't overly large, but it was in a nice neighborhood and was worth quite a lot. That was one less burden we had to worry with.

We also spent a lot of time working on my home schooling program. Meme had taught in the public schools for many years, so teaching became natural to her. It wasn't exactly hard for her or me. I watched a set of videos, took notes, and then Meme gave me a test. If I passed, I moved on to the next section. It wasn't rocket science.

I spent as much free time as possible either on the jet-ski or boat. Mike Ouzts rode with me a lot also. Part of his job as a game warden was to patrol the Mississippi River and its tributaries. He knew every nook and cranny there was. He showed me some of the best fishing spots and where important parts of history unfolded along the river. Some days we took his patrol boat and ran up and down the river checking other boaters and river barges for their compliance with water safety rules. It was all very interesting and I loved every minute of it.

I also spent a good part of my time with Dane Davenport. He took me riding in his highway patrol car. While riding with him, it was the first time I had ever been faster than 120 miles per hour in a vehicle before. He had one of those Ford Crown Victoria's that would really lie down on the asphalt and move. I got spooked more than a few times at some of his erratic driving, but it was a great adrenaline rush.

I watched both Mike and Dane write people tickets and make arrests. I also saw them let a lot of people off with just a warning. Dane taught me a very valuable lesson one day. He said that sometimes writing a person a ticket does more harm than good and that cutting people a break went a lot further than anything else you could do. Mike and Dane were both very compassionate people who believed in doing what was right, not what was going to make them look good in their boss's eyes by trying to make some ticket quota that wasn't really supposed to exist. And yeah, for all you nay-sayer's out there, highway patrolmen are given quotas that they are supposed to meet each month. That goes to explain why some of the assholes will write you a speeding ticket for doing two miles over the limit.

Even though I had left Porters Chapel, I didn't forget about the friends I had made there. I still went to all of the football games and pep rallies. I dropped in numerous times during the middle of classes to say hello to some of my old teachers. Every time I went, people always asked me to come back- it was good to be missed.

I spent a lot of time on the weekends with my friends. I was determined not to lose those friendships that I had made. I had several boat parties where I would invite seven or eight of my closest friends out onto the boat with me for a Saturday afternoon. We would ski, kneeboard and go tubing. Everyone had a blast, but the summer and warm weather were quickly dissipating. Fall and winter were just around the corner.

For my sixteenth birthday Meme bought me a computer. It was the first computer I'd ever owned and I was anxious to get it assembled and hooked up to the internet. I had to call Kenny and Wendy over to help set it up. I knew how to work computers, but I'd be damned if I knew how to put one together and hook up all the wires. Kenny did, though, and I was soon surfing the net.

I had told Kenny that summer about my sexuality and to my surprise he was completely cool about it, even supportive, as well as Wendy. They are two people who honestly don't care about things like that. They just want what's best for me and what makes me happy. Kenny even took time that day to show me some chat rooms on America Online where I could meet other gay teenagers like myself.

Having a computer opened up a new kind of world for me. For the past few years I had felt like I was the only gay teenager on the planet. Now that I had access to the rest of the world, I realized that I wasn't the only person to go through what I had. Being able to talk to other guys my age was a real comfort. I've always had a lot of friends but never that really special someone that I could talk to everyday and share together a common bond. I was getting to the point where I just didn't care to hide it anymore. I was going to be who I was whether someone else liked it or not. I was determined to do what made me feel happy.

Having friends to talk to on the computer helped, but it

still didn't replace that face-to-face bond that I craved. I needed someone that I could hold and make love to. I needed a boyfriend.

Shortly before Halloween in 1999 my dad appeared at the doorway of Meme's house and asked to speak with me. Noticing that this was something unusual, I stepped out into the garage and asked my dad what was going on.

My dad had been told by numerous people that I'd been seen hanging out with Mike Ouzts and he was concerned. Most everyone in Vicksburg knew that Mike Ouzts was gay and apparently my dad had a serious problem with me being with him. Without even asking my opinion, he ordered me not to have any more contact with Mike.

Since I had not lived with my dad in over two years, I did not feel he had a right to try and determine who I could and could not be friends with. Unfortunately, our argument that day escalated into a huge crisis and somewhere in the middle of us screaming back and forth at one another, I blurted out that I was gay. I probably said it more to shock him than I actually wanted him to know, but whatever the reason I let it slip and it had its intended effect. My dad stood there jaw dropped and eyes wide. He asked me to repeat myself, and again I told him that I was gay.

For the first time in my life my dad hit me with his closed fist. He had always been physically abusive to my mother and me, but he had never hit me as hard with his fist as he did that day. Thankfully, after he knocked me out, he got in his truck and left. Meme had been listening to the fight and heard him hit me, but before she could get outside to where I was, my dad had already left.

Sitting in the kitchen later that afternoon I refused to talk about what my dad and I had been fighting about. Admitting to my grandmother that I was gay was not something I wanted to do at that time, especially after what I had just been through with my father.

A few days later, just as I thought things were returning to normal, we received a knock on the door from two of the sheriff's deputies. When we invited them inside, they explained to Meme and me that they had a commitment order, signed by the chancery judge, to have me picked up and transported to the state hospital for juveniles in Meridian, Mississippi.

After I had told my dad that I was gay, he had gone to the courts and filed a lunacy commitment against me, citing a number of different illnesses that I was suffering from, including a "gender identity" issue. Since Meme had never officially received custody of me through the courts, my dad was, unfortunately, within his rights as custodial parent to have me committed to the mental institution.

On the night that the deputies picked me up and transported me, there was nothing Meme or I could do about it. To say the least, we never saw this coming and it infuriated my grandmother that my dad would do something so ruthless and cold. When my mother was told of what my dad had done, she became hysterical with anger. She immediately had Jerry file a motion in court to have custody of me taken away from my dad and given to her and Meme.

Meanwhile, I was taken to East Mississippi State Mental Hospital for juveniles. From the moment of my arrival, I made it clear to anyone and everyone who would listen that there was nothing wrong with me and that my dad had only had me committed because I told him I was gay.

The doctors there were very skeptical and didn't believe me at first when I told them what my dad had done and why he did it. Thankfully, my mother and Meme quickly informed the doctors of *their* opinion of why I was there, but until the courts gave my mother and Meme custody of me, there wasn't a whole lot that the doctors and psychologist at the hospital could do but keep me.

Several days after I arrived at East Mississippi my dad drove over and had his first meeting with the doctors who were in charge of my "treatment". As soon as the meeting started, my dad began demanding that I be treated for being a homosexual. It was almost comical at the farce of which he tried to perpetrate.

Up until that time, I do not think that the doctors believed me when I told them that the only reason I was there was because I had told my dad I was gay. Hearing the reason come from my dad's own mouth only reiterated what I, Meme, and my mom had been telling them since my arrival. Several times the doctors even asked my dad if there was anything else wrong with me. Laughably, my dad said no, only that he thought being homosexual was a mental disorder and something that I should be treated for. It was at this point in the conversation that the doctor stopped taking notes and closed her notepad.

Thankfully, I only had to stay at East Mississippi a little over a week before custody was granted to my mom and Meme and the doctors there released me. Before I left, one of the doctors told me how awful it must be to have a father like mine. At the time, I could only agree.

That was practically the last time I ever had any contact with my dad. He had alienated Meme so bad that she never talked to him again either. My mother, already having a dislike for her ex-husband, only came to hate him worse for what he had done and what he had put me through. Somehow, throughout this entire saga, I had managed to avoid the discussion with Meme and my mom about whether I was actually gay or not. They didn't specifically ask and I didn't mention it. Even though they knew the truth, we continued this little ruse for another year or two before I finally decided to come out of the closet. By that time, I was only confirming what everyone already knew.

# CHAPTER TWELVE

After getting out of the state hospital, Christmas came and went fairly quickly. Like the year before, I spent Christmas Eve with my Meme and then got up the next morning and drove to Kosciusko to spend the holiday with my mom's side of the family.

Unfortunately, this would be first Christmas that my dad, aunt and two uncles would not call Meme and wish her a Merry Christmas, nor would they stop by to visit. They'd finally completely frozen Meme and me out of their lives. It was hard on Meme. She'd just lost her mother and on top of that, none of her children would even talk to her on Christmas. It was a sickening experience, but one we were getting use to everyday.

There was a lot of apprehension about the 2000 Y2K bug. I had already stored away several months-worth of clean drinking water and survival rations, just in case. I didn't really think there would be any problems, but I was going to be careful nonetheless.

Shortly after getting my computer, Meme decided she wanted to get one for herself. I'd spent many long hours trying to teach and demonstrate to her how to operate a computer. She was totally oblivious and to make matters worse, she bought into the whole Y2K thing and was dreading the thought that her new computer might crash so soon after she bought it.

Nothing happened to her computer and she eventually learned how to become an efficient operator. She now spends most of her time playing card games on Yahoo with other players from around the world. She's even been able to teach me a thing or two.

I spent New Year's Eve with Dane, his wife Tammy and their five children, all boys. They would later adopt a baby girl from Russia, but for the time the boys dominated their household and they always had something going on. This year, they were throwing a huge New Year's party.

I had started becoming good friends with Dane and his family. We'd all gone horse-back riding before and we'd been out on the boat and jet-ski together. Dane really did a lot to include me in his family. I think Dane realized I needed some type of father figure in my life and he tried his best to help me out.

I was horribly embarrassed the time I had to go to him and get him to tie all the ties I wore with my suit to church. I didn't know how to tie a tie. I'd always gotten someone else to do it and rather than untie them when I was done, I'd just loosen them and slip them over my head. Dane sat me down and taught me how to finally tie a tie. It was one lesson from him I would never forget. Most boys learn from their father; I learned from a man I was only friends with.

I knew that sooner or later I needed to tell Dane about my sexuality. It's not something that I felt I *had* to tell him; rather it was something that I think he needed to know was a part of my life. It took a lot of courage to finally come out and just tell him.

When I did tell him, it caught him completely off guard. I

really sandbagged him with it. We were riding in his patrol car when I just came right out and said that there was something I needed to tell him. Then I spit it out, "I'm gay."

He must have thought I was playing a joke because he didn't believe me at first. I actually had to take another breath and then argue with him over my sexuality. He said that I couldn't be serious. I was like "Yeah, uh…I…uh…think I would know whether I liked guys or girls and I'm pretty sure that…I…uh…kinda like guys more than girls..uh…yeah uhh mmmm". I also tried to explain to him that being gay was the reason my dad had had me committed to the state hospital.

He quieted down a minute, staring at the yellow lines going by on the road. I felt about two inches tall, wanting nothing more than to get out of the car and be as far away as possible. I was waiting for him to start the religious spill about what a huge sin I was committing by being a cocksucker, but he had no malice. He simply apologized for being caught off-guard so suddenly and told me that if that's what I was then it was okay with him, and he and his family wouldn't treat me any differently. Like I said, Dane was a very sincere, honest, and compassionate person. I wished more people were like him.

After our tense little conversation, everything went back to normal. We didn't even bring the subject up again until the party on New Year's Eve. It was that night that Dane came to me and offered to introduce me to a young guy that he knew and thought was gay.

I was kind of stunned. I never thought in a million years that Dane would try to play matchmaker for me, but I guess he had good intentions. I was also intrigued. I didn't know of any other guy in the area that was gay. For so long, I had been dreaming about finding somebody like me that I could spend all my time with, somebody that I could love and hold and kiss and make love to. Had Dane found that person for me?

He quickly stopped my day-dreaming fantasy. He didn't even know whether this guy we were talking about was gay or not. He just had some suspicions and was going to introduce the two of us and see if anything touched off. I was shy and embarrassed and didn't know whether to go through with his plan or not, but he didn't leave me much choice. We were going to go meet this guy as soon as the holidays were over.

If anything, Dane is insightful. I think he knew that I needed someone like me to spend time with. I had let on a few times that I was lonely and this guy that Dane wanted to introduce me to was the only one that he knew of that I might have a chance with, provided the guy was even gay- something we didn't even know yet. I got so frustrated. Why did every damn thing have to be so hard?

A couple days after the new year, I met Dane at his house and we jumped in his patrol car with our plan intact of going to meet this guy who Dane suspected, but didn't know for sure, was gay. I felt the plan had disaster written all over it.

Up until this time I hadn't thought to ask what this guy's name was or if Dane even knew it. So, I asked and Dane told me he thought the guy's name was Kevin Southern. The name was familiar to me. I asked Dane if it was the same Kevin Southern whose family owned a horse feed and tack store out in the county. Yep, that's the one and the store was where we were headed.

I had heard of Kevin numerous times before. My ex-girlfriend, Liz Clark and Kevin were best friends, along with Liz's boyfriend, Stephen George. I had never met Kevin but had heard Liz talk about him several times. Kevin and I also had another mutual friend, Jessica Harris. Jessica and I had been friends for a long time but she'd never introduced me to Kevin. What was ironic was that both Liz and Jessica had questioned Kevin's sexual orientation. No one was quite sure whether he was or wasn't gay. It was a question that a lot of people spent time thinking about. Today, I was going to try to determine for myself.

Dane owned horses and bought most of his feed and saddle equipment from Kevin at his family's store, which they called "Total Horse". My aunt and I owned horses too, but we got all our feed and equipment from another company. After shopping a few times at Total Horse, Dane and Kevin became friends. Dane noticed a few personality "tics" that might indicate to him that Kevin was gay, but Dane wasn't sure. Besides, he didn't care one way or the other until the thought hit him that he could possibly fix Kevin and me up together, provided Kevin was gay- something he was going to get my opinion on in a few short minutes.

Within thirty-seconds of Dane introducing us, I knew Kevin was a big, flamboyant drama queen just waiting to burst out of its shell. Not to imply that Kevin acted like a woman or that he had secret desire to one day become a woman, no, that's not what I mean at all. Kevin just simply acted gay and flamboyant. He was delicate- let me put it that way. And he talked with a slight lisp. Regardless, I thought he was fucking hot!!! He had a great body and a really cute face. Besides, from the minute I met him I knew he was gay and that was all that mattered.

I couldn't just come right out and say "Hi, I'm David, I heard you were gay. So am I, want to fuck?" I would have to be a little more tactful than that, especially with his mom hanging over our shoulder. I would have to work my natural charm and try to figure out a way to get his cell phone number without looking too suspicious.

Kevin and his mom basically ran the store. Kevin's dad owned it, but he worked full-time at a ship building company down on the river. Kevin had graduated high school the year before and was now taking night classes at the local community college, the same one where Mrs. Rush was teaching. Kevin was three years older than me, but we had a lot in common. We were both country boys. We loved to fish, hunt and ride horses. Both he and I were down to earth, independent, and intelligent. I immediately thought we would make a good match....if only I could get him to quit acting so damn gay.

While Dane wandered around the store, pretending to be interested in buying something, Kevin and I sat and talked about horses, saddles, the people we knew, where we went to school and other small chat. I was trying to build up a repertoire with him so that just in that small chance he wasn't gay, I wouldn't look like a total weirdo when I asked him for his phone number and invited him to come hang out with me sometime.

To my surprise, he asked me for my phone number first! I guess I had made a good impression. Dane overheard him pop the question and as I was writing down my cell phone number, I saw a huge smile come across Dane's face. I gave him a wink and went on talking to Kevin. I definitely thought I had hit my mark.

Kevin promised to call me soon and set up sometime to hang out. I made some comment about riding horses together or something like that and then Dane and I left. As I closed the door of Dane's patrol car, I looked over at him and said that there was no doubt in my mind that Kevin was gay. We had a good laugh and pulled out of the parking lot, not thinking that ever in a million years Kevin and I would fall in love and spend the next year almost inseparable. I just didn't think something like that was possible.

Several hours after Dane and I left Kevin's store, my phone rang. Guess what? It was Kevin and he wanted to know what I was doing that night. I didn't want to sound desperate so I named some things that I needed to take care of but said that if he wanted to hang out, have dinner or catch a movie, I could find the time to do it. Catching a movie sounded great to him- my place or his? My place.

God only knows what the movie was that I rented. I think I just grabbed something off the shelf at Blockbuster. I had no intention of watching a movie that night. My thoughts were filled with lustful desires of things to come. I have to admit, I was nervous as hell. I didn't know what to do or even how to approach Kevin. I didn't even know whether he was really gay. But there was still that possibility that I could be wrong and that Kevin was just a really nice guy. How embarrassed I would be if I were wrong.

I lived a good ways out into the country and directions there can sometimes be complicated so I decided to meet Kevin in town and let him ride with me out to the house. That way I wouldn't have to worry about him getting lost and wasting precious time.

About an hour before we were to meet, I took a shower and got all dazzled up. I took extra care in making sure everything was perfect. I don't know what Meme was thinking. I'm sure she thought I had a hot date with a sexy young girl. I hadn't gotten around to completely telling her about my sexuality. Even though she suspected I was gay, especially after the fiasco my dad pulled, she never mentioned it to me and I didn't offer any details.

I met Kevin in town and he jumped in the truck with me. I had thought we would go straight to my house, but instead he asked if it would be alright if we went and had dinner first. We chose a nice family restaurant where my family and I eat all the time. Rowdy's Family Restaurant serves home-style southern fried catfish and other country-cooked entrees. It's not exactly a great place to take a date, but it would do.

Over plates of catfish and black-eyed peas we broke the ice. I had never been so engrossed in conversation. Everything about Kevin infatuated me. He seemed so perfect. I couldn't wait for dinner to be over and to be headed back to my house for the movie. I was confident of good things to come.

We went back to my house and I introduced Meme to Kevin. I'm sure she was a bit surprised to see another guy at my side. I had never brought home another guy before to "watch movies with". There had been several girls and several groups of girls and guys, but never a guy by himself. Whatever Meme thought, she was totally polite and welcomed Kevin into our home.

We popped a movie in the VCR and lay back on my bed. I didn't have any couches and I felt a little embarrassed about watching a movie in my bed with another guy, but Kevin didn't seem to mind. He jumped right up in the bed and laid down close beside me. I was too nervous to watch the movie. All I could think about was whether Kevin was gay or not.

Even though the movie was playing, we were still engrossed in conversation. Since we had met that night we had done nothing but talk. We talked about the people we knew, places we'd visited, places we wanted to go, dreams, ambitions and everything else.

Somewhere about a quarter of the way through the movie I asked Kevin if he had a girlfriend. He said no and quickly followed up with a statement that he didn't really like dating girls. My ears perked up and my heart raced. Was he hinting to me that he was gay? Did I just hear what I thought I heard? What straight heterosexual guy would ever say he didn't like dating girls? But wait a second! Did he mean that he doesn't like having long-term relationships with girls and just likes having sex with them- no strings attached, or does he really not "like" girls?

A million thoughts raced through my head. Was he or wasn't he? Should I or shouldn't I? The stress was killing me. I had to know. I took a huge leap of faith. A few more minutes went by in silence and I finally said that I didn't like dating girls either. With that, we turned our heads toward one another, stared in each other's eyes and I knew then that we were both after the same thing.

I leaned over closer to him and locked my lips with his. We embraced in a long passionate kiss. He was a good kisser. I stopped for a minute and took a breath. So much for wondering, now I knew for sure. I told him to hold on a second while I jumped up and ran to lock my bedroom door. I didn't think Meme would come back there and bother us, but I couldn't risk it. She was only seventy years old, but seeing two guys rolling around in the bed together might have been more than her old heart could manage. Some things are better left unknown.

For the next three hours we did nothing but make love. We finally rolled over and went to sleep; curled up together like we were trying to protect ourselves from freezing, never being able to get close enough. We slept that way till late morning, bathed in ecstasy. I was the happiest person in the world. I had finally found someone that I could spend the rest of my life with. But, did he feel the same way?

Sometime before lunch my phone rang. It was Meme calling from her line on the other end of the house. "Uh, what are you doing? Your door's locked!" I stumbled through some answer about accidentally locking it. I promised to be up in a minute.

What we had done this morning and the night before was not something either of us had ever really done before, but no instruction manual was needed. We stumbled through everything like two novices would. Not knowing whether anything we were doing was the right way or not. It was weird, but a good weird. We fit together perfectly, no pun intended.

I realized that if either of us were going to get anything done that day that eventually someone was going to have to be the first to crawl out of bed, though neither of us wanted to. We could have laid in bed all day without a care in the world, but we had to get up.

I threw some pants and shirt on and went out my door. I told Kevin he could use my shower and bathroom if he needed to. I was going to use Meme's to take a shower. As I walked into Meme's room she gave me the weirdest look that I ever saw. I was frozen with embarrassment. Could she have heard us last night?

To be honest, Meme probably didn't know what was going on. She probably thought we were back there doing drugs. Meme and I had always had an open door policy. She never locked any of her doors to me and the only time one of my doors stayed locked was when I was in the bathroom. Imagine how she felt that morning when she came back there to see what we were up too and found the door to my side of the house locked? I had a little explaining to do, but she seemed to accept my story and let me go on and take a shower.

After we had showered, Kevin and I drove back into town. He had to work that afternoon at the store. I was busy replaying the events of the morning and night before, over and over. I was anxious about when we could do it again.

I dropped Kevin off at his truck and we stood there a moment talking. He promised to call me after he got off work that night. I was on cloud nine. For so long, I had wanted a boyfriend. Not someone I only saw once or twice a month, but someone I could see and talk to everyday. Those first few days, Kevin and I didn't talk about dating, but that's what both of us wanted.

After Kevin left the parking lot, I sat there a minute and thought about what I wanted to do. It was the weekend so there wasn't much planned. It was too cold to go out in the boat or jet-ski, so I decided to just go ride around for a while.

Dane called shortly after that. "How was your night?" he wanted to know. I wanted to blurt out everything that had happened, but reasoning caught up with me. "Just fine" I said. I wanted to leave it at that, but Dane pressed for more details. "How about meeting me for lunch and I'll tell you all about it?" I said.

So, Dane and I met at El Sombrero, the Mexican restaurant in Vicksburg, and over big glasses of sweet tea and plates full of fajitas I told Dane about Kevin's and mine's adventuresome night. Of course, I left out most of the juicy details but Dane got the picture. He caught on real quick that I was totally in love with Kevin. Dane was happy for me and I had him to thank for setting it all up. Without him, I probably never would have met Kevin. We left the restaurant and Dane headed off to work. I decided to go home and ride my horse.

It had been about two months since I'd been horseback riding. I'd gone to several reenactments that fall, but with the holiday season and cold weather, I'd slacked off on riding. Today would be a good day. It was about fifty degrees, but with great sunshine.

I haltered the horse and tied him up at the horse trailer. I grabbed my saddle and slung it across his back. I started to cinch it up, but noticed that it was a lot looser than the last time I had used it. It would need an extra hole on the leather strap and I didn't have a hole-punch. I would have to use a knife.

Well, that worked all of about ten seconds. The pocketknife's blade folded down and split my thumb and nail wide open, slicing the flesh all the way to the bone. I was hurt, but I was also pissed. How could I have been so stupid? I had just told Kevin the night before that I had never had stitches.

I wrapped the end of my shirt around my thumb and ran inside to show Meme. Already my shirt was drenched in blood. Meme knew immediately that I would have to go to the hospital. It was a thirty-mile drive to the hospital, made quicker by the red lights and siren I had mounted on my truck from my work with the volunteer fire department. I was proud of my grandmother's skillful emergency driving as we weaved in and out of traffic and then I remembered- we'd done this several years before, when I blew myself up. The irony of it all...

# CHAPTER THIRTEEN

After I overcame the trauma of having my thumb sliced open to the bone, things greatly and quickly improved. I consider 2000 to have been the year that I really came into my own, so to speak. Everyone always remembers his or her first love; in my case I fell hard for Kevin. After our first night together, I knew that I was deeply and madly in love with him. Some people might not think that it's possible to fall in love with someone they'd only known for a few days, but the first weeks that Kevin and I spent together only confirmed my initial feelings.

To say whether Kevin felt the same way as I did would be purely conjecture on my part. In all fairness to him, I don't think that he fell for me as hard as I fell for him. Kevin was more than three years older than me and with that extra age came maturity. I was only sixteen and was in love for the first time. It's impossible to describe my feelings of that time. I'm not a romantic, but Shakespeare is probably the only person that could have described in words how I felt.

Kevin and I were virgins in the sense that we had never had total and complete sex with another guy, if that's the right words to use. Where Daniel and I were more or less two adolescent teenagers, fumbling around unknowingly, in the world of gay oral sex, Kevin and I had the advantage of knowing a little more about the "mechanics" of gay relationships, thanks to an awareness made possible by the advent of the internet.

While there will be some who will always and forever condemn gays and their relationships, what Kevin and I were doing felt more natural than anything else I had ever experienced in my life. I won't spend time sharing the many intimate details of Kevin and my personal lives, but from the beginning we were both completely satisfied with the other and that satisfaction lasted throughout our relationship.

In January 2000 life for me took a very different path than what I was used to. My life literally revolved around Kevin's. Every day he went to college classes and in the afternoons he worked at his parent's store, but as soon as he got off from work, the time was reserved for him and me. Admittedly that time was mostly spent at my house. Kevin was deathly afraid of his parents finding out about his sexuality. So instead, it made him feel better if the time we spent together was out from under the watchful eyes of his parents.

Now, before I continue, let me say this: Kevin's parents and his brother had always suspected Kevin was gay. It would be wrong for me to say that Kevin was a sissy- he wasn't, but at times he did exhibit some tell-tell signs that might indicate his sexuality was something other than straight. Not that his parents or friends cared, but still one of Kevin's faults was his fear of their knowing.

I had my own fears and doubts about my sexuality, but the possibility of people finding out never consumed me like it did Kevin and other gay men I know- which is kind of remarkable because if anyone had more to lose, it was me. But, Kevin's parents were different than mine and I feel now as I did then, that Kevin was over-reacting when it came to people knowing that he was gay. Truth be told, everyone already suspected him anyway.

I never blamed Kevin for his fear of coming out of the closet, as that's something every gay man and woman should deal with personally. I do know that I found it aggravating for the first few months we were together, over Kevin's hesitancy to allow me near his family. To the contrary though, I introduced Kevin to all of my friends and relatives. I loved him and was more than proud to introduce him to everyone I knew. At first no one was the wiser, but the two most important women in my life took immediate notice.

My mom was the first to question me about why I was hanging out with a guy who acted and talked "gay". At first I was able to easily play it off. I simply told my mom that Kevin was most certainly not gay, he just acted a little funny sometimes. Meme, on the other hand knew that Kevin came over to my house every night and we immediately went to my room and locked the door, only to emerge hours later, him going home and me dressed only in my bathrobe. Meme may have been old, but she certainly wasn't stupid, especially after finding empty personal lubrication bottles in my garbage can.

Regardless of the tell-tale signs, both Meme and Mom kept their mouths shut for the first few months Kevin and I were together. By the time they finally knew the truth, I was past caring. Again, regardless of what they felt, they treated Kevin as well as they treated me. Kevin was always welcomed and still is in any of my family's households. I won't say it was always easy with people knowing or suspecting, but for the most part people respected our privacy and we always kept our business to ourselves.

After the initial euphoria subsided from our meeting and falling in love, we developed a good routine. Weeknights were spent together at my house and weekends were spent horseback riding, at the movies, or out doing something with another group of friends. We didn't have or know of any other gay couples in our area, so most of our time was spent with the friends that he and I had grown up with.

We got along great and for the most part never argued. I remember having the feeling at the beginning of our relationship that things were going *too* well, and that it was too good to be true. Mostly those thoughts were unfounded. The first real fight that we got into was over a vacation I had planned to Breckinridge, Colorado. Almost every February, I would go snow-skiing in the Rocky Mountains. This year I wanted Kevin to go with Meme and me. Kevin was at first excited about going, but he had never traveled much and the thought of getting to go skiing in the mountains appealed to him.

For whatever reason he began to have doubts about going and then got it into his head that we were spending too much time together and that his parents were starting to suspect that he and I had something going on that was more than a friendship. He thought that the time I spent away on vacation would be a good time for him to think things over and reevaluate his commitment to having a gay relationship.

This turn of events devastated me. Thankfully, I had sense enough to know when to leave something alone and that's exactly what I did. I let Kevin have his space.

Instead of Kevin going with us, Meme and I flew out to Denver, rented an SUV and spent a wonderful ten days in the mountains. For anyone who doesn't know, Breckinridge, Colorado is a wonderful, out-of-the-way ski resort that's perfect for someone who wants to avoid the high prices and confusion in such places as Vail and Aspen. It's only a two-hour drive from Denver but has dozens of the most amazing things to do.

Although Meme was seventy years old, she was perfectly able to keep up with me in everything but the ski slopes. We spent one day taking a snow mobile ride to the continental divide where the views of the surrounding mountains are the best in all of the Rockies. We also went cave exploring in an abandoned gold mine and took a sleigh ride around town.

Several days I spent skiing on the slopes, while Meme stayed in the cabin and read or else visited one of the spas for a facial treatment and back massage. Several years earlier I had learned to ski while on vacation to Breckinridge with my mom. Snow skiing came very easy to me and I was a quick learner, but that didn't stop me from getting into a serious predicament the first time I hit the slopes.

In Breckinridge the ski slopes are classified by three different colors. Green slopes are the easiest, their inclines are geared more towards beginners and children; blue slopes are moderately difficult and should only be used by the experienced skier; and black slopes are the steepest and most dangerous. Only expert skiers should try one of the black slopes.

Of course, my luck being the way it is, the first time I ever tried to ski, I misread the sign on the chairlift and instead of getting off on one of the green slopes, I continued to ride the chairlift all the way up the mountain where the only way down was by a black slope. I remember standing there totally alone at the top of one of the highest mountains wondering how I was going to make it down.

After contemplating for a moment whether the gods of fate were playing a cruel joke on me, I decided the best way to solve my predicament was to remove my skis, hold them and the poles in one hand and use the other hand to balance myself while stepping sideways down the mountain. It was not a pretty sight and had there been anyone else on the slopes I would have been highly embarrassed at my situation.

After nearly an hour of sidestepping my way down the side of a mountain I finally came to a blue slope that I thought was half-way negotiable with my meager skiing skills. To make matters worse, it was also at this time that I noted a sign that read "Beware of snow cats". Just my luck I thought. Not only was I barely able to make it down the mountain in one piece, now I had to worry with being eaten by a snow cat. It was only later that I realized that a snow cat is a piece of machinery that's used on ski slopes, not a vicious predator that eats wary skiers.

Needless to say, my first ski experience nearly ruined me from ever wanting to snow-ski again. By the time I took the trip with Meme to Breckinridge in February 2000, I was a confident and experienced skier, although I never summoned up the courage to try to take on the black slopes.

Another predicament that I got myself into while on vacation in Breckinridge was when I made the suggestion to Meme that we drive up to Aspen one morning for a day of shopping. On the map the drive looked like it would only take two hours. I forgot to take into account the snow and ice on the mountain roads. But, before that had entered my mind, Meme and I were loaded into the SUV and off we went headed for Aspen. I guess this would be a good time to point out that I was only sixteen years old and had only been driving for eighteen months and never in snow and ice. I'm from Mississippi, where we hardly ever get snow or ice, but that didn't stop me from being confident in myself that I could make a drive through snow and across iced mountain roads.

The first two hours into our side trip to Aspen went fine. The weather was nice and the roads were in good shape. Forty miles from Aspen the road suddenly dead-ended into a snow bank and warning signs. We had come all that way for nothing and now we had to turn around. That was not the bad part. As we started heading back to Breckinridge storm clouds were forming in the sky. Another thirty minutes and Meme and I were in the worst snowstorm either of us had ever seen. I think northerners call it a whiteout.

I won't lie, Meme looked at me and I looked at her and both of us sensed the fear. But what could we do? Stopping and calling for help was not an option. My southern pride wouldn't allow it. Instead, we plowed on, never more than ten or twenty miles per hour. Any faster than that and it was impossible to tell where the road ended and the dirt began. Slowly but surely we pressed back to Breckinridge. Somewhere about halfway back we were able to get behind a snow plow and the going was easier, but by the time we got back to our cabin later that night, both of us were worn out. The events of the day had been an experience neither of us would forget.

The next day I decided to take it easy and instead of hitting the slopes or going far from the cabin, I laid in the hot tub for several hours while simultaneously watching television.

Meme stayed in the bed and read one of the slutty romance novels she always keeps nearby. If you've ever heard the phrase "I need a vacation from my vacation", that's how I felt then. But like a good sport, I quickly recovered and spent the last few days of our vacation going on a sight-seeing tour of the local wildlife.

Of course every night I would call Kevin and let him know how much fun I was having and how much I wished he was there with me. It was during one of these late night phone conversations that Kevin brought up the idea of taking a trip with me in order to make up for not coming with me to Colorado. After discussing several places we could go, it was decided that as soon as possible, after I got back from Colorado, he and I would take a weekend trip to New Orleans.

New Orleans is only three hours from Vicksburg and I had been there before, but never out of the accompaniment of either my mom or dad. The prospect of spending a weekend down there in the party capital of the world, with just my boyfriend, seemed like a dream come true. But again, I only succeeded in getting into another predicament.

About three weeks after Meme and I returned from our ski vacation, Kevin and I finally were able to get away for the weekend. I don't remember exactly what Kevin told his parents about where he was going, but it wasn't the truth. Even though he had decided that he indeed wanted to be in a relationship with me and that he loved me just as much as I loved him, he wasn't ready to face his parents with that decision. Neither was I for that matter, but as usual I have a "I don't really give a damn" attitude and the only thing that meant something to me was Kevin. I could care less who knew about our relationship. What Kevin decided to tell his parents about where he was disappearing to for the weekend was his business. As long as he was actually going to spend that weekend with me in New Orleans, I could care less.

We left Vicksburg early on Saturday morning and arrived in New Orleans around nine. I immediately had to call my mom for directions because I didn't have a clue where anything was. I had been to eat at the Café Du Monde, a world renowned restaurant that specializes in French Beignet donuts and coffee, but was having problems locating it. It is a wonderful place, very chic, and I wanted to share a meal there with Kevin. After searching for what seemed like hours, we finally found a place to park my truck, but then had to walk several blocks to where the Café Du Monde is located. It was worth it, though. Kevin and I both agreed that the beignet donuts are some of the best we had ever had.

After breakfast, we drove over to the Hilton River Walk Hotel, where I had reservations, and checked in. We didn't stay in the room for more than a few minutes before we were out the door again and headed for Bourbon Street. Kevin and I had never been in a gay bar before and before leaving Vicksburg, I had asked some of my gay friends from off the computer which were the best clubs to go to in New Orleans. Everyone recommended "Oz" as the happening place on Bourbon Street where gay men could go to drink, dance and socialize.

At one o'clock in the afternoon not much was going on there. It wasn't exactly what Kevin and I expected but it didn't look like all that bad of a place. We made plans to come back later that night and check it out when there would be more people.

We spent the rest of the afternoon going to as many places along Bourbon Street as possible and buying as many souvenirs as we could afford. By the late afternoon we had returned to our hotel room and dropped off all the goodies we'd bought earlier in the day. We were also about to starve to death, which was a good thing in this case, because I had a wonderful seafood restaurant picked out that I wanted to go to.

Again, I had to call my mom for directions. Did I mention that my mother knows New Orleans like the back of her hand? When we finally found the place, we were tickled to death. I had eaten at the Harbor Cove Seafood restaurant that's located out by the airport in Kenner, LA and I knew that the food there was some of the absolute best.

I am a huge fan of raw oysters and nowhere are they better than at Harbor Cove. Kevin, of course, had never seen a raw oyster, much less eaten one. I showed him the proper way to "prepare" the oyster, a squeeze of lemon and a dab of horseradish, with a squirt of ketchup. That's the best way to eat them, but never one to sample just one dish, I soon had also ordered boiled crawfish and fried soft-shelled crabs. As usual, the food was out of this world. New Orleans has a reputation for some of the best Cajun food in the world and it's no exaggeration. From the minute we arrived in New Orleans, Kevin was hooked.

Later that night, after spending some quality time together in the hotel room, we again ventured out to Bourbon Street. We headed straight (no pun intended) to the gay bar. The place was jamming. There were gay men everywhere. Some were obvious about their sexuality, while others were more reserved- similar to Kevin and me.

This was the first time that either of us had ever been exposed to the gay culture and club scene. The most exposure we had ever had with anything to do with homosexuality was what we read or saw on the internet or what we experienced between ourselves. The experience was somewhat frightening, while at the same time exhilarating. It was like discovering a whole new world, but being afraid of the unknowns that the world possessed.

Personally, I was thrilled at the opportunity to experience something different. I felt as though I could be comfortable in a place like Oz. It was a lot easier for me to walk into a gay bar than it was for me to walk into one of the redneck honky-tonk bars that we have scattered around Vicksburg. But before we could even make it to the entrance of the club, Kevin grabbed me by the arm and asked me whether I thought this was a good idea or not. "What if someone we know sees us going into a gay bar?" I just stopped and looked Kevin in his face and said to him, "Look around you, there are two hundred thousand flaming homosexuals dancing half naked in the street. No one is going to notice two normal looking white boys walk into a club". That's at least what I thought…

Kevin and I had been in the club for only a few minutes when we were approached by several different guys trying to strike up conversations. Kevin was petrified, but I was comfortable talking to other gay men. It didn't take these guys long to realize that Kevin and I were complete virgins when it came to the gay clubbing scene. That was okay, though, because these guys were more than happy to take us around for a tour.

First, we were shown all around Oz; the dance floors, the balconies, the couches where people went for "quiet" time, the bathrooms, and then thankfully the exit door. Not that Oz was a bad place, but there is only so much new and crazy information that your mind can process. Once out on the street, our new friends offered to take us over a couple of blocks to another gay club called "Rawhide".

Normally, the name of a club like "Rawhide" would raise the little red flags in the yonder regions of my brain, but in April 2000 my self-defense mechanisms were not as toned as they are today. Without so much as a second thought, I agreed to accompany our new friends to Rawhide.

When we first walked into the door everything looked normal. It was actually a better first impression than I had gotten when we entered Oz. The front bar was not congested with sweaty men, the music wasn't blaring and for the most part the clientele looked like the normal, everyday business men. That was until we were led through a pair of doors, into another room.

The sight that met my eyes was one of pure terror and abject curiosity. Men were all over the place wearing hardcore leather and biker gear. Some men were the "slave", others were the "master". I murmured to Kevin, "Oh my God!" I had never heard of an S and M place before. I thought that was just something that occurred in pornographies.

I think the purpose our new friends had in taking us to Rawhide was just to shock us, which of course they achieved in doing. Needless to say, neither Kevin nor I wanted to stay there long. Oz was a daycare center compared to Rawhide.

After making a hasty retreat from the S and M dungeon, Kevin and I decided that we'd had enough excitement and chaos for one night. We had both had the same sensation inside the S and M dungeon- that if we didn't start exercising better caution we might both end up tied to a chair in leather straps and chains. We quickly hailed a cab and got it pointed in the direction of our hotel.

After being dropped off at the front lobby and seeing the cab drive away, I realized that I had left my wallet in the taxicab. My night went from fabulous to shitty. We eventually tried everything possible to get my wallet back, but no one ever turned it into the police and I was never able to find out which taxi I had left it in. I was extremely disappointed in myself, but I tried not to let it get me down for long. Most everything I had could be replaced. I was having too much fun with Kevin to let it bother me for the time being.

Kevin and I went to bed around four and didn't wake up until the hotel started calling the room to rouse us later that morning. By the time we had everything packed and ready to check out, the poor cleaning lady was beating on the door to come in. We finally got everything together and were able to check out.

About five miles outside of New Orleans, my truck's transmission broke and got stuck in fourth gear. No matter what I tried I could not get it unstuck nor could I get my truck to go over forty-five miles per hour without reaching the red line on my RPM. I was furious at this latest change of events.

At the time I had a 1999 Dodge Ram and since I'd bought it, I'd had been nothing but trouble. Every eight thousand miles, on the dot, the brake pads, calipers and rotors would need replacing- not counting the other minor parts that broke down on a regular basis. The mechanics kept telling me that it was because I was an aggressive driver but I knew that was bullshit. I had a perfect driving record and never abused any of my trucks. The transmission breaking down was just another in the long list of problems I had with that truck.

Forty-five miles an hour we drove, from New Orleans, Louisiana to Vicksburg, Mississippi. A normal three-hour trip took six hours, not to mention the dirty looks and fingers that were flashed our way for driving so slow on the interstate highway. Coupled with the fact that I had lost my wallet, I was not a very happy person.

But, we made it back safe and sound. Our two-day trip to New Orleans was definitely interesting, insane and an eye-opening experience, but also one that was a lot of fun. Kevin and I got along great. We had a wonderful time and we were determined to do some more traveling in the future. While in New Orleans, Kevin had asked me to go on a cross-country horseback ride later in the summer with his family and I, of course, had said yes.

# CHAPTER FOURTEEN

Several weeks after returning from our New Orleans trip, I finally completed my home schooling program and would receive my high school diploma, a full year early. Being only sixteen years old, I was proud to graduate with honorable grades a year earlier than my regular classmates. From the beginning I had every intention of working as hard as I could to finish the home schooling program early.

The program and curriculum that I used was from a Christian school in Pensacola, Florida called A-Beka. Where most home-schooled students would spend three or four days a week doing their lessons and watching the instructional videos, I worked through the week and weekends, except those times that I was on vacation. However, because of the ease of the curriculum and the study-at-your-own-pace concept, I was even able to do a lot of my work when I was away from home.

Some people asked me if I missed the schoolroom setting with my friends, but the answer was not really. I still went to homecomings and proms and was usually always invited to all the dances and parties. What I certainly didn't miss was the homework assignments and pop quizzes and tests. Looking back, with nearly ten years of hindsight, there's nothing I regret about choosing to finish my last two years of high school being home-schooled.

Even with my new relationship with Kevin, I didn't slack on my studies. Like I said, during the day Kevin was either at college or at work. That left me all the time I needed to take care of my schoolwork and other things around our farm. But once I graduated in May, my time was drastically freed and now instead of having work to do every day, I was faced with boredom and idleness.

Instead of sitting around the house everyday doing nothing, I would usually drive across town to Kevin's store and help him with the work that it took to run his family's business. Earlier in the previous chapters I mentioned that Kevin's parents owned a horse feed and equipment store. Many of the local farmers, cattlemen, and horsemen got all of their feed from Kevin and the store. There were always bags to be taken outside and loaded onto people's trucks. Kevin never paid me for the work, but I wouldn't have taken his money anyway. I enjoyed being up there where I could spend as much time as possible with my boyfriend.

At first, Kevin didn't like the idea of me hanging around so near his parents, but Kevin's mom immediately took a liking to me and from then on I was always welcomed in their home and place of business. They even invited me to go on several trail rides with them. For anyone who doesn't know what a trail ride is, it's when a group of people get together and spend an afternoon riding their horses through the woods. It can be a lot of fun. Mostly the only thing I ever did with my horses was to take them to a reenactment, but since becoming friends with Kevin's family I had been invited to go with them on several trail rides and had loved every minute of it. Slowly and surely Kevin was beginning to feel more comfortable with me around his parents.

At the end of May, for Memorial Day weekend, Kevin and I decided to go with Mom, Jerry, Fisher and Hannah to our condo in Destin, Florida. Kevin had never been to the beach so he was excited about our trip. It would only be for a couple of days, but we had a lot of things planned. I hauled my jet ski down there with us and although I had never used it in the ocean, I was confident that we'd have a blast.

I also decided to take everyone deep-sea fishing. Since before I was born, my family had been chartering the same fishing boat every year. Once when I was about four years old, Mom, Dad and I had gone out deep-sea fishing on this boat and I had become petrified to death when we encountered some rough and choppy seas. But, twelve years later I had complete confidence in the captain and the boat, which was named "The Mindy Lou II".

The day we had chosen to go was a bright, hot day. Perfect for catching the red snapper and grouper that we were after. We spent over eight hours on the water that day and everyone had a blast. When we returned to the pier, Kevin and I took a picture together with our catch. Everyone in our group had caught their limit in red snapper and while we weren't as lucky with the grouper, we caught some amazing mackerel, barracuda and bonitos. It was really a fun experience and I always go back to Destin for a deep sea fishing trip at least once a year.

The second thing that's worth mentioning was that Kevin and I went parasailing. Neither of us had ever done it before, but it looked like it would be a really good time. Not only did we decide to do it, but my little brother, Fisher, decided to go with us. I recommend to anyone who has the chance to parasail that you put away your fear of heights and just do it. It's an exhilarating, yet relaxing experience with wonderful views of the ocean and sea life below.

I was so busy having fun with Kevin that I didn't notice the curious glances and questioning looks my mother would direct our way. This was the first time she had really been able to observe Kevin and me together over long periods of time and she began to suspect that something more than friendship was going on. For the time being though, she didn't say anything to me about it. She kept her suspicions to herself. As time progressed, as I would later find out, she shared some of her concerns with Jerry and Meme. But again, neither of them said anything to me about it.

I've spent a lot of time talking solely about Kevin, and myself, and the vacations we took together. I don't want to leave the reader with the impression that we abandoned our friendships with our other friends. There were times when Kevin and I would take a day or two off from doing something with the other and he would go out with his friends, Gina, Stephen or Liz. I, on the other hand, would hang out with my buddies, Kenny and Wendy or Jessica.

During the spring of 2000, I also went to several reenactments; one of which was my favorite, and is held every year at Fort Gaines, Alabama in Mobile Bay. Fort Gaines is a civil war era fort that never underwent bombardment in the war, and is in near perfect condition; much like it was during the war. The group of reenactors who put on the event even had two civil war era gunboats that sail around the fort firing blank-shooting cannons, while the infantry fights it out around and inside the fort. As far as reenactments are concerned, it's one of the best there is.

I had tried to get Kevin to go with me on several reenactments, but he was totally uninterested. I was a little disappointed in his refusal to go with me, but I was just as capable of having a good time without him as I was with him. Even though I say that for the year he and I were together, everything we did revolved around the other, I don't want to leave the reader with the impression that we couldn't have fun unless we were with each other. We weren't in that type of relationship.

We always gave each other space when the other one needed it. But at the same time, we were the type of couple who were so close we could finish each other's sentences. We both had the same likes and dislikes in food, movies and sports. About the only thing we did disagree on was what type of music to listen to. He was a rock and roll fan and I listened to country. But we got along almost perfectly and during the year we were together I was the happiest I'd ever been.

Besides the fight that finally ended our relationship, there was only one other big argument that we got into and it involved a trip that he had invited me to go on with him and his family out to Colorado for a weeklong trail ride. For several months he and I had planned on me going with him and his family, but on July 4th weekend, right before we were ready to leave, Kevin withdrew his invitation.

This was the first time in our relationship that I was truly hurt by something Kevin said or did. I honestly felt as though the trust had been broken between us. The reason that Kevin gave me for breaking our plans was that hauling four horses, his mom's, dad's, his and mine, would be too crowded for the long haul out to Colorado. Once I finally prodded this excuse out of him, I offered to take my truck and trailer. But again, he shot that idea down. Come to find out, after Kevin eventually broke down and told me, his younger brother had told his parents that I was gay.

This latest turn of events hit me like a sack of bricks. At the time, I didn't think anyone knew I was gay, except of course, Kevin. The stringent denials on Kevin's part did nothing to convince his parents to change their minds. Kevin didn't want to deal with the embarrassing situation and I wasn't willing to push the issue with his parents. The decision stuck.

I spent the time that Kevin was away doing something special for myself. Instead of lying around the house for twelve days, I decided to spend a week with my grandparents in Kosciusko. It'd been a couple of months since I'd seen them and it had been even longer since I'd spent any time with them. I was also looking forward to seeing my cousins and maybe even Daniel.

The day that Kevin left with his family to Colorado, I hooked the jet-ski to my truck and headed to Papaw's house. On the way up, during the two-hour drive, I called my cousins and Daniel to let them know I was on the way.

I had not talked to or seen Daniel in about six months. The previous Christmas I had seen him in downtown Kosciusko at the Sonic Drive-In and although we only saw each other for a few minutes, he seemed genuinely happy to see me. But, when I called him this time he was a little more than reluctant to go jet-skiing with me. I hung up the phone after letting him know that if he wanted to do something with me all he had to do was call…he never called back and it would be another year before we spoke again.

I later found out during that same trip that he was in a serious relationship with a young girl from his church. Finding out really didn't bother me much. I had Kevin and was happy with that, but the thought did cross my mind about whether Daniel was happy doing what he was doing.

The week spent at my grandparents was a lot of fun, but after about the fourth day I began to miss Kevin. Four days was the longest we had been apart since we started dating. It wouldn't have done any good for me to try to call him because his phone wouldn't work way out in the mountains where they would be staying. My pride probably wouldn't have let me call him anyway. I was still a little upset at him for the way things had turned out and for the insinuations of his parents regarding my sexuality. It wasn't something that I dwelled on too long, but it was really the start of a lot of problems relating to his fear of people knowing about his sexuality and relationship with me.

As everyday passed I became more and more comfortable with my sexuality and who I was, or better put- what I was becoming. Although, I didn't have the fear that Kevin did about "coming out", I still had some reservations about the potential problems that it might cause with some of my friends and family. I had made up my mind that if anyone, whether it was Meme or Mom, or someone else, were to ask me about my sexuality, I was going to tell them the truth.

During my weeklong stay at my grandparent's house, while Kevin was on vacation with his parents, I thought a lot about our relationship, my sexuality and where my life was going. I planned on starting college that fall, but I still didn't know exactly what I wanted to do with my life. I had a lot of dreams, but not the understanding of how to achieve them.

I had a wonderful week with my grandparents and cousins. Every day was spent jet skiing on the lake or fishing for bream and bass in the pond behind Papaw's house. In the afternoons I helped Papaw work in his garden. He always had a huge garden full of butterbeans, tomatoes, sweet corn, okra, squash and a myriad of other different fruits and vegetables. And although I thought about Kevin every day, I didn't let it stop me from having fun.

A couple days after I returned to Vicksburg from Kosciusko, Kevin called. He and his family were on their way home and this was the first chance he had to call me. Again, like I said before, I was still a little upset about not being able to go with Kevin, but when we talked, I didn't let it show. As far as Kevin knew, everything was fine. But I looked at that event as being the "high-water" mark of our relationship. Things just slowly declined after that.

# CHAPTER FIFTEEN

Before I started college that fall I wanted to go on one more vacation before the summer was over. Meme and I talked it over and decided that spending a few days in the mountains of Tennessee might not be all that bad of an idea. My family and I had been to Gatlinburg, Tennessee many times before and we never tired of vacationing there. We usually went once a year during the summer, but sometimes we'd get away during the Christmas holidays as well.

Gatlinburg is a small resort town situated on the Tennessee and North Carolina border of the Great Smokey Mountains. There are all kinds of things to do there for all age groups. There's a Ripley's Believe It or Not museum, a large saltwater aquarium that would rival any in the world, trout fishing, mountain biking and gobs of other things to do that would keep a person busy year round. In the next town over, Pigeon Forge, the two biggest attractions is the Dixie Stampede, a "dinner and show" type entertainment and Dollywood, being a large theme park owned by country music legend Dolly Parton.

We always rent a cabin in Gatlinburg, but this year I went all out. Kevin still felt bad about not being able to take me with him when he went to Colorado, so when I asked him if he would go with us to Gatlinburg he readily agreed. Also going with us was my grandfather Atwood's sister, my Aunt Geneva.

Even though Aunt Geneva and Meme are exsister-in-law, they get along very well and have before and after Meme and Pop's divorce. We'd spent many weekends with Aunt Geneva at our lake house in Kosciusko, but this would be the first time we all took a trip together. Everyone was excited, especially me. The prospect of spending a week in the mountains with Kevin was not only romantic, but was probably just what we needed after having the fight about the trip to Colorado. We never really had a "making-up" after that. But, I was hoping that this trip would do it.

I went onto the internet and searched for cabins that I thought would be sufficient for the four of us. I wanted something that was big enough so that Kevin and I could have plenty of privacy without being interfered with by Meme or Aunt Geneva. That probably sounds bad to the average reader, but I was an out-of-control teenager whose hormones were racing like crazy. Besides, it was probably best that Meme and Aunt Geneva not know what we were doing.

After searching what seemed like hours, I finally found a very nice, two-story, three-bedroom cabin with a pool table and upstairs hot tub. Kevin and I were set.

It's not a long drive from Vicksburg to Gatlinburg and we arrived in time to get our key to the cabin and drive up to it before the sun settled for the evening. Even though we'd been on the road most of the day, we decided to spend the evening dining together at Damon's BBQ, one of the finest pork rib joints in the country. While waiting around for a table, Kevin and I looked at some of the brochures outside the restaurant. We saw two things that caught our eye. The first was a brochure for white water rafting. That was filed away as something to do on the day before we left. The next thing I saw that caught my eye was a brochure advertising a museum dedicated to Sheriff Buford Pusser.

After reading the brochure and digesting the focal points of Buford Pusser's life, I was astounded at what I saw. First off, I'd never heard of Pusser and second, I didn't know that there were three movies about the man's life. The "Walking Tall" sheriff, as he was known around those parts, was a legend unto himself. Whether people look at Pusser as a hero to a crime-riddled county or an over-aggressive sheriff who took too many liberties with the law, there is no doubt that the man has an amazing story.

Pusser was sheriff of McNairy County, Tennessee during the late sixties and was elected on the platform of cleaning the county of the organized crime ring known as the "Dixie Mafia". During the course of his tenure as sheriff, his wife was killed in an ambush; he himself was shot and stabbed dozens of times; he killed numerous people, but was eventually successful in fulfilling his promise of ridding the county of illegal moon-shining, gambling and prostitution. Perhaps the most famous thing Sheriff Pusser was known for, was a four-foot hickory stick carried with him at all times, and used more than once to intimidate a reluctant criminal.

Sheriff Pusser's policing tactics quickly earned him the status as the most hated law enforcement officer throughout the south by many in the organized crime world. This probably led to his eventual death at the hands of a suspicious and never-solved car accident. His death only added to the legend and lore surrounding his life. Three amazing movies were produced about his life and are so popular they are still in production today.

When Kevin and I visited the Buford Pusser museum in Pigeon Forge, Tennessee, I was so enthralled by the man I immediately bought the book "Walking Tall: The Life and Times of Buford Pusser" and all three of the movies. Over the next few days the book was read and the movies watched. The movies and book would help me eventually form a solid and infallible opinion of corruption and the police tactics used to combat that corruption.

The lessons that I learned from studying the life of Buford Pusser would later help in combating the police and organized corruption that I faced in my own hometown and state. But, that's a story for a later chapter. At the time I was only interested in Kevin and myself. But, I never tire of watching the "Walking Tall" movies.

In addition to touring the rather small Pusser museum, we also went to Dollywood and the Dixie Stampede. On the third day of our trip, we took an hour-long helicopter tour of the Smokey Mountains, which was to say the least, a very beautiful ride. At night, after Meme and Aunt Geneva had gone to bed, Kevin and I stayed up, sitting in the hot tub, until the early morning hours. We spent a lot of time talking about ourselves and our relationship and where we thought we would be in another year. I shared some of my anxieties about starting college. He talked about his difficulty dealing with his sexuality.

Kevin and I had many such talks while on our vacation and it was during one of these talks that he first broached the subject of us moving down to Hattiesburg together and going to school at the University of Southern Mississippi. To say the least I was a little bit dumbfounded. I knew that sooner or later Kevin would have to leave the community college he was attending (and the one that I would be starting in the fall), in order to continue his education at a university, but the thought didn't really occur to me how that would affect our relationship.

The University of Southern Mississippi, or USM as it is called, is a fine school with a wonderful criminal justice program, which was one area of studies that I was becoming interested in. However, I never really considered going to school there. My entire family is Ole Miss fans, and it was taken for granted that that would be where I would go. But, when Kevin asked me to move down to USM, it changed everything.

Sitting in the hot tub that night, I was non-committal towards making a decision, but in my heart the thought of getting an apartment and living together thrilled me to death. I had not given much thought as to what would happen to us when our two years were finished at the community college. Kevin had started college the year before I graduated, so somewhere in the back of my mind I knew this would present an eventual problem. But now that Kevin had asked me to move down there with him, the problem was solved and at the time I couldn't have been happier with the outcome.

On the way home from Gatlinburg, Kevin and I brought up the subject with Meme. I was driving, Kevin was in the passenger seat and Meme and Aunt Geneva were in the backseats. When I had finished my story and Kevin had thrown his two-bits in too, I looked into the rearview mirror and noticed that Meme was giving me one of those looks that said she wasn't all too happy. I decided to wait and think on it some more before I brought the subject up again.

In August 2000, a week after we'd been home from vacation, I started college, at sixteen years old. The classes I signed up for were the usual for any college freshman: Western Civilization, English Comp, Psychology I and Introduction to Spanish. But as my first class started, I didn't know what to do or what to expect.

College, even though a small community college, was quite different from high school. Although the atmosphere was more relaxed, the responsibility was double that of a high school student. I had not been in a class with other students and an instructor for over two years, and although I had a little difficulty at first getting readjusted to a classroom atmosphere, I quickly became an astute student.

Probably my initial favorite class was criminal justice. It was taught by our local sheriff, Martin Pace. Sheriff Pace, as I described in the prologue, was a man of dubious character who came into office on the coattails of the outgoing sheriff who'd been convicted in federal court of perjury and sent to prison.

I had known quite well who Sheriff Pace was. He was a dear friend of my Dad and Pops. They practically helped him get elected soon after the former sheriff left office. Whenever there was a need to involve the cops in a situation, my dad and Pops didn't dial 911, they called Sheriff Pace and he immediately, and personally, handled the matter.

Some might say that this was just the result of a concerned and dedicated sheriff, but very few people had the sheriff on speed dial twenty-four hours a day- my dad and pops happened to be two of them that did. No matter was too big or too small for the sheriff's personal attention. Whether it was investigating an embezzlement crime at the dealership or handling a routine trespassing complaint on their property, Sheriff Pace was more than willing to see to matters himself. Even at sixteen years old, I recognized the immense power and sway that my family had over the sheriff and his deputies.

But at the time, when I was a student of Sheriff Pace's, he and I both were pleased with me being there. I looked forward to gleaning the useful knowledge from the course that only someone actually in law enforcement could offer. Kevin had taken Sheriff Pace's course the previous year. It was viewed by the students as being one of the better courses to take. Sheriff Pace was an excellent and easy instructor, who kept the students enthralled with tales of police work.

Like I said, after a bumpy start, I soon got into a good routine and good grades followed. Kevin and I both went to school during the morning and the afternoons were usually spent at his store. Apparently, his parents had given up the notion that I might be gay. I was seen with enough girls and had several of my "girl" friends stop by the store when I knew his parents would be there, and for the time being, it seemed to satisfy his parent's curiosity. I'd even begun staying at his house at night rather than mine, but not much, less we rouse his parent's suspicions again.

It wasn't very many weeks after we started college that I had my first car accident. I still had my Dodge Ram and one night as I was driving home from Kevin's house, I was speeding along a gravel road and instead of having the traction to make a turn, my truck skidded up an embankment and rolled over onto the side before slamming into a large oak tree. The airbag deployed, and having the air knocked out of me and a few cuts from the broken glass, I was otherwise okay. I was in quite a bad situation though, because of the way my truck was positioned. I was unable to get out.

Instead of waiting for someone to spot the accident and call for help, which might have been forever because I was in a deserted area of the county, I was finally able to locate my cell phone, which had been tossed around, and called 911. Within ten minutes, several friends of mine from the volunteer fire department had arrived, along with an ambulance and they helped me out of my truck. I didn't want to go to the hospital, but was convinced by the paramedics to go just in case.

Let me be the first to say: I hate hospitals. I've never had a good experience there and I certainly didn't like going for what I considered to be a minor traffic accident. I expected the doctor to tell me what I already knew- that I was fine, take two aspirin and get plenty of rest. Which, of course, is what he did.

By the time I was released from the hospital later that night, everyone and their mother had turned out to see if I was going to live- everyone except my father, of course. Meme had called to tell him that I'd been involved in an accident, but his only response was to call him back if it was serious. I wasn't concerned and his absence didn't really bother me. Kevin and his parents were there, along with Mom, Meme, and numerous friends of mine from the fire department. It was kind of aggravating having everyone fussing over me when there wasn't anything really wrong- that was until I saw the damage to my truck.

My truck was a Dodge Ram 2500 4x4 with the Cummins Diesel engine. In addition, I had a lift kit and mud tires. On the road it dominated everything but the eighteen-wheelers. Yet, when I saw it at the body shop it looked as if a can opener had been taken to it. Literally, it was crumpled and destroyed. I stood there in amazement wondering how I walked away from it. Somewhere in the back of my mind, I filed away for future thought the lesson I learned that night about speeding on gravel roads.

# CHAPTER SIXTEEN

Several days after my truck wreck and after I'd recovered from the aches and pains associated with the crash, I went up to my dad's dealership and looked for a new truck. Because of my horses and trailer, I had to have a three-quarter ton, heavy-duty truck and the only thing my dad had available on his car lot was a brand new 2001 Chevy 2500 four-wheel drive, for an astonishing price of $34,000.

Even though my dad and I weren't exactly on good talking terms, we arranged for me, with Meme's help, to buy the truck at the cost that my dad paid for it from General Motors. I think the total ended up being about $25,000, which surprised me seeing as how I was not aware of the normally high mark-up associated with new trucks. But nonetheless, for the third time in as many years, I had a new truck.

A few weeks after I'd gotten my new truck, Kevin and I took it to Jackson to the after-market truck store and picked out several accessories that I thought would look good and serve a purpose on my new truck. Together we picked out the style brush guard and roll bar that we thought would look best, along with a winch, new rims and mud tires. I also had the shop install a three-inch lift kit. This raised the truck slightly to increase the ground clearance, but unfortunately I couldn't put anything bigger on there because it would have prevented me from hooking up my gooseneck horse trailer.

Even though I had nearly been killed in a serious car accident, after I bought my new truck, I spent the next several weekends showing it off to all my friends and anyone else who wanted to admire it. From the first truck I'd bought, I'd always had a one-of-a-kind truck that no one else had.

It wasn't long before I decided that I wanted to try out my new winch. North of Vicksburg, about ten miles outside of town, there's a place that we call Long Lake. It's about two thousand acres of farmland that forms a peninsula between a large horseshoe-lake. There are all kinds of mud trails and pits that are always ready to test the limits of any four-by-four truck. New truck, new mud tires and a new winch- I was ready to go.

After spending the first few minutes making my way through some of the less difficult mud holes, I decided to press the limits of my new truck. Kevin was with me that night along with several of our friends, and they all warned me not to try to take my truck through one mud hole that was notorious for swallowing trucks in its thick, soupy mud.

I had a few second thoughts until someone issued a challenge. Never to shy from a dare, I backed my truck up about two hundred feet and got a quick running start. I hit the water-filled mud hole at about forty miles an hour. Mud, water and debris went everywhere and even though I had a good start, my truck never traveled more than a few yards before becoming bogged down up to the hood and doors, in gunky mud. To say that I was stuck would be an understatement.

In order for me to extricate my truck and myself, I had to crawl through my window and ease myself off into the water and mud. Before I could make it to the front of my truck, I was up to my waist. I had to reach under the water and unhook my winch and then struggle with the cable through the messiness of the mud hole to the nearest tree, all the while undergoing the laughs and jeers of Kevin and my friends.

True to the guarantee of my winch manufacturer, it pulled my truck flawlessly out of the mud. However, there was not a single spot on my truck or me that wasn't covered in thick, caking Mississippi mud.

Having lost the dare, but spirits still intact, I was insistent on giving the mud hole another shot. I reasoned that if I had a little more speed and kept the RPMs up, then maybe my truck would make it through. Kevin, on the other hand, knew my ego was bruised enough and convinced me that sometimes discretion is the better part of valor. Needless to say, I didn't try to make my way through the same mud hole twice that night. The only place that Kevin would agree to go next was the nearest carwash.

Many times, Kevin and I spent weekends and nights together, such as the previous one. At sixteen I was still wild and crazy and was constantly looking for a party. Thankfully, Kevin was a little bit older and more mature and on numerous occasions kept me out of trouble.

The one and only time that I have ever tried to outrun the police was indirectly Kevin's fault. In his defense, I will say that Kevin obeyed the law to the letter. He always drove the speed limit and would not even consider doing something wrong. But, when it came to preventing his being outed as a homosexual or being caught, quite specifically in the act, he was more than willing to justify our course of action.

About a month after I'd gotten my new truck and about two weeks after I'd started college, Kevin and I decided to spend a night eating fast food and driving around Vicksburg, which was becoming one of our favorite things to do. During the course of the night, we found ourselves at Long Lake, except this time we hadn't come to mud ride.

Usually, Long Lake is abandoned. The only time a person might encounter a vehicle is either during the day or on the weekends. It was highly unusual to see another vehicle there late at night, which, I guess, is the reason we chose the spot to have sex.

Before I go any further let me say this: it was completely Kevin's idea that night, to go to the deserted area of Long Lake, for the purpose of having sex. I didn't like the idea of having sex in my truck and had never done it before. But somehow, Kevin convinced me that it would be fun. I vaguely remember something being said about my sense of adventure.

We pulled off the side of the gravel road and shut down the engine. It was a moderately cool night and we were comfortable with the windows partly down. After a few minutes of routine kissing, we climbed into the backseat and removed our clothes. The only noise was from my radio. I had a Tone-Loc CD playing his hit favorite, *Wild Thing*.

I'll spare the reader the intimate details of what Kevin and I were exactly doing other than to say that a cool night quickly became hot and sweaty. But before our steamy night could be concluded, the red and blue lights of a deputy sheriff's car appeared behind my truck. There was no way that Kevin and I could clothe ourselves in time to beat the officer as he approached the window. Even if we did, I don't think that anything could be said to the deputy to explain what we were doing on a deserted road, and why we were there. It was quite obvious.

What was worse was that I knew every deputy on the sheriff's department and they knew me. What they didn't know was that I was gay. I could only imagine the rumors and innuendo that would flood the ears of everyone in Vicksburg after the deputy had made known that he caught me and another man having sex together in a deserted part of a cotton field. I wasn't scared of going to jail because I knew that the deputy would not arrest us. But more importantly, I was afraid of the embarrassment. So, instead of trying to talk my way out of a very compromising situation, I ran.

No sooner had I looked up from the back seat and saw the deputy emerging from his car, than like a bold of lightening, I was back in the driver's seat and had the engine cranked and the transmission in gear.

I stomped the gas pedal and watched as a rooster tail of dirt and rocks were flung from my tires at the deputy and his car. Finally my truck's tires caught traction in the deep gravel and I was able to put some distance between the deputy and ourselves before he could make it back inside his car and give pursuit.

During these first initial seconds, Kevin remained naked lying on the floor of the backseat. It was only after I'd made the decision to flee and the truck was in motion that he decided to speak. "What are you doing!!!" he screamed. To this day I don't remember what my response was, but I think he realized that the alternative to fleeing was worse than fleeing itself.

Thankfully the outlaw gods were on my side that night. I had never driven so fast or so reckless, as I did on that curving and winding gravel road. Because it had not rained all summer, the road threw up a torrential cloud of dust, which to my advantage prevented the deputy sheriff from closing within fifty yards of my truck. But nonetheless, he kept up with everything I tried to do. I didn't have a plan, but I knew that I would soon have to shake him or else risk having other cops join the chase.

I knew every mud trail and back road that ran through Long Lake and my only hope was to lose the deputy on one of them. But nothing I tried seemed to work. Just when I thought all my options had been spent I decided to go off-road completely. Without missing a beat, I swung my truck from the road and off into a cotton field and without stopping or slowing down to shift into four wheel drive. I made for the other side in hopes the deputy would follow and perhaps get stuck in his effort- which is exactly what happened.

When I made the turn from the road to the cotton fields, the deputy turned with me. My truck would easily make it through the soft plowed fields, but his Crown Victoria immediately bogged down and became stuck. As I put more and more distance between us, I realized that he wasn't moving anywhere, anytime soon.

After a nearly five minute chase, his backup must have still been a good ten minutes away because when we made it to the other side of the cotton field, Kevin and I immediately made for the main highway and from there to the nearest dark hiding spot that I could think of.

I parked my truck about thirty yards off the highway and on a piece of land that my dad owned that was thankfully very close to where Long Lake Road met the highway. I quickly shut off the engine and killed the lights. We were parked behind a grove of trees and it was impossible to see us from the road and with a little luck, no one would find us.

My heart was still racing nine hundred miles-an-hour and the adrenaline level in my body was so high that I was shaking uncontrollably. But, for the moment we were safe. It was only then that I fully realized that I was still naked except for a pair of socks. Poor Kevin was walking round and round my truck exclaiming how he just couldn't believe that I just outran the sheriff's deputy.

After a few minutes we finally calmed down enough to talk. During the chase Kevin had remained in the backseat and watched out the rear window for every move the deputy made. Come to think of it, he wasn't a bad wingman that night. He quickly agreed that under the circumstances we had no choice but to run. The other scenario of having to explain to the cop why we were naked and in the middle of nowhere was far less appealing. Our main predicament at the moment was finding a way to make it back to my house without being seen on the road.

I was very worried about the fact that the deputy might have seen and recorded my tag number, seconds before we drove away and it wouldn't be until a few days later that I could find out for sure from my godfather, Kenny, whether or not the deputy had recognized my truck or gotten my tag number. I did have a unique truck that was easily recognizable, but thank goodness luck was on my side. The deputy had neither recognized my truck nor had he been able to get my tag number before the chase began. How he missed that is still unknown to this day.

Kevin and I remained at our hideaway until the next morning. I knew after a chase like that and the embarrassment handed to the sheriff's deputy chasing me, that they would be out looking everywhere for a truck that closely matched mine and I didn't want to take the chance. We decided it was best to stay put until daylight. That didn't stop me from becoming paranoid as hell on the drive home that morning.

Several days later, after the paranoia subsided, and I found out for sure that the cops were not after me, I was able to reflect on our unfortunate and totally preventable incident.

As I stated before, I had not wanted to have sex with Kevin that night in my truck. I had begged him just to go back to the house with me, but he had persistently declined. Instead he had wanted a "quickie" and then a restful night sleep in his own bed. His desires, and my reluctance to decline, had nearly cost us severe embarrassment at the least and a trip to jail or our lives at the most. It was an important lesson that I learned about responsibility and positive decision-making that I would never forget. Unfortunately, it was a lesson that I would have to be taught again and one that would nearly cost us our relationship.

# CHAPTER SEVENTEEN

There comes a time in almost every relationship when the two people involved face a certain crisis that tests the strength of their relationship. For nine months, Kevin and I had managed to get along very well, keep our relationship private, all the while maintaining an image of two straight heterosexual guys. Up until that time we'd mostly succeeded. Sure, there were some questionable looks and quiet whispers, but no one had openly accused us of being gay. But that was about to change.

Saturday, September 30, 2000 was a day that began like any other in our relationship. We had decided earlier in the week to eat dinner together at one of my favorite restaurants in Jackson called Shapley's, followed by going to the theatre to watch a late movie. Kevin was then going to come back to my house and spend the night. The next morning we were going to saddle two of my horses and go for a trail ride. But we never made it that far.

After dinner, we drove over to the Tinseltown theatre in Pearl, Mississippi and barely arrived in time for the opening credits of the movie. We chose a seat in the back where we could have a little privacy. I don't want to leave the impression that we were fooling around in a theatre, because we weren't. We always chose the back because it just looked better when two guys attended a movie together if they were seen by as few people as possible, or so our thoughts went at the time.

After the movie, which didn't end until almost midnight, we left and started the drive home. We had left Kevin's truck at his parents' store, which was along the interstate. It was actually a convenient spot to meet and a lot of times Kevin and I had our friends meet us there before all going over to Jackson for a movie or a trip to the mall.

When I pulled up to the front of the building, Kevin jumped out and closed my door. We were planning on him following me back to my house, but before Kevin got in his truck he said to me through my truck window that he needed to go inside the store for a minute and wanted me to come along.

I didn't think much of his request and with my truck's engine still running, I climbed down from the cab and followed him inside. The place was deserted and all the lights were off. As soon as we were through the doors, Kevin flung himself on me like a human projectile. There was no doubt as to what his immediate intentions were. Kevin wanted sex and I was the means to that satisfaction.

We didn't normally do things like this and it occurred to me that we were playing a dangerous game, but I also knew that no one ever came around the store at 1:00 in the morning. I thought we were safe and I didn't let my paranoia stop me from obliging our sexual desires that night.

After kissing and groping one another passionately for a few minutes, I removed a portion of Kevin's clothing and we moved over to a stack of 50-pound horse feed bags to lie on. In another few minutes we were almost entirely naked and so engrossed in each other that we didn't hear the vehicle pull into the parking lot, or Kevin's three friends Gina, Stephen and Liz, get out of their vehicle and open the front door to Kevin's store.

It was only when the door chime sounded and they were fully inside the store, that Kevin and I both realized we'd been caught. Standing there were Kevin's three best friends. Whatever assumptions and private beliefs they had about mine and Kevin's unusual relationship ended right there in the feed room of Total Horse.

The look on their faces expressed abject horror. They had just witnessed two of their friends, naked, on a stack of feedbags, having sex, and who up until this point had maintained their absolute conviction that they were straight. Any doubts should have ended right then and there.

Before Kevin and I fully grasped the compromising situation we had just been caught in, he literally threw me off of him, flung his clothes on and ran out the door after Gina, Stephen and Liz, who had turned on their heels and left out the door seconds after they'd come in.

No sooner had they left than Kevin was dressed and running out the door after them. I just stood there in stunned silence. Five minutes went by, then 10 and finally after almost thirty minutes Kevin came back inside. Even though I knew Gina, Stephen and Liz well enough to call them friends, (hell, I'd even dated Liz two years before), I didn't have enough guts to walk out there with Kevin and try to explain to them what they'd just seen. So, instead I just stayed inside Kevin's store alone and in the dark wondering what in the world Kevin could be saying to them to minimize the damage that they'd caused that night.

What in God's name were they doing driving around at 1:00 in the morning and why were they cruising past Kevin's store? None of them lived even remotely close and the road that Kevin's store is on is not on any of their normal routes. Supposedly, they were just bored and riding around that night when they just happened to pass the store, saw our trucks there and decided to stop by to say hello. No doubt, they got the surprise of their lives.

When Kevin did come back inside the store, he was a

totally different person. Defeated and depressed, and almost in tears, he didn't have much to say to me. I was full of questions about what they had said and what he had told them. The only thing that Kevin was willing to tell me was that he had convinced them that we weren't gay.

As if the shock of getting caught right in the act of having sex wasn't bad enough, the shock of what Kevin said brought home all the tragedy of the night's events. My mind raced as I tried to contemplate how three people, who had just witnessed two guys having sex, could be convinced that those two guys weren't gay. That didn't fly with me, but somehow Kevin had convinced himself that they believed him.

During the course of his conversation with Gina, Stephen and Liz, he had told them that we weren't really gay, but had only been drinking alcohol that night and were horny, which was the cause of our lack of judgment in choosing each other as a sexual partner in lieu of a woman. Apparently, this excuse had worked because Gina, Stephen and Liz had bought it and had assured Kevin that they would never tell anyone what they had seen that night.

When Kevin had finished telling me all of this, I just stood there, dumbfounded that he could be so stupid as to believe such garbage. Surely, he didn't really believe that he had convinced his friends that he wasn't gay. I mean, my God, they had just caught us right in the middle of having sex.

I don't remember the exact moment when I had decided that I was no longer ashamed of being gay, but it was probably a few months before that night. I knew who I was and I didn't see a reason to be ashamed of it. I knew what kind of family I'd come from and I knew what some of my family members would say. Worse, I knew that some of my family would be embarrassed to know that I liked men over women. But that was something I was ready to deal with. So, on the night that Kevin and I were caught, it actually, in some weird way, came as a relief to me. I wouldn't have to pretend any longer. Kevin and I could be who we really were. Kevin didn't see it that way, though.

Standing there in the darkness of Total Horse, I tried everything I could to get Kevin to see the positive side of this situation. He would not have to lie to his friends anymore. If they were his true friends, they wouldn't care one way or another, I reasoned. But, homophobia was so ingrained in Kevin's brain, it was impossible for him to see anything but shame and embarrassment.

Our conversation was short that night. I tried to get him to come home with me so we could talk more about what had happened, but he refused to even look me in the eye. All he wanted to do was be alone. I did manage to get him to talk to me on our cell phones while we both drove to our own houses. Before we left the store, I tried to kiss him and give him a hug and reassure him that everything would be okay, but he refused to even touch me. He just pushed me away and slowly climbed in his truck and drove off.

I stood there for a moment and watched him leave before, I drove away myself, but as soon as I got going I called him on the cell phone and tried one more time to get him to talk to me. The only thing he said was that our relationship was over and that we couldn't see each other anymore.

By this time I was almost in tears. I thought it was so unfair that this would be what ended our relationship. I had had a dream at one time that Kevin and I would be able to live together happily and openly without having to worry about what people thought, but now it seemed like that was only a fleeting memory. No matter what, Kevin was determined to protect his secret, even at the price of losing someone he was supposed to love dearly. I was crushed and was on the verge of going home and confessing everything to Meme. Surely, she would understand.

But, I didn't go home that night. I drove around for what seemed like hours. At daybreak, I was still driving around with no clue of what to do or where to go. I didn't want to go home alone and face the reality that this was probably the end of Kevin and me. That wasn't an option, but I knew it was something that I would have to face.

The thought occurred to me that Kevin might do

something stupid. I knew he was emotional and didn't make good decisions during stressful times. I hoped he would have enough sense not to try and kill himself. As I continued to drive that morning I wanted to pick up the phone and call him. It took every bit of discipline that I could summon to prevent my hand from picking up my cell phone and dialing his number. I knew that he needed to be alone at a time like this and I knew that I would have to give him his space to sort things out in his own mind.

Personally, I didn't consider our friends knowing about our sexuality as that big of a deal. I'm sure they suspected already. But Kevin had denied being gay and had lied to them for so long that when they finally did discover the truth, the shame was too much for him to bear. Instead of standing up like a man and dealing with the facts head-on, he chose to seclude himself and ignore the problem. But sticking his head in the sand solved nothing- it only made things worse.

For six days I stayed glued to my phone. I wanted to be near it at all times should Kevin decide to call. Every day we went to class at the same college, but never did he try to make eye contact with me or even acknowledge my existence. The silence was killing me, but I just couldn't bring myself to pick up the phone and call him. I'd made up my mind to leave him alone until he called me.

Finally after six agonizing and emotional days, Kevin wanted to talk. He called my house late Friday afternoon and wanted me to meet him secretly, at the same place where he and I had hid from the police the night we ran from them. I don't have any clue why he chose that spot, other than it was remote and no one would be able to see us from the road. But at the time, I could have cared less where he wanted to meet. We could have met in the stall of a woman's bathroom for all I cared. The only thing I was concerned about was finally getting to talk to him again. Six days may not seem like a long time to most people, but when you are separated from the person you love and are not sure if you'll ever see each other again, six days can seem like an eternity.

When I arrived at our hideaway spot, Kevin was already there and was sitting on his truck's tailgate. My heart beat with anticipation at what I was getting ready to hear. I didn't know what Kevin was going to do or say. I got out of my truck and went and sat down beside him on his tailgate. We just sat there for a few minutes before either of us spoke. Finally the silence was no longer bearable, and I asked him what was going on.

Like the floodgates of a dam opening, Kevin burst into tears and apologized over and over for the way he had acted. He was profusely sorry for having wanted to break up with me. He had missed me terribly during the past week and had had time to think about a lot of things. He didn't want us to break up and he was finally ready to be honest with himself and his sexuality. He wanted me to take him back.

I sat there in stunned silence. I just sat with my arm around him, listening to everything that he was saying. I sat there taking it all in and wondering how this all could be happening. Kevin didn't need to apologize to me; I was never really upset with him. I was upset at the thought of our relationship being over. As we sat there, I did my best to convince him that everything was okay and that I would never stop loving him. This had been the single most traumatic thing that Kevin and I had been through together and it looked like we might have made it.

We lost count of the number of hours we stayed there, sitting on his truck's tailgate talking about everything wrong with the world, the plight of gay men and women everywhere and how given the opportunity, we could make it right. It was so damn unfair how straight couples could enjoy the openness of their relationships without the ridicule of their parents and friends.

Even though Kevin had made the decision to stay with me (damn what his friends think), he wasn't ready to bring his sexuality to his parents, but he wasn't going to lie to them if they asked. I made the same decision myself. It was better if we tried to keep everything private, but we wouldn't lie anymore if anyone asked. That seemed like good logic at the time.

I didn't know whether it was a good time to bring up the subject of moving in together down in Hattiesburg, but decided that that would be the true test of Kevin's promise of not being concerned about what people thought about the two of us. For the past two months, the subject had been brewing in the back of our minds and we discussed it on occasions, but no firm decision had been made. I only gingerly broached the subject to him again, and to my surprise he still readily agreed.

It was both of our beliefs that our relationship would improve and things would be easier if we lived together outside of the prying eyes of gossiping Vicksburgians. Both of us knew too many people in Vicksburg to keep our secret forever. But in Hattiesburg, at college, the cover would be easier. There were still those thoughts in the back of our minds that just couldn't deal with the possibility of a totally open relationship. It was one thing having your best friends and family knowing; it was quite different living an open and out homosexual relationship in southern, conservative Mississippi.

Nonetheless, throwing caution to the wind, we planned on moving full steam ahead with our plans of finding an apartment, registering for classes at a new college and then moving in together. After what we had just been through, this small victory seemed like a dream come true. We could finally be together, really together, in a real relationship, almost just like a straight couple.

There was one last obstacle to overcome- Meme. I guess Meme thought that eventually I would have to be turned loose and given room to let my wings spread, but that didn't mean she would willingly let me go. It took some argument and persuasion, but I was soon able to win her over to my side. However, there was one stipulation: she had to go and pick out the apartment with me.

# CHAPTER EIGHTEEN

Kevin never did particularly recover from the unfortunate episode of getting caught having sex with another man by his three best friends. Yes, he still talked to them and on occasions went out on the weekends with them, but he was never comfortable having them and me together with him. For Gina's, Stephen's, and Liz's parts, they played the role of the believing and sympathetic friend that Kevin had hoped they would be. Privately though, they had many concerns.

About two weeks after Kevin and I patched things up, Liz called me and wanted to know if I could meet with her and talk. When I agreed to drive over there, I knew in the back of my mind that she was going to want the truth- the real truth from me- and I didn't know whether I would be able to lie to her or not.

No sooner had I walked in the door than Liz brought up the subject about what happened that night at Total Horse. I let Liz say her piece and ask the million-dollar question- are you and

Kevin gay? I respected Liz and felt as if there was no way possible that I could lie but I still felt an obligation to Kevin.

Even though I had dated Liz for a few months and was intimately close with her, I didn't feel as if I should be the one to explain to her our relationship and I told her such. It was not my place and if she wanted that kind of information she would have to ask Kevin.

Of course, that didn't satisfy her curiosity and she only pushed harder. Why did it matter, was my question? Truth be known it shouldn't have. I was a firm believer then, as I am now, that Kevin should have sat his three friends down and explained to them the truth. The truth will set you free, so they say, but Kevin only confounded the situation by his silence. Too many questions were left unanswered and it was making his friends turn to me for the answers, answers that I wasn't ready to give. That was Kevin's job and one that he would eventually have to do.

I was able to get Liz to promise not to bring the subject up with Kevin. I didn't think it would help the situation if Liz or anyone else pushed Kevin for the true story. Yes, Kevin had made up his mind to tell them the truth, or anyone else, if they asked, or so he said, but that was not an option that I wanted to test. I really felt that if everything just died down and went back to normal that Kevin would forget about the whole thing and quit worrying about it. That was the purpose of making Liz promise not to hassle him about it. I told her that when Kevin got ready to officially come out to his friends then he would do so, but not a day sooner.

While Kevin was dealing with his inner demons, outwardly things returned to some resemblance of normalcy. We still went out on the weekends, we still spent the night at each other's house and together we were extremely happy. Unfortunately, because of Kevin's wishes to avoid his parents' and other friends' suspicions, he gradually became more and more isolated from them, which subsequently drove him closer to me. It was a pattern that I quickly recognized and brought to his attention, but one that he seemed to care nothing about.

It was easier for Kevin to avoid his parents and friends than to possibly face their questions and scrutiny. The day was coming when he would have to confront his sexuality openly with his parents and friends but he wanted to delay it as long as possible.

As the days passed, the more he pressed for a decision by me about whether we could get an apartment together in Hattiesburg. Going to USM and moving in with me was the escape from Vicksburg that Kevin so desperately craved, anything to get away from the gossip and nosy people who were so concerned with our lives.

Finally, at the end of October I had made my decision. I would get an apartment with Kevin in Hattiesburg and move out of Meme's house, change colleges and live two hours away from home.

In making this decision, I knew that I was doing something that would possibly change my life forever. Moving out of the home that I'd known for so long, away from the care and guidance of my grandmother, and into a place where for once I was totally on my own, to make my own decisions, and handle my own household. It was a big step and although I knew that Kevin would be there, I felt as if I was doing this alone.

On Halloween day, Meme, Kevin and I loaded up in my truck and drove down to Hattiesburg to look for a place to live. I had found several nice apartments on the internet that I thought would be sufficient for Kevin and me, but once we got down there and saw them, I began to think differently.

We were not impressed with anything we saw. All of the apartments that I'd chosen to look at were old, shabby and less than the quality of housing I was used to. Even if I had wanted to live in one of the older, less expensive apartments around Hattiesburg, Meme would not have allowed it. In her words, she wanted something that was nice enough for her to stay in and not be embarrassed, or to worry about pests and insects.

For the next hour we continued to drive around town looking for a better set of apartments. We finally saw the Foxgate Apartments off Westover Road, two turns away from the interstate. Foxgate was clean, new and upscale. After touring one of the units, we were thoroughly impressed. This was the place.

We sat down with the landlady and signed a twelve-month contract for a two-bedroom apartment at six hundred dollars a month, starting in January 2001. To say the least, Kevin and I were thrilled to death. We actually were going to move into our own place. Meme was happy because I'd be living in a very nice part of the city, practically no crime and in an upscale luxury apartment. Kevin and I were happy because we finally had a place of our own; close to the college campus and right in the middle of where we needed to be. The only thing left to do was pick out our furniture.

Our next stop was the furniture and Pier 1 Imports stores. There we bought a plush blue leather living room set that included a couch, sofa, love seat and ottoman. We got coffee tables, lamps, silverware, new mattress and pillows and everything else it takes to furnish a new dwelling. In all, we spent over six thousand dollars that day on furniture, washer/dryer and other household items.

Meme and I went all out on our choice of furnishings. Kevin just sat back. I think he probably could care less about what our new apartment looked like. It's funny because Kevin was the feminine guy in the relationship and you would have thought he would have been the one to want to pick out all the furnishings and decorate the apartment, but instead the chore fell to Meme and me- which was fine, of course. My apartment, when we were finished, looked just as masculine as any other bachelor's place.

I'd always wanted to decorate my own place in a civil war-type motif and now given the chance, I went all out. I ordered dozens of civil war paintings from my favorite artists, Don Troiani, John Paul Strain and Mort Kunstler. Thousands of dollars were spent just on the paintings alone, but during the two months before we were planning to move in, I poured money, artwork, and paint into our new apartment to make it look as beautiful and unique as possible.

When I finally finished and the stores had delivered everything and set it up, my apartment was a walk-in museum and living history of memorabilia of everything pertaining to the American Civil War. Some might have said that I'd overdone it for such a small place, but I was proud of it. Kevin just shook his head. He was planning to bring his bedroom suite from his house in Vicksburg and although it probably wouldn't ever get used, he felt it was necessary in order to keep up the appearance of two single, straight, bachelor men living in the same apartment.

By the Christmas holidays we were completely finished and our new apartment was ready to be moved into. I'd even stocked all the shelves and pantries with non-perishable foods. I'd had the phone lines set up, hell, I'd even bought a new computer and had turned Kevin's bedroom into our computer and multimedia room. The only thing left for us to do would be to move our clothes into the closets and we'd be set.

At the time, Kevin and I had put everything that had happened behind us. We were happy and were looking forward to the future when we would move in together. Even Meme was excited about me going to a new college and starting out on my own. At first she had been a little reluctant, but she soon came around when she saw how excited I was about it. It was a good thing too, because if I were going to be able to concentrate on my studies, I would need all the help I could get from Meme-financial and moral.

After finding, leasing and decorating our new apartment there was only one thing left to do and that was to go and register for our spring classes at the University of Southern Mississippi. We knew that Kevin would not have any problem- he had graduated with all A's from Warren Central High School and had more than a year under his belt in classes from the local community college in Vicksburg. I, on the other hand, would probably have some difficulties because I had home schooled my last two years of high school and only had one semester of courses.

True to our suspicions, the USM Registrar's Office was going to require me to attend one more year of junior college before allowing me to enroll at their university. I tried to appeal their decision, because after all, I was a superb student. I had always made A's and B's and had scored a 21 on my ACT. I felt just as capable as any other student, but nothing could be done. I would have to take additional junior college courses and demonstrate a history of high test scores.

This news was a bit devastating to me. Kevin and I had just spent dozens of hours and thousands of dollars preparing our apartment so we could live in Hattiesburg and go to school at USM. The only alternative I had, if I was still going to move there, would be to drive twenty miles one way, every day, to the nearest junior college in the area.

I had heard of Jones County Junior College. It was the largest junior college in the state and had an excellent reputation both in the academic and sports curriculum. I wasn't exactly keen on going there. I would much rather go to school with Kevin at USM, but under the circumstances, it wasn't a bad choice. I would do anything, and go to school anywhere, to be able to stay in Hattiesburg and live with Kevin in our new apartment. A year there wouldn't be bad and then I could go to USM.

# CHAPTER NINETEEN

During the late fall, soon after we had picked out our apartment, something happened in my life that changed my course of thinking forever. I had become interested in law enforcement through my introduction to Buford Pusser, along with the criminal justice classes I had been taken in college, and was certainly beginning to think that I might be going to spend a career as a law enforcement officer. I was soon given an education, however, about how in reality, law enforcement in my town truly worked.

One night after class, I drove over to Kevin's house so I could sit down with him and study for a test the next day. Kevin had taken the same course a year before and knew the subject well. He always offered to help me study and even though at times we were distracted from the task at hand, due to our attractions to one another, I seemed to always do better on my test after having spent time studying with Kevin.

When we were done studying, it was past eleven o'clock and the only reason I didn't stay the night was because we both had class the next day and I didn't have a change of clothes. I would have to drive home and stay in my own bed and wait to see Kevin the next day.

I said my goodbyes to Kevin and his family and left their house for the thirty minute drive back to mine. About ten minutes after leaving Kevin's house, I turned onto Highway 61 South and headed for the interstate. When I hit the city limits of Vicksburg I slowed my speed down, but it apparently wasn't slow enough because a city patrolman turned his blue lights on and motioned for me to pull over in the nearest gas station parking lot. This time, I didn't flee.

I wasn't nervous, just agitated. I didn't think I had been speeding and if I had, I certainly wasn't going much over the speed limit. I was very familiar with Hwy 61 and knew all of the speed limit signs. I knew when I could speed up and when to slow down. I was convinced I had been within the confines of the law. The police officer that came to my window wasn't so convinced.

"I need to see your driver's license," the officer said. I already had it ready and politely handed it over. "Do you know why I stopped you tonight?" was his next question. Again I politely told him that I did not know why, but was certain that I had not been speeding. "I clocked you doing 72 in a 45 mph zone."

I knew that was bullshit, and if indeed he had clocked that speed, it had to have been somebody else. I'd spent enough time riding with my friend Dane Davenport, in his highway patrol car, to know a thing or two about how radar guns worked. There are times when they will lock onto a car going away from them rather than the intended target coming towards them. This is called "radar ghosting".

I tried talking courteously to the policeman who was a young and inexperienced officer. I later learned that these were the most difficult to deal with because the vast majority of them are rookies and have something to prove. I didn't have this knowledge at the time and the most plausible thing to do, it seemed, was to argue with the cop.

The more I tried to explain that I had not been speeding, the more irate and arrogant he became. Never once did I raise my voice, shout or cuss at him, but he continued to get more out of control.

After he had taken a moment to go back to his car and check my driver's license against their criminal database he returned to my truck window. "Can I have permission to search your vehicle?" he asked.

I had only been pulled over by a cop one other time and it was to tell me that I had a broken taillight on my horse trailer. I'd never dealt with an officer who was so arrogant and demanding and I'd certainly never been asked to let one search my personal property.

In the nicest way I could, I told the officer "Under normal circumstances, I would let you search my vehicle, but it is late at night. I'm trying to get home and get to bed because I have a college test in the morning. I don't have anything to hide, but I feel that your search would be unreasonable." Apparently, this was the wrong thing to say to the asshole.

"Ok then, step out of the truck, I'm placing you under arrest for reckless driving." I was speechless. "This is just fucking perfect," I thought. Without further argument from me, I stepped out of my truck and was placed in handcuffs and escorted to the back of my truck and told to stand there and not move. The officer then proceeded to search my truck, being not too careful in his endeavor.

About this time, a second officer arrived on the scene. It was Joe Adams, an officer I knew very well and was happy to see. As I would later find out, he had heard my name broadcasted over the police radio, when the asshole officer had run my license, and decided to come to the scene to see what the problem was.

As soon as Joe got out of his car, I started blabbing my mouth ninety miles an hour about how I'd done nothing wrong. I wasn't speeding, but yet was being treated like a common criminal. Joe listened to what I had to say and then went and talked to the patrol officer who had pulled me over.

A few seconds later, another officer showed up. It was the night shift lieutenant. Although Lieutenant Jeffers knew my family, I had never met the man, but when he got out of his patrol car and came over and told me he was here to help clear up the problem and that he knew my dad, I was happy to meet him.

Lieutenant Jeffers immediately took me out of handcuffs and had me explain to him what had happened. I told him the same thing that I had told Joe Adams. I had not been speeding, the officer was mistaken and that he had become rude, arrogant, and offensive when I wouldn't agree with him and had arrested me because I wouldn't let him search my truck.

The lieutenant promised to get everything cleared up quickly and get me back on the road. While I was sitting on my truck's tailgate, watching Joe Adams and Lieutenant Jeffers talk to the patrol officer, several more cops showed up including the deputy chief of the department, Jack Dowe. It began to register in my mind that when the top level of the police department's administration had heard on the police radio that I'd been pulled over, and was having some problems with the officer, they all responded. I knew my family had power and influence with the local cops, but never like this and never at 12:00 midnight. I was beginning to get a little embarrassed over the big fuss.

It didn't take long for the deputy chief, lieutenant and the other officers on scene to explain to the rookie cop that I was the grandson of a prominent businessman in town, Emmett Atwood, and the stepson of a very successful attorney, and as such was not to be treated in the fashion that I had been.

Deputy Chief Dowe brought my license back to me and offered an apology for his officer's behavior. He explained to me that the guy was a new officer and didn't have much experience. Deputy Chief Dowe assured me that no citation would be issued and that I was free to go, again apologizing for the inconvenience.

I climbed in my truck and through the window offered my

thanks and appreciation to Joe Adams and Deputy Chief Dowe. I drove away from the gas station parking lot sincerely grateful for their help, but in the back of my mind I had serious apprehensions about the officer's conduct. I wondered what would have happened had I *not* been the grandson of a prominent businessman and stepson of an attorney. Would I have been arrested on a false and trumped-up charge, solely for the purpose of helping a rookie cop make his arrest quota for the week? If this happened to me, was it happening to other people in the city?

The gears in my head wound into action. That night was the first time "police corruption" flashed in my mind. What was going on and just why was that officer such an asshole? If he treated me that way, then surely he treated everyone that way. It wasn't right, and I was more than a little curious as to whether other people had gone through the same thing I had that night.

After I left the parking lot and while driving home, I was more than a little shaken about what had happened. In fact, it downright scared me. That officer might have punched me in the jaw if I had decided to cuss him back. That wasn't my idea of how the police should operate and I made up my mind to do something about it.

I learned two very important lessons the night I was rough-handled by the rookie police officer- some police officers are corrupt and never do anything to piss them off. It was two lessons I learned, but would be bound to repeat several times over.

Not content with letting the matter die and thanking the deputy chief and Joe Adams for helping me out, I started looking for a way to retaliate against the corrupt officer who had so rudely and arrogantly treated me with such disrespect. Committing a crime was out of the question, but the more I thought about doing something, the more the picture became clear.

The following Sunday I picked up my local newspaper, The Vicksburg Post, and turned to the editorial section. The thought came to me one night while lying in bed- I would write a letter to the editor and explain what happened that night, thus exposing the officer as a potential liability to the police department and a threat to the citizen population. No one deserved to be treated the way I was and no one should be arrested on false charges. I hoped to bring some exposure to this injustice. What I did instead was to cause animosity and outright hostility by persons in the Vicksburg Police Department.

In my letter to the editor I stated the facts as they occurred that night and then went into a short rendition of the abuse of power and quasi-military type mentality of some of our local police. I pointed out that we have a very strong constitution in this country whose purpose is to protect innocent citizens from the same abuse of public power that I experienced at the hands of an untrained rookie cop.

I went on to call for higher standards of training among law enforcement and pointed out that law officers in the state of Mississippi are not required to attend the training academy until after they've been on the force for a year. That means that potentially thousands of men and women are given guns and badges every day and turned loose to police our streets with little or no training. As unbelievable as it sounds, it was and is occurring every day in Mississippi.

I took the opportunity to criticize the police chief for hiring untrained officers which probably contributed to the highly unethical conduct I encountered on the night of my confrontation with the officer. I left no stone unturned as I finished my letter with the admonishment that higher standards in their hiring procedures, along with increased pay, and training, would decrease the likelihood of having corrupt and/or unethical police officers. My letter was printed in the following Sunday paper. I signed it "Police brutality victim, David G. Atwood, II."

I normally sleep late on Sunday mornings. I know I definitely intended to on the Sunday morning that my letter to the editor was printed. Kevin and I had stayed out late the previous night and I was tired. Soon after eight o'clock though, my phone began ringing off the hook. People, some I knew and others I didn't, were calling to congratulate me on writing such a nice and informative letter. These people, too, were concerned with some of the local trends they'd been seeing in regards to how the cops treated people, both innocent and guilty.

I was beginning to enjoy my newfound popularity and support, when for the umpteenth time, the phone rang. I answered with a polite "Hello". The other voice on the phone was clearly upset and mad, "Just so you know, I am a police officer and I read your little letter and every time we get a chance to fuck with you, you are going to be pulled over, searched, written tickets and generally just treated like the piece of shit you are. From now on, you aren't going to be able to hide behind your family." Then the phone went "click".

The thought never occurred to me that my letter might offend someone other than the rookie cop who I had the problem with. It was stupidity on my part not to foresee the potential problems it would cause. Several more phone calls throughout the day, from anonymous and irate police officers, only confirmed the first call's lethality. I was a wanted man and I had pissed the entire police department off and they were not going to let me forget about it.

Not knowing what to do, I called up my two closet friends in law enforcement- Mike Ouzts and Dane Davenport. Both of them had read the letter and heard the hostility about it from officers all over the county. They, too, were incredulous that I would risk so much ridicule by openly criticizing the police.

Dane gave me the best piece of advice, "You can't fight city hall in this town". Those words have stuck with me to this day. But at the time, I paid him and his advice little heed. I had quickly uncovered a severe problem in my town and I was determined to do something about it. The numerous threats and irate phone calls that I received from police officers after my letter was printed only convinced me that there existed on a much lower level, an underworld of police corruption and an all-out effort to cover it up.

Probably the most difficult phone call I had to deal with that day came from my Pops. He was extremely upset that I had written the letter to the editor of the local newspaper. He believed that I had embarrassed the family name and myself. He told me that I should never have involved the media or the press in that manner and that our family had "friends" in the police and sheriff departments that handled situations like that for us.

I was quickly reminded how Deputy Chief Jack Dowe had responded to the gas station when I was stopped by the rookie officer and had cleared everything up for me within a matter of minutes. That is how we handled things in our family, not by running to the newspaper.

It was a sober conversation and I didn't like being chastised for something that I felt totally justified in doing. Pops seemed to be missing the point entirely, and that was that there were corrupt cops who were making false arrests on trumped-up charges, treating people harshly and brutally, and without any fear of punishment from the administration.

That is what I had witnessed myself, but what about all the other things that were probably going on that I didn't see? Surely if the cops were doing petty things like arresting people on false charges, then they were certainly taking more extreme liberties with the law. That wasn't right and I wasn't happy knowing that it was taking place. The only reason that I wasn't taken to jail that night and placed in juvenile detention was because my family had political connections and practically owned the government administration. But what about the average citizen, who is being hassled by the cops; what protection do they have? The Constitution and Law certainly weren't going to protect him in Vicksburg. Something had to be done.

At my next criminal justice class, I spoke with Sheriff Pace about what had happened that night. He had heard the story off the grapevine and had read my letter to the editor, but I wanted him to hear my side of the story. By this time, I had set off a certain firestorm of controversy surrounding what I wrote to the newspaper. Like a slow burning fuse that finally hits the gunpowder, the episode with the rookie cop, and my decision to write about it in the newspaper, stirred the emotions of cops and citizens alike. To the best of my knowledge, I was the only one in a long time to so openly criticize the local police and I was curious about Sheriff Pace's thoughts and reactions.

I don't know why I thought I might get sympathy from Sheriff Pace, but I didn't. Instead he seemed unconcerned about what I thought was a total abuse of police power. "Look kid, you got stopped by a cop that was having a bad night. You obviously did something to arouse his suspicions or he wouldn't have wanted to search your vehicle. That's all there was to it. Now, here you go making a mountain out of a mole hill and accuse the entire police department, from the Chief on down of corruption and incompetence. There's nothing there. No conspiracy and no blue wall of silence."

Sheriff Pace was a very believable person. I left his classroom feeling dejected and defeated. Maybe I had gone too far. Maybe I did overreact to the situation. I certainly had provoked a serious backlash from the police, but what about all the people who had called me after my letter was published and shared similar stories of police harassment and abuse. Surely, there was something going on with how people were treated by the local police and sheriff. I couldn't let it drop.

# CHAPTER TWENTY

The Christmas holiday was fast approaching and even though Kevin and I were busy preparing for the move into our new apartment, we still had a lot of other things going on.

During Thanksgiving, I'd spent time at my grandparents' house in Kosciusko and stayed around long enough to get reacquainted with all my aunts, uncles and cousins that I hadn't seen much throughout the year. But as soon as our turkey dinner was over, I immediately drove back to Vicksburg so I could at least spend part of Thanksgiving Day with Kevin and Meme.

Before I left to go to my grandparents', I made arrangements with Meme and Kevin to have a small supper at my house later on Thanksgiving Day. When I came back from Mamaw and Papaw's house, I met Kevin in town and we rode together to my house where Meme had another big dinner fixed for us. Twice in one day, Kevin and I ate very well, but he especially swore that Meme's cornbread dressing and giblet gravy was the best he had ever had.

It was at this dinner when the three of us started talking about a possible Christmas vacation somewhere. Several ideas were tossed around before we finally settled on going to Gettysburg, Pennsylvania, Washington, D.C. and Richmond, Virginia during a one-week trip to the area.

I quickly checked the computer and discovered that the tickets were fairly cheap and that hotel rooms were available. We even called Aunt Geneva to see if she wanted to go with us. We would leave the day after Christmas and come back on January $2^{nd}$. Aunt Geneva said she'd be more than happy to go.

Without much more discussion, the reservations were made and the itinerary planned. On December $27^{th}$, we would fly to Baltimore-Washington airport, rent a car and then drive to Gettysburg where we would stay five nights. Then we would leave and drive down to Richmond where we would stay two nights and then on the last day drive to D.C. where we would tour the White House before catching a late afternoon flight back to Mississippi. I was extremely excited that once again Kevin and I would be going on another trip together.

Prior to Thanksgiving and prior to making plans for all of us to take a big Christmas vacation, I had been planning all summer and fall to host a civil war ball dance at one of the local antebellum homes. This was an idea that I had tossed around several times in my own mind and to other civil war reenactors that were friends of mine. Everyone thought it would be an excellent idea.

Even though I had school classes to attend and study for, an apartment to decorate and a dozen other things that needed tending to, including a relationship with Kevin that always demanded attention, I was very capable of planning, what in my mind, would be one of the biggest and best civil war ball dances ever.

The first thing I had to do was contact one of the string bands I knew from the reenactments who could come and play civil war era style music. You can't have a dance without the right music. I then had to find a place. The most beautiful and extravagant antebellum home in Vicksburg is Cedar Grove Mansion. I only wanted the best and I set out with the intentions of getting it.

Although it took some hassling, and earnest promises of a cordial and non-rowdy party, I was able to secure the mansion for the day at a fairly low cost. I printed hundreds of invitations, hired a caterer, bought decorating supplies, and managed to get the best civil war band in existence at that time- the 12th Louisiana String band from Rayville, Louisiana.

I had been to several reenactments where the 12th Louisiana played for the ball dance and they always knew how to throw a good party. I was certain that they would be perfect for what I wanted and thankfully they were available for the first weekend in December.

By the time the first weekend arrived, I was all jitters. I had mailed out over two hundred invitations to everyone I knew. Over a hundred promised to come. I spent the day before the dance decorating the entire place similar to what it would have been decorated had we been in antebellum times. When I was finished, the place looked fabulous. Everyone who saw it was impressed. Most importantly, I wanted to have a good dance, with lots of people and lots of fun.

Finally the big day was here. Everyone showed up on time. The caterer arrived first and got everything set up. We had tons of hors d'oeuvres, cheese and crackers, little tuna fish and pimento cheese sandwiches, crab claws, wine, punch and all the other trimmings. I was thoroughly impressed.

The band showed up an hour or so early and got all of their gear and instruments set up and then changed into their period uniforms. At the designated hour, people started coming through the door. Most of the people I had invited were not civil war reenactors and did not have period uniforms, so I instead requested that they wear semi-formal attire. Those friends of mine who were civil war reenactors came dressed in their civil war uniforms and giant hoop skirted ball gowns. It was really turning into a great time.

Kevin and his parents showed up, along with my godparents, Kenny and Wendy. Mrs. Rush and her husband were there, my grandparents from Kosciusko came too, and of course, Meme and Mom were there. They wouldn't have missed it for the world. When I took a rough headcount, there were over a hundred and fifty people.

After about thirty minutes of idle chatter and introductions, I took the stage area of the ballroom and motioned for everyone to quiet down. I made a short speech and offered my thanks and appreciation to everyone for showing up and making me feel like I was giving them a wonderful time. I introduced the members of my family, especially my mom and Meme. Notably absent from the crowd was my Pops and his wife. They had refused to attend. However, I made no mention of them in my speech.

After I finished, I invited everyone to choose his or her partners for the first dance of the evening, the grand march. Most of the men took their lady partners by the hand and led them to the center of the ballroom and formed a double-file line in front of the band, one couple behind the other. When the band started playing, I led everyone around the room and directed them through the steps of the dance.

For the next three hours, I talked and danced and talked and danced some more. When the night was finally over, everyone had danced enough Virginia reels, patty-cake polkas, Carolina promenades, military two-steps and waltzes to be thoroughly exhausted. All the wine and punch were consumed and the food eaten.

Everyone had had a wonderful time, but before the dance concluded and everyone went home, one of my dear friends, Mike Harper, gave me three rousing cheers and then launched the crowd into a rounding rendition of "For He's a Jolly Good Fellow". It was the ultimate tribute for a lot of hard work and preparation. The ball dance had been a resounding success!

On the way home from the dance I thought about what a wonderful night it had been. Over a hundred of my best friends had turned out solely on the invitation of a seventeen-year-old.

# INTO HELL I RODE

No one really knew what to expect or what was going to happen.

Frankly, I don't think anyone thought that I could pull it off. But, the night had gone so well that all doubts in anyone's mind had to have been assuaged. I was very, very happy. It was Christmas time, I had a wonderful boyfriend with whom I was in total love, and would be living with in less than a month in our own place, but before then we would go on another wonderful and romantic vacation together. I had so much, so very, very much, to look forward to. Everything was going perfect, so perfect that I didn't see the catastrophe that was about to erupt.

# CHAPTER TWENTY-ONE

The weeks leading up to Christmas were very busy and my schedule was filled. The civil war ball dance had come off splendidly and I was still extremely excited that it had been such a success. With only a few short weeks left until Christmas Day and then our planned departure for vacation, I had a million different things to do.

I always buy my friends and family some type of gift for the holidays, but because I had been so busy with the dance, planning our vacation, and with school, I had neglected to find time to go shopping. When I finally got around to it, the lines at the mall and the crowds were outrageous. I spent hours and hours trying to find the perfect gift for everyone.

I had a pretty good idea what Kevin wanted for his present, but he pretty much left it for me to decide. I got him an automatic door lock with remote keypad and alarm for his truck and paid to have it installed. Anything for his truck he was more than happy to have.

The last week before Christmas, Kevin and I practically never saw one another. We were both too busy studying for our final exams to find time to be together. I was determined to earn the best possible grades that I could feasibly get and I devoted hours of time studying. This had been my first semester of college and if I was ever going to go to a university, I would need a history of positive grades to reflect my commitment to academics.

My concerns were unjustified; as usual I came out doing just fine on my final exams. I was also able to get all of my shopping completed and get nice, individual gifts for everyone. By the time the big day rolled around, I was able to lie back and relax and enjoy seeing the family again.

I spent most of Christmas Eve with Kevin before we both went to our own houses. Meme and I stayed up well past midnight talking and watching TV. It was just the two of us and we had a lot to talk about. So much had happened in the past year, and so much more was yet to come, that it left both of us with a vulnerable feeling of unknowing.

On Christmas morning I woke up and Meme and I exchanged gifts. Soon after, my cousin Julie, her husband, and kids came over to exchange presents too. After they had been there for a while, I said my goodbyes and loaded up my truck and drove to Kosciusko. For as long as I could remember I had always spent Christmas Eve with Meme and then driven to my grandparents' on Christmas Day. All of the family on my mother's side was already there and I would arrive just in time to eat lunch.

When I got there everyone had already opened presents and the only ones left under Mamaw's tree were mine. I made sure to say hello to everyone and give them all hugs before I started opening my gifts. As always, I usually got my best gifts from Mamaw and Papaw. This year they bought me a very finely crafted Remington 870 twelve-gauge shotgun. Since I was a little boy, I had always used my papaw's twelve-gauge to hunt with, but they finally bought one for me. I immediately went outside with my cousins, Scott and Andy, and shot a few rounds. But we didn't stay outside long because Mamaw soon called us to the table for the big Christmas dinner.

And a big dinner it was. She had turkey and dressing, Virginia ham, homegrown butterbeans, corn, squash, peas, potato salad, string beans, mustard greens and cornbread. There was so much food there, we never could have eaten it all. Three days later they were still trying to finish off the last of the leftovers.

I spent the night with my grandparents and family. There were so many people at their house that my two cousins and I had to sleep on pallets on the floor. The next morning I got up early and drove back to Vicksburg. I had to get everything ready for us to leave.

Kevin came over later that afternoon, after I had made it back home, and brought his suitcase and everything else he was going to take with him on the trip. Our plan was for him to spend the night and then the next morning Meme, Kevin and I would wake up, get ready and then drive over to Jackson to the airport where we would meet Aunt Geneva. From there, we would board our plane and fly to Baltimore-Washington airport.

Everything seemed to be going fine until we got to the airport and Aunt Geneva was nowhere to be found. Kevin and I searched all over the Jackson airport but could not find her. We checked with the ticket agent and discovered that she hadn't even checked in. We tried calling her house but didn't get an answer. We didn't know what to do.

We waited and waited until the very last minute before we had to board our plane, but she never showed up. Just as they were about to shut the door to the plane, one of the ticket agents came up and told us that Aunt Geneva had just arrived at the airport but wouldn't have time to catch this flight, but would be on another one later in the morning.

Meme and I quickly made the decision that we should go on without her. We could always wait on her at the Baltimore-Washington airport. The ticket agent promised to inform Aunt Geneva of our decision and to give her the information she would need to rendezvous with us in Baltimore.

Meme, Kevin and I then flew to Cincinnati where we changed planes before flying on to Baltimore. Our two flights were uneventful. When we arrived at Baltimore airport and got off the plane, we inquired about Aunt Geneva and her status. We were told that her flight would not get in to Baltimore until late that night. Rather than sit around and wait, the three of us decided to go ahead and rent our car, and drive on to Gettysburg and get Meme situated in the hotel room. Kevin and I would then drive back to the airport and pick up Aunt Geneva.

It was a two hour drive to Gettysburg, but the weather was beautiful and the scenery great. It was cold and a fresh snow had fallen and covered the ground, but the sky was clear and the sun shining. When we arrived on the outskirts of Gettysburg, the civil war battlefield immediately dominated the area and the sights and history intrigued me. I immediately wanted to go tour the battlefield. I had not been to Gettysburg since I'd come to the reenactment there back in July 1998. It was almost the same as I remembered it, just cold and with snow.

We quickly found our hotel, the Best Western Battlefield Inn, right in the heart of Gettysburg. We checked in and got situated in our rooms. Kevin brought our luggage up while I got Meme's situated in her room. I had reserved two separate rooms, one for Meme and Aunt Geneva and one for Kevin and me. When I had made the reservations, I had made sure that our room was a little special. It was the corner suite, third floor, overlooking the town square. It also had a wet bar stocked with every kind of alcohol imaginable, and a gigantic jacuzzi in the bathroom. Kevin and I were set for a romantic and sex-filled New Year's.

Before we got comfortable though, we had to turn around and drive back to Baltimore-Washington airport and retrieve Aunt Geneva. She didn't have a cell phone and we weren't sure where to find her or even where to start looking, but between the both of us, we were sure to find her.

It was a quick drive back. Kevin and I were so happy together, and we spent the whole way talking about our future.

Both of us were extremely anxious to move into our apartment as soon as we got back from our trip. We held hands the entire time and I don't think we had ever been happier in the entire time we'd been together. So much had happened and we'd dealt with so much drama and crisis, but we overcame all that and it had just made us stronger. We looked to the future with hope and great expectations.

When we finally arrived back in Baltimore and had found a place to park our rental car, we quickly discovered that we didn't have to look far for Aunt Geneva. She was posted right out front where everyone could see her- sitting on a passenger bench in the chilly night air. When she had gotten off her plane she called Meme at the hotel and told her that she had finally arrived and where we could find her. Meme then called me and told us where to look at the airport. If Aunt Geneva was not relieved, I for sure was. I was beginning to worry that we were going to have a bad trip.

When we got Aunt Geneva to the car and started heading back to Gettysburg, she explained what had happened to her earlier that morning. She had gone out to her car to come meet us at the airport, but discovered that her door locks had been frozen shut. Instead of going inside and getting a pitcher of hot water and pouring it on them to dissolve the ice, she called the police for help. Being that the Jackson Police are notorious for taking long amounts of time to respond to legitimate crimes, they took even longer to come to Aunt Geneva's house to help her get her car locks melted.

By the time the officer had come and gone, and Aunt Geneva had gotten her car up and running, it was too late for her to make it to the airport on time to catch the flight. Instead, the Delta ticket agent had been able to put her on another flight several hours later that went to Atlanta instead of Cincinnati. In Atlanta, she had to change planes and then fly up to Baltimore, where she arrived an hour before Kevin and I arrived back to pick her up. That gave her just enough time to get her baggage and call Meme at the hotel.

It was an interesting story, being told by an interesting

lady. Aunt Geneva had traveled all over the world in her lifetime. She was widowed at a young age and left a considerable fortune in which to spend any way she chose. She decided it would best be spent seeing the world, and for more than twenty years she traveled to every continent except Antarctica, crossed the ocean by both boat and plane, traversed the Serengeti Plains of Africa, braved malaria in the jungles of Asia and ate at the finest restaurants in Paris.

Aunt Geneva fascinated Kevin and me with her stories of travel, and we had never gotten bored or aggravated with having an old lady with us on our trips. We especially loved to hear her stories and the whole trip back to Gettysburg was filled with her reminisces of the world.

By the time we got back to the hotel, it was almost midnight, but Meme was still awake and waiting for us. But not long after we got Aunt Geneva situated in the room with Meme, did Kevin and I go to our own room and pass out. We were exhausted and the only thing we felt like doing that night was going to sleep and getting some rest. We'd been up since four o'clock that morning and sadly to say, neither of us had any energy for intimacy.

On our first full day in Gettysburg we woke up around eight o'clock and started getting ready. We had coffee and breakfast in the hotel lobby before loading up in the car and going to tour the Gettysburg battlefield.

I started the tour about fifteen miles outside of town on the Cashtown Pike road. I had spent weeks beforehand studying everything I could about the battle of Gettysburg and felt fairly confident navigating the area. We began at the Cashtown Inn where General Lee and one of his lieutenants, A.P. Hill, had had an early morning conference on the morning of July 1st. We then went back down the Cashtown Pike, following the route that portions of the Confederate army took to reach the outskirts of Gettysburg, and where the first day of battle commenced at a portion of the area called the "railroad cut".

From there we drove through town, past our hotel and down Seminary Ridge to the Mississippi monument, which faces

Cemetery Ridge, the wheat field, and peach orchard. It was at this spot that my great-great grandfather's regiment had begun their assault on Union positions. From there, we rode around to Little Round Top, one of the most famous civil war spots other than where Pickett's charge occurred. At Little Round Top a person has a full view of the battlefield and we could easily see the difficult terrain that the confederates would have had to assault.

Kevin and I then walked down to a spot called "Devil's Den", which was an area of extremely large and complicated maze of boulders and rocks that the Union and Confederate armies had to fight their way through for much of the second day of the battle. As we walked among the rocks, I could almost get the sensation of having been present at that great battle. The hairs stood up on the back of my neck at such a sacred and hard-fought-over piece of land. I've never experienced such a feeling as I did then, that day in the Devil's Den.

We finished the day with a quick tour of the visitor's center run by the National Park Service. I had been to the visitor's center at Vicksburg and many others, but none were as insightful and moving as the one at Gettysburg. The amount of information to be gleaned, and the number of artifacts on display from the battle, is overwhelming. It was definitely something that I especially enjoyed on our trip.

That night we all sat down together and ate a wonderful meal at a little place next to our hotel that served hamburgers and steaks. We planned to do some shopping the next day. After we left the restaurant, we went back to our hotel rooms. Meme and Aunt Geneva wanted to go to sleep, but Kevin and I had a romantic night planned in the jacuzzi.

I didn't drink alcohol, but Kevin did, and it wasn't long before the whiskey from the wet bar had been opened and Kevin was drunk. It was actually an amusing sight-seeing my boyfriend drunk. But, when we got ready to go to sleep ourselves, the laughing and giggling stopped and everything turned serious again. Suffice it to say we didn't get much sleep that night.

The next morning everyone was up and ready by nine and

after we had our breakfasts we were out the door of the hotel by ten. There was an art gallery that I desperately wanted to check out. It featured two of my favorite civil war artists, Don Troiani and John Paul Strain. Even though I had ordered several of their prints online, to decorate my apartment with, it was nothing compared to actually being in their gallery and seeing their artwork up close.

Right off, I saw four prints that I just couldn't live without and promptly had the kind salesmen package them for me to mail back to Mississippi. I didn't like any of the frames so I just got the prints. I would have them matted and framed when I got back home. Up until this point Kevin had not bought me anything for Christmas, but when he saw how much I loved those civil war prints, he bought a small one for me and included it in with mine. I was beginning to think he hadn't or wasn't going to get me anything for Christmas, but when he finally bought that print for me, I was more than satisfied.

The rest of the stay in Gettysburg was fairly uneventful. We visited as many shops and museums as possible and tried to see everything that we could in the so little time we had. On the second to last night, we walked down to the local movie theatre and watched Sandra Bullock in "Ms. Congeniality". It was actually a pretty good movie and we rather enjoyed it.

Since this was my second trip to Gettysburg, I was able to try and catch all the things that I had missed two and a half years before when my reenactment group had come up for the 135th anniversary reenactment battle. What I was especially keen on seeing were the other battlefields in Maryland and northern Virginia that we planned to tour after we left Gettysburg.

The last day of our time in Pennsylvania we took it easy. Meme and Aunt Geneva wanted to stay in the rooms and rest. Kevin and I decided to take a drive through the Pennsylvania countryside. I had wanted to go back to the old battlefield that we had used, and fought on, when we were at the reenactment in 1998. I was curious to see it again and felt like this would be a good time.

All day we drove around and just looked at the scenery

and talked. By the time we got back to the hotel it was almost dark and Meme and Aunt Geneva were waiting for us in the lobby. Apparently they were hungry and had been waiting on us for a while. Kevin and I laughed about it and just turned around and loaded the two old ladies up in the car and went and found a restaurant to eat.

Kevin and I didn't really have any plans for our last night in Gettysburg. The plan was to get up around five in the morning, pack up, and drive down to Maryland and tour the Antietam battlefield, then drive to Manassas, Virginia and see the military park there, before driving down to Richmond and checking into a hotel. We would then spend two days in Richmond before driving to Washington, D.C., touring the White House, and then catching a flight later that evening out of Baltimore and back to Mississippi.

Meme and Aunt Geneva turned in and went to sleep around nine o'clock that night, while Kevin and I stayed up watching television. Around eleven, Kevin decided to start drinking again. His drink of choice was Kentucky bourbon with coke, and unfortunately, the hotel stocked plenty of bourbon in our wet bar. By 12:30, Kevin was thoroughly intoxicated, drunker than I had ever seen him before. He had consumed about eight of the shot-sized bottles, not to mention the couple of vodkas he had drank when the bourbon ran out.

The amusement wore off at two o'clock in the morning when he started throwing up and puking his brains out in the bathroom toilet. Normally I wouldn't give a shit, but considering we were supposed to be awake and ready to check out of the hotel in another four hours, and I hadn't had any sleep all day, I was getting very perturbed.

Finally at three o'clock, I got Kevin cleaned up and put to bed. I made sure we had a wake-up call at five thirty, and then I went to bed to try and get what little sleep I could. Before I had even closed my eyes it seemed like the phone was ringing to wake us up. After I answered the phone and crawled out of bed, Kevin didn't move. He was dead to the world.

I went ahead and took a shower and got our luggage

together. Meme and Aunt Geneva were already up and ready to go by six. They were standing in the lobby waiting on Kevin and me whenever I came downstairs with the suitcases. All I had to do was go back up and get Kevin.

After trying several times to wake Kevin and him not wanting to get up, I finally got frustrated and jerked the covers off the bed. I knew Kevin was not a morning person, but I had to get him up and down to the car so we could leave. I told him he could sleep in the car on our drive down to Maryland, but he just wouldn't crawl out of bed.

Getting angry now, I walked into the bathroom and picked up the ice bucket and filled it with cold water. I walked back into the bedroom and threw the water right at Kevin. Thankfully, it did the trick and Kevin sprang out of the bed, but unfortunately he was madder than a nest of hornets. Kevin had never swung at me before, but I believe if I had not run out of the hotel room, he probably would have tried to knock my head off.

I went down to the hotel lobby to wait for him to dry off and come down so we could leave. Finally after about another ten minutes, he popped out of the elevator, still madder than hell, but at least ready to go so we could get under way. I had told Meme that I had to throw cold water on him in order to get him out of bed, and although she thought it was kind of funny, she immediately realized that Kevin was still drunk and was madder than hell at me.

As soon as we got in the car, Kevin went back to sleep and I started heading south, back to the Mason-Dixon line, and hopefully back to a good vacation. After driving for about two hours we arrived in the town of Fredericks, Maryland, about an hour from D.C. and Antietam. Meme and Aunt Geneva had seen an advertisement for an outlet mall where they wanted to stop and do some shopping, so after I finally found it, and pulled into the parking lot, they got out while Kevin and I stayed in the car.

Soon after we stopped, and Meme and Aunt Geneva got out to go inside, Kevin woke up...still mad at me for throwing cold water on him and from the smell of his breath, still drunk. I had teased him about it earlier that morning, but decided that now wasn't the best time. I had dropped my cell phone in the snow the previous day while Kevin and I were outside the car looking at a civil war monument and it had quit working. The only cell phone left was Kevin's and I needed to borrow it to confirm our reservations to tour the White House.

Because Kevin was already in a shitty mood, he was hesitant to allow me to use his cell phone. We got into an argument because his phone was "roaming" and he didn't want to pay the high long distance charge. It was a stupid thing to argue about, but by this time I wasn't in the mood to listen to anymore of his crap.

Kevin went from complaining about the phone, that he still had not let me use, to complaining about the whole trip, and how much he was ready to get home. I certainly felt like he was being very ungrateful. Meme and I had paid for everything, including his plane ticket and meals. We always treated him like a member of our family, but yet, here he sat next to me, complaining about how awful the trip was going. For the most part, I just sat there and listened to it and didn't say much back, but then he started complaining about having to sit and wait while Meme and Aunt Geneva were inside shopping.

I don't remember exactly what I told him, but I made it very clear that I thought he was still drunk from the night before, or either he was having a bad hangover, and that he needed to lie back down and sleep it off. I said that he was being totally unreasonable about the phone and that if he was so worried about the cost of a ten-minute phone call, that I would be more than happy to pay him back whenever he got the bill. The last thing I said to him was that he was being a total, ungrateful little bitch.

When I said that, Kevin just stared at me in unbelievable disgust and then reached right over and slapped me in the face. It didn't hurt, and he didn't even hit me that hard, but the thought of another person laying their hands on me absolutely infuriated me-boyfriend or not. Without really thinking I reached back with my fist and throwing as much weight as I could into it, punched him right in the nose. I felt the bone crunch beneath my knuckles before I pulled away.

Kevin and I had just come to blows over a stupid argument about a cell phone. This was the first time in my life that I had resorted to violence in that way. Kevin's nose was broken and it immediately started gushing blood. I was horrified at what I had done. I immediately felt guilty and regretted it as soon as I had done it.

Kevin started screaming as soon as he realized what had happened. Instead of sticking around and trying to help him, I decided the best thing to do was run and get Meme. Besides, I don't think Kevin would have allowed me to help him anyway.

With Kevin in hysterics, I left the car and walked inside the outlet mall in hopes of finding Meme- I knew she would know what to do. I didn't have to look long for her or Aunt Geneva, they were both in the check-out line and very quietly I tried to explain to them what had happened. Apparently Meme didn't seem too concerned or she didn't quite grasp the seriousness of it, because she wanted to get checked out with her shopping items before she would leave and come outside.

When we finally made it back to the car, about ten minutes later, Kevin had the doors locked and was on his cell phone with someone. I didn't have the key and Kevin wasn't letting us into the car. He kept screaming at me to leave him alone. I thought that it was actually a little bit melodramatic myself, but Meme finally coaxed him into opening the door.

As he was opening it and letting Meme and Aunt Geneva look at his nose, I realized that he was talking to his dad on the phone. The thought horrified me, not because I was afraid of his dad, but because he had called him in the first place. When I first introduced Kevin several chapters ago, I figured the best way to describe him was as "delicate". I understand having your nose broken could probably be a traumatic thing to go through, but I wouldn't call my dad or mom if it happened to me, and I thought Kevin was only making matters worse by including his parents.

We were starting to attract a crowd by this time and several people offered their assistance, but I quickly turned them down. I was praying and hoping that no one called the cops. That was the last thing I needed. My concern at the moment was getting everyone into the car and Kevin to the hospital where we could have his nose looked at by a doctor.

It took some cajoling and promises of no more violence, but I finally got everyone loaded up. Kevin was in the backseat with Aunt Geneva and Meme up front with me, as we went looking for a hospital. I knew, though, that there wasn't much that could be done for a broken nose. The bleeding had stopped and Kevin said he wasn't in any pain, but he insisted on going to a hospital anyway. So much for our day trip to the Antietam and Manassas battlefields, I thought.

# CHAPTER TWENTY-TWO

In the few short minutes before Kevin and I had become violent, something happened that I couldn't explain. Kevin had never acted that way before and we had never even come close to becoming physical. We had always had small arguments, but they could always be worked out and the thought never crossed either of our minds to assault the other. But yet we had, and it hadn't ended so well.

Kevin was hurt, and from what he told his parents, it made me look like I was at fault. Meme and Aunt Geneva were mad at me because I broke Kevin's nose and up until the time we arrived at the hospital, and Kevin went back to the emergency room, they hadn't heard my side of the story.

I have replayed that incident in my mind over and over again. I've tried to blame it on the alcohol and maybe it was. Kevin was extremely drunk the previous night and was still drunk that morning, or was at least having a serious hangover. Regardless, Kevin had never acted that way before or talked to me the way he did.

Looking back, I wonder now, if that single act of violence wasn't some type of pent-up aggression being released for unresolved issues dealing with our relationship and him being outed as a homosexual to his friends. Indirectly, that was my fault, and I wonder whether or not he somehow blamed me for getting us caught. His life had significantly changed since we'd met and I just don't know whether he was comfortable yet with that. Maybe subconsciously he was lashing out at me. The alcohol is maybe what lowered his inhibitions and that is all it took.

Whatever the reason, our relationship effectively ended that day, in the parking lot of an outlet mall in Fredericks, Maryland. No matter what I tried to do in the future after it happened, Kevin was insistent that our relationship was over. He even went so far as to say that I had jarred him into realizing that he was in actuality "straight" and liked women. He even said that he wouldn't fool around with guys anymore, because truth be known, he didn't like it anyway.

I didn't believe that shit for a second. I don't know what was going on in Kevin's head, but he had serious issues that he had to deal with concerning his sexuality. I can sympathize with a person, to a point, who has issues dealing and coming to terms with his sexuality, but to try and totally depress your feelings, and deny who you are, is wrong and will only make your life harder.

To this day, I feel like Kevin has made things a lot harder on himself than what was necessary. There was never any need to hide who he was or try to deny it. Actually, from sixth or seventh grade, everyone had serious suspicions that he was gay. Kevin just wasn't the type guy who could hide it easily. When he denied his sexuality to people who knew otherwise, it only made them resent him for his dishonesty. It wasn't a good cycle.

As I was sitting in the hospital waiting room, waiting for Kevin to get his nose cared for, I thought back to the different episodes of our relationship, and no matter what I did, I never thought I could foresee the end happening like this. I figured he and I would break up one day, but not that it would be so soon. Without discussing it with Kevin, I knew that this was the end, especially after he had told his parents. I didn't think I could ever face them again.

After waiting for over three hours, we were finally able to leave the hospital and head towards Richmond. Kevin's dad had called and talked to Meme several times about getting Kevin on a flight back to Mississippi that night. The problem was, it was going to cost over six hundred dollars for us to get Kevin a new ticket, and Meme and I were just not going to pay that.

This started the second argument of the day between Kevin and me. Kevin and his dad felt as if we owed it to Kevin to pay the full cost of the plane ticket. Unfortunately, I wasn't going to do that and Meme wasn't either. We offered to pay half and if Kevin wanted to go home so bad, he had to pay the other half of the cost.

Dealing with money is the first thing that will determine how well a couple is at problem-solving their dilemmas. Kevin and I failed miserably. And for the second time of the day, we almost came to blows over who would pay for the plane ticket.

Finally, Meme got Kevin's dad to agree to pay the other half and a seat was quickly reserved on a late evening flight out of Richmond International back to Jackson, Mississippi. The way I figured, if we left Fredericks, Maryland immediately, we would have time to reach the airport in Richmond before the flight left. Unfortunately, we would not have time to visit any of the battlefields that I had wanted to. It would have to wait until another trip.

We left the hospital and quickly headed towards D.C. and from there we would catch the interstate, south to Richmond. We hit Washington right at five o'clock rush hour and the interstate was packed with slow moving cars and lots of congestion. After finally getting away from the Capitol, the traffic finally cleared, but we were running very behind. If I didn't hurry, we would miss Kevin's flight and he would be stuck with us.

At this point, I'd been through so much, and had dealt with another side of Kevin that I had never seen before, I was ready for him to leave. It wasn't the Kevin that I was used to dealing with. The Kevin that woke up that morning was hateful and bitter.

I pushed our rental car to the limit that day. It was sprinkling snow and the roads were probably icy, but my speedometer never lowered below eighty until I reached the airport exit. I quickly pulled into baggage drop-off and jumped out of the car and grabbed Kevin's suitcase and travel bag and tossed it to the corner.

The airport security would not allow the car to stay there so everyone said their goodbyes to Kevin. The last thing I said to him was that I was sorry it was ending this way. He wouldn't let me hug or touch him, so I just got in our rental car and drove away, leaving him to fend for himself through airport security, the ticket counter and finding his gate.

I didn't look back at Kevin as I drove away. He didn't want me or anyone else to help him administer the airport intricacies. He wanted to be left alone. I was certainly saddened to see our relationship end this way. But, I was thoroughly pissed off at the way he had acted. Not only that, but I was also extremely embarrassed that all of this had happened in front of Meme and Aunt Geneva.

Up to this point neither of them had asked many questions. I guess they knew that it was probably best not to talk about it until the two of us had been separated. Even after we dropped Kevin off at the airport and drove off to find our hotel, neither Meme nor Aunt Geneva had much to say. The entire day had been so stressful, coupled with the fact that none of us had had much sleep. I don't think anyone was ready to discuss what had happened. All we wanted to do was find a bed and get some rest.

It wasn't until the next day that Meme brought it up. The three of us had slept late the morning after. I don't think anyone wanted to get out of bed. We certainly didn't have much of anything planned and although we were sleeping in separate rooms, my phone didn't ring until almost ten o'clock. It was Meme and Aunt Geneva and they were hungry and wanted me to take them to get some breakfast.

On the way to get something to eat, Meme was the first to bring up the previous day's episode. She wanted me to explain, step by step, what had happened and how Kevin and I had come to blows. I'm sure Meme had a good idea already, and I didn't try to embellish or exaggerate my story. I told her exactly what happened. Satisfied that I was to blame just as much as Kevin, she asked me if I thought we should call to see whether he made it home alright. I didn't think it was a good idea. If he would have had any problems, I felt like he or his parents would have called. Then I remembered that my cell phone was broken.

We only stayed in Richmond for two days before ending our trip and flying back to Mississippi. But before coming home, the three of us stopped by the White House and took one of the guided tours. It was snowing heavily the day of our tour, and a portion of downtown D.C. had been closed pending the inauguration of the newly elected president, George W. Bush.

Up until that time, I had not really been interested in politics other than to the extent of the local and state leaders in my hometown. The 2000 Presidential Campaign was the first campaign that I intently followed, and I went all out for Bush. I considered myself then to be a conservative Republican and I believed Bush was a moral and upstanding candidate who would lead our country into the twenty-first century.

As we drove around Pennsylvania Avenue looking for a place to park, I was saddened with the loss of my relationship with Kevin. My cell phone was broken and I didn't want to pay long-distance charges on the hotel phone, so I didn't try to contact him to see if he had made it home okay. In the back of my mind, I didn't really care.

Meme, Aunt Geneva and I were running late and it was impossible to find a place to park close to the White House. Finally, I spotted a truck pulling out of a parallel parking spot, or so I thought, and without any second thought I pulled right in. I got the old ladies out of the back and we headed towards the

White House. It was pouring snow and freezing cold, but the lines to get inside were short and we didn't have long to wait.

This was Meme and Aunt Geneva's first time to tour the mansion, but I had been there when I was in sixth grade. I had, however, forgotten a lot of things. Because of the Clinton-Lewinsky scandal, everyone on the tour was especially interested in seeing the Oval Office- our tour guide did not disappoint us.

We spent an hour in the mansion and then left to head back to our car. Our plane was leaving out that afternoon, and with the weather as crazy as it was, we would need all the time we could spare to drive back up to Baltimore-Washington Airport.

After we had walked down the sidewalk that I thought our car was parked beside, I realized something was amiss. At first, I thought we were lost, but there had been a large Bank of America building close by where we had parked. The building was still there, but the car was gone. The first thing I thought was that it had been stolen, after all, this *was* downtown D.C.

I went inside the bank and used their phone to call the police and report my rental car stolen. It took over an hour for the police officer to arrive and when he did, I pointed out where my car had been, and that we'd gone down to the White House for a tour, and when we came back, it was gone.

The officer pointed to where my car had been parked and asked, "Your car was parked right there?" and I answered in the affirmative. "You say that your car was parked right there, at that exact spot?" The officer asked a second time and had a quizzical look on his face and for the second time I answered yes.

"Well, your car probably wasn't stolen. I think it was towed. Your car was parked directly in front of a fire hydrant." Sure enough, when I looked over at the parking spot I'd used, it was right beside a fire hydrant, and it was at that moment that I realized my mistake.

"Officer, I'm from Mississippi and we don't have fire hydrants down there. I didn't know I wasn't supposed to park in front of one." Amplifying my deep southern drawl, I tried to elicit some sympathy from the big-city cop. It didn't work.

Meme and Aunt Geneva had gone inside the bank to sit down and keep warm, and left me out in the cold to deal with the Capitol Police.

The police officer explained to me that I would have to go down to the court and pay the towing fine and then catch a cab out to the city impound lot and retrieve my car. Meme and Aunt Geneva decided to stay and wait inside the bank while I traveled around D.C. and got our car back.

Several hours later, and two hundred dollars shorter, I had finally paid the fine, retrieved the car and found my way back to the bank where Meme and Aunt Geneva were patiently waiting. It was after five o'clock and the bank had closed, but one of the security guards was nice enough to allow Meme and Aunt Geneva to wait inside the lobby until I'd returned.

Our plane departed at 7:30 that evening, which left us with two hours and thirty minutes to drive from downtown D.C. to Baltimore-Washington airport. I never thought we would have time to make it, but I drove as fast as possible in the snow and ice and we arrived in our assigned seats with only minutes to spare. A person could not comprehend how happy I was that this vacation was finally over and that we were on our way back to Mississippi. This trip had probably been the worst ever, and everything that could go wrong did, and I was glad it was finally over.

I had a window seat on the flight home and as I glared out at the dark sky and lights below, I sat there and wondered how different my life was going to be. I was able to recognize that a new chapter in my life was beginning, but I was very sad to see the old one go. This trip was supposed to be an anniversary celebration of mine and Kevin's one year together. Instead it turned into chaos, mishaps and the catalysts to the end of our relationship.

I had had so many hopes and dreams for our relationship, but that was now over. As our plane started the descent into Jackson, Mississippi, I was determined to make the best out of a bad situation. I didn't know whether it was a good idea to go ahead with the move to Hattiesburg, and leave everyone and everything I knew behind, and practically start a new life, but I knew I didn't have any choice. I wasn't going to let this break-up prevent me from pursing my education and striking out on my own.

At seventeen years old I was determined that I could make it by myself. With pride and ambition I walked off that plane ready to face the future. Whatever life had to throw my way I was determined to meet it and overcome it.

# INTO HELL I RODE

# PART TWO

# CHAPTER TWENTY-THREE

I moved into my new apartment around the first of January, 2001. I had already enrolled for classes at Jones County Junior College and was excited about starting my new life. I was grieving constantly over the break-up with Kevin and I knew it would be a very long time before I recovered emotionally from my loss.

Many times, I laid in bed at night and dreamed of us being together again. Waking up in an apartment devoid of life, except for my own, was hard enough, but waking up and realizing I was no longer with the only guy I've ever loved was terrible.

Several times after our break-up, I'd tried calling Kevin, but he never would answer. I thought about calling him at his family's store, but the thought of having to talk to his mother petrified me. So, for the first few weeks in Hattiesburg, I was on my own.

Around the third week my mother came down to help me decorate the apartment and get things unpacked and in their proper places. My college classes were going good but I was finished by lunch every day and had the rest of the time to myself. My mother's presence was welcomed and appreciated. In several days' time, we had my apartment looking great. It was during this visit that my mother suggested I look into joining the local volunteer fire department.

I'd been a firefighter on the department in Vicksburg, but had lost interest during my relationship with Kevin. Now that I had lots of time on my hands, it sounded like a good idea. Later that day my mother and I rode out to the Northeast Lamar Volunteer Fire Department and met with the Chief, Scott Knue. I also met another firefighter there named Paul Leslie Amacker, Jr.

The chief took an instant liking to me and we soon became close friends. It wasn't long before I was hanging out at the fire station most of the time. After meeting Paul for the second or third time, he invited me out to dinner with him one night. At dinner, I learned that Paul's parents owned a debt collection agency where he worked full-time. Paul was also a part-time deputy with the Forrest County Sheriff's Department. Paul and I soon began doing everything together. Never did I suspect Paul was gay.

I was taking around sixteen hours of course work at Jones Junior and one of those classes was criminal justice. I had a wonderful teacher who had spent nearly thirty years in law enforcement before deciding to get his graduate degree and teach school. What I quickly was learning in his criminal justice class was not what I saw in action on the streets of Vicksburg and Warren County. It was becoming apparent that the officers in Vicksburg operated by their own set of rules that certainly were not written in any book.

The more I learned in his class, the less respect I had for the officers and administrators in Vicksburg and how they operated. It was becoming clear that I had a lot to learn about what was taught to potential law enforcement officers in school and what they actually did on the streets.

Not long after Paul and I met, I began discussing with him what I was learning in my criminal justice classes. I refrained from talking with him about what the cops in Vicksburg were doing or what I knew about them, but I was especially curious about how he acted when he was working as a deputy. Paul could tell I was very interested in becoming a law officer and he soon invited me to ride with him in his sheriff's car when he was working.

On the first ride-along I did with Paul, he showed me the different areas he patrolled in Forrest County. During this first ride-a-long, Paul asked me if I smoked marijuana or did any other kind of drugs, to which I responded I didn't. Shortly after that Paul volunteered that although he was a part-time law officer, he occasionally smoked weed himself. This revelation at first shocked me, but at the time I was beginning to develop a slight crush on Paul and I was willing to overlook it.

Around the middle of February, 2001, Paul invited me to go to a dance bar called Roper's in Hattiesburg. While we were there Paul offered to buy me alcohol. I had never really drank before and wasn't very keen on doing so, but like I said, I had a crush on Paul and wanted to impress him. It wasn't long before Paul had me drunk. I didn't notice at the time, but Paul wasn't drinking anything but coke and water.

Later that night Paul took me back to my apartment and helped me get into bed. Instead of leaving, like I expected him to do, he got undressed and got in the bed with me. Even though I was still a little drunk, I was surprised that Paul was going to stay the night and sleep in the same bed with me.

I had never expected Paul was gay or had any intentions of being anything more than friends with me, but soon after getting in my bed, Paul began rubbing on me and trying to kiss me. We were soon having sex. The fact that I was seventeen-years-old, drunk, and not in any condition to be making coherent choices didn't seem to bother Paul, but it's not like I didn't want to anyway.

Kevin and I had been broken up for almost two months,

and although I still loved him more than anything, I was glad that someone new had wandered into my life. I was just totally surprised that that person happened to be Paul Amacker.

The next morning I skipped class and slept in. Paul had gotten up early and gone to work. Meeting someone new had actually changed my feelings regarding Kevin. In one night, I had found a renewed interest in someone besides Kevin, and I was beginning to feel like I would recover from our break-up in one piece. Meeting Paul had done wonders for my outlook.

Paul and I quickly developed a strong relationship and we began to spend as much time with one another as possible. Many times Paul spent the night with me at my apartment, while other times I stayed with him. Paul had made it very clear from the beginning that no one could ever know about our relationship. Neither one of us were out to anyone about being gay and I was okay with keeping it that way.

Paul did introduce me to another gay law officer he knew who was a detective on the Warren County Sheriff's Office in Vicksburg. I had known of this officer, he had two adoptive parents who were friends with my family, but until Paul introduced us, I had no idea this deputy was gay. Through my connections with Paul I was able to eventually meet several other gay law enforcement officers. One gay officer who I became very good friends with was Ron McClelland, who worked for Jackson Police Department.

About a month after we started dating is when I first began to notice some of the illegal things that Paul would do. This would eventually lead to our break-up. On numerous occasions while I was riding with him in his patrol car, I would notice him take weed and drugs off of people and not arrest them. Numerous times I also watched Paul smoke marijuana and snort cocaine. I never criticized him for this, but in the back of my mind, I certainly had issues dealing with it.

If Paul had not have been a law enforcement officer, I doubt my conscience would have bothered me as bad, but as time passed and the more illegal things I saw Paul do, the less I wanted to be a part of it. On several occasions I confronted Paul with what he was doing and every time I did so, Paul would play it off as inconsequential. A part of me really liked Paul- I could never love him like I had Kevin- but another part detested seeing him use illegal drugs that he had stolen off of people he had pulled over in his patrol car.

At the end of the spring semester, I had to make a decision about whether to stay in Hattiesburg or go back home to Vicksburg for the summer. I was enjoying my time in Hattiesburg, but my relationship with Paul was beginning to suffer. Almost every night he would get stoned on weed or get so drunk that he'd pass out and I'd be left to fend for myself. I was starting to believe that I would be better off without Paul than with him.

I chose to go back home to Vicksburg that summer, partly to have an excuse to get away from Paul and partly to take a break from having to live alone in my apartment. In order to stay busy through the summer months, I reenrolled at Hind's Community College and took two courses that my good friend, Shirley Rush, was teaching. It would be the first time since I'd left Porter's Chapel Academy that I would have the pleasure of being taught by my favorite teacher.

About two weeks after I moved back to Vicksburg, I finally summoned enough courage to call Paul and tell him I wanted to end our relationship. I had threatened to do so before, but every time I did, Paul would begin yelling and screaming and start threatening me. I could tell Paul had an abusive personality and it was only after I made it home to Vicksburg and felt far enough away from him to be safe, that I finally decided to end our relationship once and for all.

As expected, it did not go well. Paul screamed, cussed me, threatened to hurt me and threatened to out me to my entire family if I broke up with him. For the first time since moving away from my father, I was genuinely scared and didn't know what to do. Paul was acting like a maniac and I had no one to turn to for help.

I finally consulted my friend, Mike Ouzts, and asked him what I should do. The only thing Mike could think of would be to call the sheriff of Forrest County where Paul was a part-time deputy and explain to him the situation and ask for help. Unfortunately, that was the last place I should have turned to for help. Sheriff Billy McGee was absolutely incredulous at my story and refused to believe a word I said. When I mentioned that I had been seventeen-years-old when Paul got me drunk and had sex with me, the Sheriff hung up the phone.

The one effect that my phone call to the Sheriff did have on Paul was to cause him to threaten and harass me more. I was genuinely afraid for my safety and I was more afraid that Paul would somehow out me to my entire family and friends. I began to look for other avenues of relief.

Most people don't understand what it is like to be harassed by a well-respected law enforcement officer. Because of the badge they wear, law officers are automatically given higher authority and are more believable than common citizens. This has opened the door to countless dishonesty and abuse everywhere that it's tolerated. Getting someone to listen to me about the threats and harassment from Paul was like trying to pull teeth from an alligator.

After contacting the FBI, Mississippi Highway Patrol, and DEA, and getting no help, I finally ran across someone who seemed genuinely interested and concerned. Richard Cox was an investigator with the Department of Integrity at the State Attorney General's Office. His job was primarily investigating corrupt law enforcement officers.

Agent Cox met with me, took my statement and information, and promised something would be done soon. I also provided Agent Cox with several phone recordings of Paul threatening and harassing me. I left Agent Cox's office feeling, for once, relieved that someone would finally listen to me.

Thankfully, Agent Cox and his team of investigators moved fast. The harassing and threatening calls from Paul stopped immediately and when Agent Cox followed up with me a week later, I learned that Paul had been fired from the Forrest County Sheriff's Office, had failed a polygraph examination, and that criminal charges would probably follow.

This now presented a problem. Even though Paul used illegal drugs that had been stolen off people he had pulled over, threatened and harassed me nonstop for almost a month, and had gotten me drunk to have sex with me, I didn't think I was ready to go in open court and testify to that- which is something that Agent Cox said I would have to do if criminal charges were filed against Paul.

Agent Cox assured me that Paul would never be a law enforcement officer again regardless of whether I decided to pursue criminal charges or not. After considering my options and what would be expected of me in a criminal trial, I decided not to pursue any charges against Paul. Agent Cox later told me that an investigation would continue against Paul for the drug use, but since I decided not to pursue charges and testify, that my involvement would be over.

Years later I would terribly regret this decision. Agent Cox and his team of investigators were never able to bring a strong case against Paul for his illegal drug use and several months thereafter, their investigation ended. Paul used his family's money and influence to secure himself another part-time law enforcement job with the Lamar County Sheriff's Office. Paul would later become a constable and then an FBI agent even though the FBI was aware of his threats and intimidation against me and his illegal and illicit drug use.

Throughout this entire ordeal, that I later referred to as the "Paul Amacker Affair", I became disgusted with the procedures and red tape a person had to hurdle himself through to report a dishonest and corrupt law enforcement officer.

The problem is that law enforcement officers refuse to believe that such a thing as a corrupt cop can exist. This mentality has led to a problem of such immense proportion that corrupt and dishonest cops have become the norm rather than the exception. The entire ordeal left me even more jaded and disheartened in our criminal justice system than did the officer in Vicksburg who had pulled me over and tried to arrest me the fall before. I was becoming more determined to try to do something about it.

# CHAPTER TWENTY-FOUR

I started fall classes again at Jones County Junior College in August of 2001. I had reservations about coming back to Hattiesburg after the fiasco with Paul Amacker. I had been assured by Agent Cox that I wouldn't have any further trouble from Paul, but I was still unsettled by the experience.

Shortly after starting fall classes, I decided to summon the courage to go to the local gay bar in Hattiesburg. I'd never been to a gay bar before, except for the quick walk-through that Kevin and I had done in the Oz, in New Orleans. I was extremely nervous and hesitant but finally decided that I should experience it at least once.

The bar was called Odyssey and after my first visit I began going every Saturday night. At first I just stood in a corner by the dance floor, or sat on a stool by the bar, but before long I began making friends and loosening up.

I'd never considered myself a party person, and I definitely didn't drink alcohol, but being at the bar was the only way I was going to be able to meet other gay guys. There were several websites that a gay guy could go to meet other guys, but I wasn't really into doing online hook ups- the gay bar was really my only alternative.

I quickly made several new friends and for the first time was exposed to a gay culture. There were a group of guys in Hattiesburg, mostly young, good-looking, and all gay, who were known as the "Hub-City Honey's". I was invited into their circle and before long I was learning how to dress more "stylish", how to "dance", and how to "party". It was an eye-opening experience and one that I sorely needed.

Every Labor Day weekend, New Orleans hosts an event known as Southern Decadence. It's basically a "gay" Mardi Gras. Several of my new gay friends from Hattiesburg were going and invited me to go along. I had never been to a gay pride event and the only experience I had had, being around a lot of gay guys, had been at the gay bar. But going to Decadence was something I wanted to do.

Going to New Orleans and being surrounded by two hundred thousand gay men made me realize that I was not alone in this world and that there were many others just like me who were gay too. I had no idea until then, just how prevalent gay men were. On reflection, maybe I was a little naïve to think there weren't that many gay guys out there, but going to Southern Decadence really opened my eyes.

My friends took me dancing to the Oz and Bourbon Pub- the two most popular gay clubs in New Orleans. We also went to Good Friends and the Corner Pocket. For the first time ever I saw male strippers and was envious of how perfect they looked. Trying to scare me, my friends took me into the club known as the "Rawhide" and showed me the "dark room" where men could have uninhibited sex and orgies. At first I was horribly appalled, but morbid curiosity won over and I became intrigued at such decadence.

Labor Day weekend of 2001 opened my eyes to a whole

new world of gay culture, but more importantly I made many new friends- guys my age who looked normal, acted normal, and came from normal backgrounds- just like me, I felt. One guy I met who I became close friends with was John Cofield. John was from Oxford and came from a deep, southern-rooted family that included a U.S. Senator and a personal photographer of William Faulkner. John and I would stay close friends for many years.

When I returned from New Orleans, I felt a renewed faith in my sexuality. A faith and understanding that being gay was not something that I felt I should be ashamed of. I began to feel like there was nothing wrong with being gay and that continuing to hide who I was from my friends and family was not something I should be doing. Putting theory into practice, though, was an entirely different matter.

Meme had begun to suspect I was gay during the year that Kevin and I had dated and on occasions had dropped innocuous comments but never out-right asked. My mother, to the best of my knowledge, had no clue. I was determined to come out to both Meme and my mother as soon as I could figure out the best way to do it. Summoning the courage to actually do so was harder than I expected.

I was too much of a coward to do it face-to-face, so I ended up calling both Meme and my mother. As expected, coming out to Meme was a lot easier than doing so with my mother. Meme was understanding and said she didn't care and would love me regardless. When I told my mother, she freaked.

I don't know what reaction I had expected from my mother, but from the beginning of the conversation, until the end, when she slammed the phone down, I somehow managed to get my point across. My mother's acceptance of my sexuality began that moment on the phone when I said, "Momma, I'm fucking gay and if you don't like it you can go fuck yourself." It's been a work in progress ever since, but she has now fully accepted my sexuality, and has become a caring and understanding mother. There is nothing that we can't talk about.

After coming out to my mother, our relationship took on a noticeable chill. The phone calls came less often and conversation was strained when we did talk. I finally decided that acceptance of my sexuality was not something I would receive from my mother overnight, but the fact that it was such a big deal did hurt me considerably. I didn't know how long it would take, but I wasn't going to push the issue. I assumed we would be like so many other mothers and gay sons who knew what the circumstances were, but never talked about it.

Shortly after my crazy weekend in New Orleans, and a few days after informing my mother and Meme that I was gay, the terrorist attacks on September 11th occurred. I was still in bed the morning of the attacks when Meme called me and told me to turn CNN on and that there had been a plane crash in New York City.

As most people, I initially expected the crash to be an accident, but as I turned CNN on, the second plane was crashing into the World Trade Center building. Immediately, I knew that something was terribly wrong. A few minutes later came the warnings that America was under attack.

I was at my apartment in Hattiesburg that morning and I was alone- by myself without anyone to turn to for comfort. I wanted to leave and go somewhere I felt safe, but that meant driving two hours to Vicksburg. As much as I wanted to leave, I didn't want to miss seeing anything on the television. By this time the third plane had struck the Pentagon and across the country, all hell was breaking loose. I decided not to attend classes that day- I felt history was occurring and I didn't want to miss it.

Until the day of the terrorist attacks, I'd been mostly ambivalent towards politics. During the 2000 presidential race, I'd naturally supported George Bush because at the time, Republican politics mostly reflected my own. Gay issues and gay rights were not important to me then. After the attacks on September 11th, I, like many Americans threw our whole-hearted support behind Bush, Cheney, Rumsfeld and Colin Powell.

Admittedly, my first concern was whether I would be drafted in a war that I knew was to come. September 11th changed my life, but it did so in a way that I became more involved in politics than I'd already been. Fox News and CNN replaced CMT and HBO. I subscribed to the local newspaper and USA Today and read them front to cover. The attacks awakened my senses to the world around me.

One positive effect the attacks had on my immediate life was putting my mother and me back into closer touch. After coming out about being gay, she and I had not spoken much and when we did, it was mostly arguing and fighting. Seeing and hearing of so many dying and suffering made petty differences seem trivial. We soon broached common ground and agreed not to discuss my sexuality- if I didn't bring it up, she wouldn't bring it up- and it stayed that way for years.

Christmas of 2001 was spent at my grandparent's house in Kosciusko. The entire family was there as usual and I enjoyed visiting with everyone. I had asked for and received a shotgun for my present from my grandparents and I couldn't wait to get out and go hunting with it. As always I planned to stay my entire holiday break in Kosciusko.

When New Year's came and went, I couldn't help but reflect, as I always do, on the previous year and what had transpired. At the same time the year before, Kevin and I were breaking up and I felt as if my world was coming to an end; I'd started college in a new town, a new apartment; made many new friends; went through hell with Paul Amacker; experienced a gay pride event; came out to my family; lived through the horror of 9/11; and still somehow managed to keep good grades and finish out my third semester of college in fine shape. Whatever the following year had to throw at me, I felt ready for. Never in a million years could I ever have honestly been prepared for what did happen.

# CHAPTER TWENTY-FIVE

In January of 2002, I enrolled back at Jones County Junior College, but also decided to take several night classes at the University of Southern Mississippi. Going to a real university was both exciting and more demanding. While at JCJC, classes were small, teachers more helpful, and the atmosphere more like high school. At USM, I was in classes with over a hundred students and if you couldn't keep pace, you missed out.

One benefit of going to USM was having access to their gym and weight-lifting facility. I'd never been one to pay much attention to how my body looked. I assumed and was always told that I had a nice body, but for the first time in my life, I decided to start a work-out program.

Every morning I would go to the gym at USM and work out for an hour before going back to my apartment and getting ready for class. I made several new friends at the gym and thankfully found a wonderful workout partner. The only unfortunate issue of the situation was that he was straight.

I began watching my diet and eating healthier foods. It wasn't long before I started noticing better changes with my body and attitude. When a person eats better and exercises regularly, it improves their entire outlook on life. Working out became an obsession with me. While I was not a big weight lifter, I enjoyed the cardio workouts more.

Even though I was taking a big case load and working out every day, I still found time to hang out with my friends. Although I didn't go to the gay bar regularly, I still hung out with my friends as much as I could. Several weekends were spent in New Orleans and it wasn't long before I knew the city fairly well. My mother and I were still getting along but she avoided talking to me about anything remotely gay. Like they say in the military, it was a "don't ask, don't tell" situation.

When spring break began approaching I decided to take a road trip. I'd never been on a trip by myself but the thought of taking out on a cross-country vacation appealed to me. I ran my idea by Meme, checked my finances, and began planning my trip. I wanted to go back into Pennsylvania, but I also wanted to go to St. Louis. It wasn't long before I had my trip planned on my Rand McNally atlas and was preparing to go.

On the Friday of my last day of school, before recess for spring break, I had one quick test to take and then I'd have to drive back to Vicksburg, spend the night and leave out early Saturday morning. I was letting a friend of mine stay in my apartment while I was gone out of town and I diligently removed my guns from the apartment before I left that morning. I also had my dog in the truck with me, but wasn't worried since it would probably take less than fifteen minutes for me to take my test and then be on my way to Vicksburg.

When I arrived at JCJC, I parked my truck near the administration building and quickly grabbed my book bag and headed to my classroom. The test was easy and I breezed right through it. As I left and headed back for the parking lot, I noticed something was out of order. There were cop cars and police officers standing around my truck.

At first thought, I assumed something had happened to my dog, but as I got to my truck, the officer asked me if I minded stepping off to the side and talking to him for a minute. Patiently and calmly, the officer explained to me that someone had passed by my truck and noticed the firearms I had in the back seat and then gone to campus police and reported them. The officer said that he would have to confiscate them and take down my information.

At first I thought I was going to be arrested, but the officer merely informed me that the local district attorney, sheriff, and school administrators would have to be consulted and then make a decision on whether to prosecute. I was told that it was normally not illegal for a person to carry a weapon in his vehicle on a school campus unless that person was a student there- then it became a crime.

I was astounded. My attempts to explain to the officer the circumstances of why I had the guns in my truck were met with patience and understanding, but the officer said he had a job to do. I was basically told to go home, enjoy my spring break vacation, and report back to the campus police on the first day of regular classes.

Driving away from the JCJC campus, I was petrified of being arrested and not knowing what the outcome would be. I was hesitant about telling Meme or my mother, but I felt it might be necessary to prepare for it, just in case.

When I got back to Vicksburg, I explained to Meme what the circumstances were and I hoped she wouldn't judge me too harshly. I explained that I didn't want to leave the guns in my apartment over the week because my friend was using my place and I didn't want to have to drive all the way back to Hattiesburg from Ellisville, where the JCJC campus was, since JCJC was semi on the way home.

Meme and I both came to the conclusion that I did the right thing, but that I should have exercised better caution and not left the guns in plain view. We decided to hold off on telling my mother since she was already so critical of me. We did go ahead and tell my stepdad and try to get some legal advice from him, but the most he could do was place a call to the local district attorney there and try to convince them not to pursue charges. Unfortunately, it did little to put my mind to ease.

Deciding whether to continue with my road trip was the next pressing concern. I'd already made reservations at several hotels and canceling them meant losing money. Meme's opinion was that I go ahead and try to have fun. My opinion was middle-of-the-road. I finally decided that nothing could be hurt by taking the trip and that whatever was going to happen in Jones County would wait till school started back.

I left the following morning and drove from Vicksburg all the way to Richmond, Virginia. I spent the night and the following day toured several historical areas before leaving and driving to Washington, D.C. I had always wanted to visit Ford's Theatre and several other places in our nation's capital and this was the first opportunity to do so. Less than a year after the 9/11 terrorist's attacks, D.C. was filled with armed national guardsman and police officers. It was almost a surreal experience.

After spending a day in D.C., I drove up through Maryland and toured the Antietam National Battlefield before ending my day in a hotel room in Gettysburg, Pennsylvania. I'd planned to spend two days in Gettysburg and devote most of it to walking the military battlefield there.

Since first coming to Gettysburg several years before, I'd experienced a connection to the place, but I'd never had the chance to really explore the entire battlefield. Using my two days there, I was able to see a lot of the battlefield and experience things that I normally wouldn't have been able to had I been with other people. I believe that to understand what our American soldiers experienced at Gettysburg, whether Union or Confederate, one must take the time and devote himself to studying and learning about that tremendous battle- which more than anything else saved our country from splintering.

After leaving Gettysburg, I drove across the vast state of Pennsylvania and down into Ohio. I spent the night in Cincinnati before driving on down to Louisville, Kentucky. I'd always wanted to watch a horse race at Churchhill Downs, but unfortunately they were not hosting any races while I was there. I did get to see the race track and was more than satisfied with the small glimpse.

On the seventh day of my road trip, I left Kentucky and drove to St. Louis. Being able to see the Arch was an exhilarating experience and one that I will never forget. I also went to see the Anheuser-Busch factory, and although I'm not a beer drinker myself, I enjoyed learning and seeing how beer was made.

On the last Saturday of my vacation, I left St. Louis and drove to Memphis, Tennessee where I met up with my good friend, John Cofield. John had wanted me to visit with him in Memphis ever since we had met in New Orleans several months before. I'd never been to Memphis before and I had been looking forward to our visit since planning my trip.

John and I went to eat BBQ ribs at the famous Rendezvous restaurant and then went and partied at a local gay bar, called Backstreet. Every gay club has its own unique identity, separate from others, and Backstreet was no different. I thoroughly enjoyed being there and meeting new people. Sometime, during the partying and fun, I remembered that in another day I could very well be arrested and incarcerated.

During my road trip, I had chosen to block out the possibility that when I went back to school at JCJC I might face going to jail. But as the days passed, and that eventuality became closer to reality, I couldn't help but let it depress me. In fact, the thought of going to jail downright terrified me.

I left Memphis Sunday afternoon and drove back to Vicksburg. The past week had been one of the best in my life. I will always recommend to young people that in some point in their life that they take a week long road trip by themselves. The things that you experience, and the quiet time that you have to think, opens up a whole new world in thoughts, sights and sounds that a person wouldn't normally be able to experience while traveling with other people. It had all been so great, but unfortunately it was overshadowed at moments by the looming dread that I knew was waiting for me at JCJC.

I stayed in Vicksburg the night after returning from my trip. I got up early the next morning and drove to the JCJC campus in Ellisville, Mississippi. Meme and I both were prepared for the possibility that I would be arrested, even though we both hoped it wouldn't happen.

When I got to the JCJC campus, I was told to meet the campus police in the dean's office. When I arrived, I was also met by two investigators, one from the Jones County Sheriff's Office and one from the Mississippi Highway Patrol's Investigation Division. I was presented with a warrant and told I was being arrested for possession of a firearm, by a student, on a school campus. Not only was I going to jail, but I also was told by the student dean that I was being expelled from college. My worst fears had been realized.

When I got to the Jones County Jail, I was booked-in, finger printed, and had my picture taken. It was an embarrassing and demeaning process. I was then placed in a holding cell to wait for a bondsman to come bail me out. At that moment, sitting in that tiny, cold, concrete holding cell, I don't think I could have ever felt more depressed and low in my life. I thought everything had been going so well, but at that point, all I could think about was what a failure and disappointment I had become.

After waiting over three hours, the guards finally approved my bond paperwork and allowed me to leave. Even though I had only spent a very short time behind bars, walking out of jail was a fabulous feeling. It was certainly not something I ever wanted to have to go through again, but as my bonds agent warned me, the fight was still ahead of me. I was facing up to fifteen years in prison if I was convicted of that crime, and that thought scared me even more. At the moment though, I had choices to make- none of which were going to be easy.

# CHAPTER TWENTY-SIX

After my arrest in Jones County there were certain decisions to be made that would affect my immediate future. I had been expelled from the Jones County Junior College campus but I was still taking night classes at the University of Southern Mississippi. I also still had an apartment and many friends in Hattiesburg.

I ultimately decided to stay in Hattiesburg and finish out my semester at USM. I'd purposely not told any of my friends about my arrest and I tried to carry on as though things were still normal, but in the back of my mind, I was very worried.

Finally, at the end of the spring semester, I packed up all of my property and moved back to Vicksburg. It was a tough choice to make. I enjoyed my freedom and independence but at the same time I felt that being back home in Vicksburg was a better choice for me. Meme was especially pleased that I was coming back home but I still was worried about what I would do with the rest of my life.

I had been on my own for a little over a year in Hattiesburg. Personally I thought I had done a very good job. I was only seventeen-years-old when I moved down there but I had managed to go to school, maintain good grades, keep an apartment and juggle a social life. I was pleased with my time that I'd spent there; I just wished that it didn't have to end on such a sour note.

Soon after returning to Vicksburg, I was told by my stepdad that the district attorney in Jones County had indicated that they probably would not be pursuing an indictment against me. It was relayed to my stepdad, that since I had not brandished any firearms, or threatened anyone, that there was not really a point in prosecuting me for the crime. We were told that they would eventually file a motion to dismiss with the circuit court judge. The news was gratifying and relieving. Everyone told me just to sit tight and not to worry about it- so that's what I did.

Early in the summer I decided to take my godparents, Kenny and Wendy, down to Dauphin Island, Alabama and camp out on the beach. We also took my horse and trailer. While they wanted to swim and lay out on the beach, I planned to ride my horse and fish. Once down there, it was an exhilarating feeling running the horse up and down the beach and along the water. It really gave me some time to think and ponder what I was going to do with my future.

I ultimately came to the conclusion that I would have to go to work until I could reenroll in college classes again and continue my education, but before I could implement this plan, the political history of Vicksburg changed course.

While we were on the beach in Alabama, the Mississippi Attorney General's Office arrested one of the Vicksburg/Warren County Constables for extortion. J.L. Mitchell had been the central district constable in Warren County for several terms and had generated himself a terrible reputation for corruption, but neither the Sheriff nor the district attorney would ever investigate the complaints. So for years, Mitchell was able to extort and accept bribes from people unhindered.

Finally, in May of 2002, the same investigator who had worked with me on the Paul Amacker case, began an investigation on J.L. Mitchell and soon thereafter arrested him. It wasn't long before he had resigned from public office in disgrace and was convicted of felony extortion.

Now that the constable's seat was becoming available for the first time in several years, I seriously considered filing my candidacy and running for it. I would be nineteen years old when the special election would be held later that fall, but several other former and current constables had been elected at a young age. My friend, Mike Ouzts, had been elected at nineteen years old in the early eighties, and the current constable of the northern district of Warren County, Glen McKay, had been elected when he was only twenty. The thought of being constable fascinated me.

I began to slowly develop a plan for entering my name into the constable's race and trying my best to win in November. Most of the people I quietly consulted about making a run for the constable's seat were supportive of my idea, but cautioned me against running at such an early age. Many told me that a white man could never get elected in the central district of Warren County because it was a majority African-American district. I felt, on the other hand, that honesty and integrity would overcome any racial prejudices.

As the time came nearer for me to make a choice on whether to run or not, the more I believed that I should do it. At the time I didn't fully realize the sacrifices I would have to make, or the burden of exposure that I would be placing on myself by running for public office. I assure my readers that had I known then what I know now, I never would have run for the constable's seat.

The rest of my summer I spent preparing to make a run for constable. Even though I had made up my mind that I was going to do it, I had not yet committed to it publicly. Half of my family was against it, the other half for it.

My grandfather Atwood and the rest of the Atwood

family were totally against me running for any kind of public office. My grandfather even went so far as to tell me that the Atwood's do not enter public life, they quietly "manage" things from the outside. What my grandfather meant by "manage" was to quietly influence politicians with the right amount of money, slipped quietly under the table. Unfortunately, I was receiving quite the lesson in government corruption from my own family. Thankfully, I didn't let the Atwood's discouragement stop me. I plowed on ahead.

The catalyst that finally sealed my decision to run for office was when a deputy sheriff on the Warren County Sheriff's Office illegally and horribly shot and killed a young man. As bad as it was, the shooting and the events leading up to the murder were quickly and successfully covered up by the Sheriff, his detectives, and other members of law enforcement desperate to protect a fellow comrade.

Once I realized the depravity and corruption of law enforcement in Vicksburg and Warren County, I quickly decided that a run for constable, on an anti-corruption platform, and a promise to clean up the malfeasance of those in public office would propel me to do this. There was only one thing left to do.

On August 13th, 2002, two things happened. The first, I turned nineteen years old. The second, I officially filed to run for constable of the central district of Warren County, Mississippi. In my public announcement I said: "A constable must be honest and trustworthy and never disgrace the badge he wears. I will uphold the duties of the office with honesty and integrity. I have the ability to do the job and the integrity to do it right. Some law enforcement officers in Warren County would rather handpick the next constable, one who will play ball and not rock the boat. I will not be intimidated by any politicians or deputy sheriffs. Public office is a public trust. Elections are about choosing the best candidate. I will not back down from my convictions that Warren County deserves nothing less than a law enforcement officer who is impartial, incorruptible and beyond reproach. I shall strive to meet the needs of all citizens fairly, efficiently, and equitably."

The die had been cast. And once I made my announcement to run, I took upon myself the burden of declaring war on those who held the keys and weapons to power in Vicksburg and Warren County.

# CHAPTER TWENTY-SEVEN

As news of my candidacy and anti-corruption crusade spread, the citizens of my county responded by volunteering their time and financial contributions. By Labor Day weekend, I had over three hundred campaign signs placed throughout the district, and had a small group of dedicated and loyal volunteers working with me every day, canvassing my district's neighborhoods and garnering the vote.

When the deadline for filing to run for the constable seat ended, there were a total of six candidates. My strongest competition was Rudolph Walker. He was a city police officer and the brother of the former mayor of Vicksburg. He had been hand-picked by the political machines and law enforcement community of Vicksburg. Rudolph Walker was known as a person who had no higher political ambition than that of constable and could be counted on not to be an influential future candidate for sheriff.

Martin Pace was always careful to choose and support political candidates who did not pose a future challenge to him and his grasp on power in the Sheriff's Office. My unfortunate mistake at the beginning of my campaign was to state freely and fully to anyone who would listen that the constable's seat was only a stepping stone to my political career. I made it very plain that one day I planned to run for sheriff.

Upon hearing this, Sheriff Pace and his deputies at the Sheriff's Department rolled out every big gun they could find in an effort to defeat my candidacy and ruin my reputation. Some of their tactics were covert; others were quite obvious. It wasn't long after the start of my campaign that I realized I was not only working to defeat the other five men running against me in the election, but I was also out to defeat an entire collaboration of corruption that permeated almost every political office in Vicksburg and Warren County.

My biggest campaign issue was the fact that if elected, I would be filling a seat vacated by a law enforcement officer who had used his elected office for private gain and had extorted and abused the citizens of his district for years. Furthermore, he had been allowed to operate freely, and almost openly, under the eyes of a Sheriff whose duty it was to prevent such activity. It was no secret that J.L. Mitchell was corrupt. It was also no secret that Mitchell was allowed to continue with his illegal shenanigans unhindered by any law officer in the county. Why he was allowed to do this is still unknown. I have always been told it was because he provided monetary kick-backs to the Sheriff and other members of the Sheriff's Department. But these rumors were never confirmed.

My second campaign issue was the illegal shooting and murder of a twenty-two year man by deputy sheriff Lionel Johnson and the cover-up which ensued. Because of the lengths the law enforcement community went to, in order to cover-up and hide the true facts surrounding the murder, this issue became known as "Sheriff-Gate".

Many people in our county were outraged, especially

when initial reports suggested that the boy had been handcuffed and shot in cold blood by the deputy. People were further disgusted when the deputy changed his story to fit with the evidence coming out of the Mississippi Crime Lab.

My efforts in my campaign were to direct people's attention to the fact that the cover-up originated directly out of Sheriff Martin Pace's office. But without any inside witnesses or direct evidence, I could only use suspicion and innuendo.

The district attorney of Warren County, Gil Martin, assured not only me, but also the newspapers and citizens that the investigation would be thorough and that the case would eventually be presented to a grand jury. In practice though, there never was a thorough investigation and there never was an honest attempt by the district attorney to have a legitimate grand jury investigate and consider the evidence of the case.

Unfortunately, an indictment was never returned against Lionel Johnson. I honestly believe though, that had an honest and thorough investigation been done and the grand jurors presented with all of the evidence, they would have been prompted by conscience to return a criminal verdict against the deputy.

My efforts during the campaign not only drew upon the fact that government corruption was rampant throughout Vicksburg and Warren County, but it also promised solutions to these problems. Some people, tongue-in-cheek compared, me to a modern-day Elliot Ness.

My only intentions were to rid my city and county of what I considered to be an illegal consortium of politicians and law enforcement officers bent on personal greed and personal advancement of power at other people's expense. Bad judgment or not, I didn't parse words when describing to my constituents the corruption and malfeasance of those in elected office. More than once I encouraged my people that a vote for me was also a future vote to end the corruption.

As the first month of my campaign drew to a close and October approached, I was well under way to feeling confident that I could at least make it into a run-off election instead of being defeated outright. I knew at the very beginning that

Rudolph Walker was my toughest competition. He had the money and the full support of the political machines and law enforcement community. Overcoming that amount of power, I knew, was going to be very difficult.

Every day I would wake up around five a.m. and begin my day by having coffee and donuts at one of the small breakfast shops around town. I was never pushy or confrontational, but before leaving I would always pass out a few of my campaign cards and stop to talk to those who seemed interested.

The rest of the day was spent walking on foot, knocking on doors throughout every neighborhood in my district. I had always been a connoisseur of maps and in this case I had compiled a detailed map of every house and neighborhood in my district. I planned out, every night, exactly which houses I would hit the next day. If someone wasn't home I would place a "X" mark on top of the house on the map, so that I would know to come back to it again before election day. If someone was home and I was able to speak with them I would place a "H" mark on top of their home.

Every time I was able to place a campaign sign in someone's yard, I would place an "S" mark on their home. Using this method I was able to keep track of where I had visited, who I had talked to, and where my signs were being placed. My volunteers followed the same method. About twice a week I would ride around to every place that I had posted a sign to check and make sure it was still there. After several weeks I realized that some of my signs were being stolen.

Stealing the campaign signs of your opponent is an old trick that has been used since the beginning of elections. Old as it may be, it's still aggravating and a waste of money. In certain locations I would place a campaign sign only to have it removed and stolen overnight or sometimes in as little as a few hours. When this happened repeatedly, I decided to do something about it.

There was one particular spot, off of Highway 61, near Sherman Avenue School, that is a prime location for the placement of political signs. However, I never could keep one of my signs there without it being stolen. After the third one went missing in as few days, I decided to play dirty and rig one of my signs with sewing needles and treble fishing hooks. I also decided that I would try to catch the thief in the act.

After rigging my sign with enough hooks to catch Moby Dick and enough sewing needles to supply a seamstress shop for a month, I placed it at dark near the spot where my previous signs had always been stolen. I then moved my truck about 50 yards down the road and pulled it into the tree line. From my vantage point I could easily see any vehicle which pulled off the road to mess with my signs.

After about two hours, a sheriff's patrol car pulled up. My original plan was to confront the person who was stealing my signs, but once I saw it was a deputy sheriff, I became immobile and could only stand by and watch through my binoculars as the deputy jumped out of his car, ran to my sign and quickly grabbed it. Even though I was half a football field away, I could plainly hear the deputy cussing and screaming as he dropped my sign and quickly got back into his patrol car and pulled away.

I sat in my truck giggling for a moment but the exhilaration at what I had just witnessed gave way to anger and frustration. I had been told by several of my campaign volunteers that different cops and deputies had been seen removing my campaign signs but I wasn't ready at the time to take those accusations to the Sheriff and City Police Chief. But now after witnessing it with my own eyes, my fury knew no bounds. I was determined to stop this interference by the sheriff and his deputies. Thankfully, word must have spread that my campaign signs were booby-trapped, because after that night, fewer and fewer of my signs were removed or stolen.

# CHAPTER TWENTY-EIGHT

Three events so thoroughly shook the very foundation of my belief system during the last month of my campaign that I almost withdrew from the race and disappeared from Vicksburg. It was bad enough that I had deputy sheriffs and city police officers stealing my campaign signs, but I also had to deal with them starting and circulating rumors about me that were inaccurate and totally untrue.

As the first of October came and went, people could look around Vicksburg and see the presence of my campaign. Most notably were my signs, with black and yellow colors, that had thankfully finally stopped disappearing. Second, were my radio advertisements that were playing on the local radio stations every hour, every day. And thirdly was the chatter around town. People were responding to my message of ending the corruption.

For the past year, the citizens of Vicksburg and Warren

County had dealt with one corrupt cop or politician after another. In addition to Lionel Johnson shooting and killing the unarmed, handcuffed boy, and J.L. Mitchell getting arrested and convicted of extortion, Vicksburg had also seen one of its long-serving county judges, Gerald Hoseman, get arrested for the beating and attempted murder of his mistress. People were tired of it and they responded to my campaign with gusto.

This caused an unsettling feeling amongst those members of the sheriff's department who were so intent on clinging to power. While never seriously considering me a contender to run for sheriff, they were immensely afraid of the exposure I was forcing upon them and the media coverage my campaign was generating with its anti-corruption platform. Winning an election was not only my biggest objective; just as importantly, I was intent on bringing to light the illegal and unethical behavior of those in public office. And at the time, no one could say that I was not accomplishing that goal.

Every Friday night that there was a home football game, I would always attend and stand at the entrance to the stadium to pass out my campaign cards. Once everyone had entered the stadium I would usually go to the parking lot and place more campaign literature on all the vehicles.

It was while doing this one night that I was approached by Mike Traxler, a detective on the Warren County Sheriff's Office. In a nonthreatening and polite tone, Traxler asked about my campaign and how things were going. He even commented that he thought my campaign looked really good, especially to be run by someone as young as myself.

Suspicious of his motives, but intrigued by his behavior, I played ball and went along with his charade. After exchanging a few pleasantries, Traxler asked me what it would take for me to withdraw from the race. Traxler patiently explained that no matter what I did, I would lose to Rudolph Walker and that it would be better to withdraw from the race now and save face, rather than remain in and continue to antagonize everyone that was in a position of power in Warren County.

Recognizing the underlying threats in Traxler's

admonitions, I explained that win or lose, I had a message that needed to be delivered to the people of Warren County and that I intended to give it. I also told Traxler that I had already spent far too much money to withdraw from the race at this late hour.

Without missing a breath, Traxler quickly informed me that if it was only a matter of money keeping me in the race, he and his "boys" could easily reimburse me for whatever expenses I'd had.

For a moment I was thunderstuck. I could not believe that Mike Traxler, a detective on the Warren County Sheriff's Office, was offering me a bribe to withdraw from the race. Suspicious of whether it was merely a personal offer from Traxler or whether it represented an offer from the Sheriff and the entire law enforcement community was something I would never know. Regardless of where the offer came from, I didn't think twice about rejecting it.

Before Traxler walked away, he left me with a warning. Looking dead into my eyes, without blinking and without so much as a hint of compassion, Traxler told me that I would never be allowed to finish out my term as constable even if I was elected. He made very clear to me the fact that if elected, I would be shot and killed. He said that I could expect nothing less than open hostility from then on and that I had best seriously consider withdrawing from the race immediately because from then on, it was open war. The last thing Traxler told me was that I could no longer hide behind a powerful, wealthy family.

I stood in that stadium parking lot dejected, scared, and without any emotional feeling except negativity. It was only at that point that I realized what a tremendous mountain I had decided to climb by running in this race. It was an obstacle I wasn't sure I could overcome.

I knew from the very beginning that I would have to achieve a miracle to win this race. Even with the support I was garnering with the anti-corruption platform, I still had many more issues working against me that would have to be dealt with. Having almost every law enforcement officer and politician against you in a political race is a sure sign of defeat, but I had come too far to give in. Too many people had also stepped out on a ledge to support me and I couldn't let them down. I couldn't let myself (and what I believe in) down. I was determined to push forward to the end.

Several days after Traxler tried to bribe and threaten me out of the race, I received notice from the courts that my father, my own father, was suing me in Chancery Court, asking that the courts force me to change my name to something other than David Garland Atwood, II.

As silly and as frivolous as it was, my father had decided that I'd become such a disgrace to the family name that he was going to try to force me to change it. Never mind that this was the name that he had insisted on calling me since birth. This was the same name that everyone in the family insisted on calling me, from even before I was born. To change my name now, after nineteen years, and only because I was running for public office, was absurd and ridiculous. (Being gay probably had something to do with it, but my father was not about to bring that up in a public forum, no matter how much he hated me for it.)

As stupid as it was, my father insisted that an emergency hearing be held and that the judge issue a ruling and impose an emergency injunction stopping me from using the "Atwood" name in any further campaign literature. Thankfully, the judge saw what ridiculousness this was and dismissed the lawsuit without giving it further credence.

It seemed as though the more support I received from the community and the more coverage I got for my campaign, the more people I seemed to piss off and the more my family hated me. One of my family's close friends met with me one day and explained the situation.

He said that the Atwood's never ran for public office or injected themselves into public debate. Their methods were to secretly control and manipulate politicians through influence and money. When I came along and caused a stir, accusing almost every politician and law enforcement officer in Vicksburg and Warren County of corruption and illegal behavior, it severely pissed them off, especially coming from a kid whose family had been personally involved in that illegal consortium for years.

It was pointed out to me that a large percentage of every politician and law enforcement officer in Vicksburg drove a car or truck that had been purchased at Atwood Chevrolet. My grandfather and dad had, for years, been providing cars and trucks at extremely discounted prices, sometimes even free of charge, to anyone and everyone who was in a position of power or elected office.

It was because of this arrangement that my family had been so easily able to maneuver themselves around the political scenes of Vicksburg, influencing policy where needed, and defeating opposition. It was also made evident to me that because of this arrangement, my grandfather and dad had amazing influence with the cops and deputies. Both sides enjoyed the benefits of this illegal compact.

In my campaign for constable, I was not only threatening the bread and butter of many of the law enforcement officers and politicians, but I was threatening to unravel the very fabric of corruption that my own family had worked for decades to build. Unwittingly, I was taking on a lot more than I had initially thought possible. The fabric of corruption which permeated all of Vicksburg and Warren County was woven with thread from the blood of my own family- and the knowledge of that gave me pause to what I was doing.

The final straw that unraveled my campaign race occurred about two weeks before the November 5th, 2002 election. I was wrapping up a long day of campaigning and was driving home when a sheriff's patrol car pulled in behind me and turned on its blue lights. I had been waiting for something like this to happen and was prepared by always keeping a voice-activated recorder within reach. As I pulled over into a gas station parking lot, I turned the recorder on and placed it out of view by the door.

The deputy who came to my window was Jay Ghrigsby. I had known that he had at one time been a Vicksburg Police officer, but had been in trouble there and was forced to resign. He was then hired by Sheriff Pace and had been at the Warren County Sheriff's office for only a short time. His reputation had preceded him and I thought I was well prepared for whatever garbage he might sling my way.

Deputy Ghrigsby was formal and polite. He requested my driver's license and insurance information. After returning to his car to check my information, he brought my license and insurance card back and threw them into my vehicle along with a citation for "following another vehicle too closely".

Deputy Ghrigsby then informed me that my days were numbered, and win or lose on election day, the sheriff's department would take revenge on me for what I had done. He told me that there were numerous ways that I could be killed and that they could make it look like an accident. For a solid five minutes Jay Ghrigsby did nothing but berate, and scream at me. In some sick way, I think Jay Ghrigsby achieved some sense of sexual gratification from acting like a military drill instructor that night in his treatment of me. Thankfully, my only consolation during the entire scene was the fact that my voice-recorder was getting it all.

After Deputy Ghrigsby had threatened and cursed me without any provocation for over five minutes, he got in his vehicle, spun his tires and left. I sat on the side of the road flabbergasted at what had just occurred. Before I left, I rewound the tape and listened to everything that Ghrigsby had just said. Somewhat elated that I finally had proof of the threats and intimidation that the sheriff's office was exerting on me, I couldn't help but bask in the joy.

I immediately drove home and played the tape for Meme and my friend John Cofield, who had come down from Memphis to help with the campaign. They were just as shocked. Even though it was almost 10:00 at night, I called the district attorney at his home and made him listen to the tape as well. Gil Martin's only comments were that if it truly was Jay Ghrigsby whose voice was on the tape, then the Attorney General's Office would have to investigate the matter.

The last person I called and made listen to the recording that night was Sheriff Pace. After twice letting the sheriff listen to the tape, I informed him that I would be taking the tape to the

FBI and to the Mississippi Attorney General's Office in the morning and would insist on a prosecution of Jay Ghrigsby. I also informed the sheriff that I would be filing for a restraining order against Deputy Ghrigsby and the entire Sheriff's Department. The last comment caused the sheriff to slam the phone down in such a fit of rage that I expected my phone to shatter.

I had big plans to not only insist on a prosecution of Jay Ghrigsby with the proper authorities the following day, but I also had plans to air portions of the tape on the radio even if I had to pay for all the air-time to do it. I finally had the proof I needed of a conspiracy to threaten and intimidate me into withdrawing from the constable's race and I was going to exploit it in every way possible.

Shortly after going to bed that night, I heard the doorbell ring. Unsure of whether it was coming from the front or back door, I quickly looked out the windows to see if I could see a car or anything in the drive-way. Seeing nothing, I met Meme and John in the living room and the three of us went to the front door and opened it, but there was no one there.

We then heard someone banging their fist on the back door, but before we could walk the length of the house, the banging stopped. Unsure what was going on, and somewhat scared, we remained in the living room. A moment later someone began banging on the front door again. This time when I opened the door, there was someone there.

Deputy Jay Ghrigsby raised his pistol and pointed it directly in my face and pushed his way into the house. When he saw Meme and John Cofield, he pointed his pistol at them also and told everyone not to move or say anything.

Returning the pistol to my face, he asked very calmly for the tape recording. Finally realizing what was going on, but in no mood to cooperate, I tried to mumble out an excuse for not being able to produce it. Unsatisfied with my answer, Deputy Ghrigsby became enraged and grabbed me by the neck and forced me to the ground. Stating that he would blow my goddamn brains out if I didn't turn over the tape recording to him, Deputy Ghrigsby gave me one hard kick before holstering the pistol. Before I could get up off the ground, Deputy Ghrigsby was going through the house, overturning furniture, slinging stuff off shelves and demanding to know where the tape was.

Scared and unable to do anything but acquiesce, I told him where the tape was in my room. Meme had already dialed 911 and was on the phone with the emergency operator. I took the phone from her and explained to the emergency operator that Jay Ghrigsby had broken into my house and was basically holding us at gunpoint. Neither the emergency operator, nor anyone at the Sheriff's Office knew what was going on, or what to do to stop it.

Once obtaining the tape, Deputy Ghrigsby was satisfied with his destruction and left as quickly as he had come. Unfortunately, neither the Sheriff nor anyone else that night was interested in investigating the break-in and assault. The Sheriff wouldn't answer his phones, and the 911 center patiently explained that they had been instructed not to dispatch any law officers to our house to take a report. I realized that being victimized by a law enforcement officer was a lonely and painful experience. I also realized that getting anyone to care or investigate illegal conduct by a law enforcement officer was next to impossible.

The next day and for the next few weeks I tried everything I could to file charges on Jay Ghrigsby and have an outside law enforcement agency investigate the crime. According to Sheriff Pace, he had never heard of any tape recording. District Attorney Gil Martin became uncooperative and claimed the tape recording he heard was inaudible and undecipherable. And even more mysteriously, the 911 recordings of our emergency call that night vanished.

The cover-up was so systematic and complete that the only record and evidence of the tape recording and of Jay Ghrigsby breaking into our home and holding us at gun point was our own memories of the event.

I was later informed that after receiving my phone call and listening to the recording, Sheriff Pace contacted Jay Ghrigsby and ordered him to recover the tape "by any means necessary". When Deputy Ghrigsby broke into our home and ransacked it, he was doing so at the behest of the Sheriff in an attempt to destroy, what up until that time, was the best piece of evidence I had collected that proved a conspiracy of corruption and intimidation by the Warren County Sheriff's Office.

Losing that evidence did more to sink my morale in the last weeks of my campaign than any other event I had so far had to deal with. I literally felt trapped on all sides. If I wasn't forced to deal with my own father dragging me into court and trying to force me to change my name, I was having to deal with bribery attempts and break-ins by sheriff's deputies. If it could have gone wrong, then it did go wrong in my campaign.

Regardless of the difficulties I faced, and the terror that I knew was waiting on me, I always rebounded and continued to press forward with my fight to end the corruption in Vicksburg and Warren County. The last two weeks of my campaign I worked harder than I had ever worked in my life. Even if I wasn't going to win the race, I was going to at least tell my story, and what I was forced to overcome, to any and every person who would listen.

# CHAPTER TWENTY-NINE

On election day, November 5$^{th}$, 2002, I began by having a McDonald's Big Breakfast and reminding the cashiers and cooks there to vote. My district was comprised of five different voting precincts and I made sure that within view of every precinct, I at least had three or four campaign signs visible.

I was not allowed to pass out campaign literature in or around a voting precinct, but I made sure my volunteers were nearby and could talk with voters as they came in to vote. Some very smart people had predicted that I would make it into a run-off election with Rudolph Walker, but then would be beaten after that.

Because this was a special election, a candidate had to receive fifty percent, plus one, in order to win, rather than a simple majority. It was explained to me that because I was running in a majority African-American district that I didn't have much chance of getting elected. My response was that regardless of skin color, people were tired of corrupt cops and politicians and would vote regardless of the ethnicity of one's background.

It was also pointed out, that regardless of district demographics, Rudolph Walker had the full support of the police and sheriff's department and was the "chosen" one to fill the vacant constable's seat. This was made apparent earlier in the summer when the Board of Supervisors had unanimously appointed Walker to the constable's seat rather than wait until a special election could be held.

By being appointed to the constable's seat, rather than at first earning it by election, Walker already had a step-up on any other candidate. Regardless of whether you become the incumbent by election or appointment, it gives you an unfair advantage. The political machines in Warren County knew this, and they wasted no time in appointing Walker to the constable's seat soon after J.L. Mitchell was convicted and removed from office.

Thirdly, it was obvious that the law enforcement community and political machines were not going to sit idly by and let the voters make informed decisions about the best candidate. Gossip, rumors, and innuendo always play a part in election campaigns, but that still doesn't mean it's right or fair. Responding to rumors and gossip was an ordeal I chose to ignore at the very beginning of the race. Doing so would only tie me down with issues I couldn't defend against.

Fourthly, I was only nineteen years old. Dozens of times I was asked how old I was when I would be out knocking door-to-door asking for votes. Many people saw my race as a good thing and age was not an issue. Some people questioned whether at such a young age I would have the ability to do the job. I assured everyone I met, that age would not hold me back from serving the citizens of my district honorably and fairly. One advantage to being young was having the gusto and energy to do a good job.

Regardless of what my setbacks were, I felt it was still possible to achieve a large enough percentage of the vote to at least prevent Walker from achieving a fifty percent or more majority; thereby throwing the election into a run-off. If I could then garner enough support and votes from the other four defeated candidates, my logic was that I could win the election.

Shortly after the polls opened that morning, I traveled down to my precinct and for the first time in my life voted, and of course, the first person I voted for, was myself. Very few people in this country can honestly say that the first time they got to vote in a government election, they were able to vote for themselves, but I did, and I was very proud of that vote. I just hoped that more people felt the same way and chose me as their candidate.

When the polls closed at 7:00 that evening, my entire campaign team and all my volunteers went to the courthouse to await the results of the election. I had considered just going home and going to bed- after all I was utterly exhausted, but there was such a good feeling among my campaign staff, that to abandon them would have been disappointing. My volunteers had risked so much and worked so hard for me the past two months, I owed them at least enough to stay out and await the voter returns.

After seeing about half of the votes from my precincts counted, it was apparent that no one would be earning enough votes to win the election out right. When the counting ended, Rudolph Walker was in the lead, with me in second. The other four candidates barely made a showing. Just as expected from the beginning, Walker and I were the strongest candidates, and just as I had hoped, I made it into the run-off election that was to be held two weeks later.

Most of my campaign staff and volunteers were exuberant that night. Of course I was too, but the strain and stress of having pulled through one of the toughest obstacles in my life was finally catching up with me. Regardless of whether I won or lost, I was honestly ready for the race to end.

After leaving the courthouse that night, confident in my small victory, but knowing there were two weeks left of campaigning, I couldn't help but breathe a sigh of relief knowing that it was almost over.

The next two weeks were a whirlwind of nonstop operations designed to get every supporter I could to go back to the polls and vote for me again. Curiously absent was Rudolph Walker. Maybe he was utterly confident in his victory at the run-off election, but whatever his motives, I never saw any of his campaign staff or volunteers during that two weeks.

On the Sunday before the run-off election, I received a call from a friend of mine bringing attention to the fact that negative campaign literature was appearing around town accusing me of being under indictment by a Jones County Grand Jury for the possession of firearms on a school campus.

Earlier in the election race I had made the decision not to tell anyone about my arrest in Jones County. My stepdad had been assured by the district attorney in Jones County that they were not going to indict me and would soon be dismissing the charges. Feeling free of the obligation and under no moral conscience as to any wrong-doing, I proceeded with my campaign. Learning of an indictment at this late hour smelled of corruption and illegal influence.

My stepdad quickly made a few calls and was able to ascertain that the district attorney of Jones County had indeed gone back on his word and had recently indicted me. We later learned that after I had earned enough votes to remain in the run-off election, certain members of the Warren County Sheriff's Office discovered the details of my arrest from earlier that year and vehemently pushed the district attorney in Jones County to immediately indict me.

My indictment in Jones County was a direct result of members, probably including the Sheriff, influencing the district attorney to indict me on a charge which we had been assured would be dismissed, solely to influence an election in which the Sheriff's Department was terrified of me winning.

Once they had secured an indictment against me, the sheriff's office wasted no time in disseminating that information to the public. They purposefully waited until one day before the run-off election so I would not have time to adequately respond to the accusations and do damage control.

Predictably, I ended up losing the election to Rudolph Walker, but not as badly as I feared I might. Some people chose to ignore the news of my indictment and vote for me anyway. Some probably didn't even know about it and voted for me because they knew it was the right thing to do. But I honestly believe a lot of my supporters just stayed home that day and didn't vote at all.

Regardless of the reasons for my defeat, I was left with a sickening feeling for the entire election process. Beginning what I thought was an honest and meaningful campaign to end the corruption and malfeasance of those in public office, ended in a disgraceful defeat, given to me at the hands of those I had worked so hard to uncover and expose. No amount of comfort, or excuses from those close to me, could rid my conscience of the fact that I had lost. The ideals of a perfect society, free of corruption and personal greed, were defeated.

Being defeated in an election humbles you. I had worked, dreamed, and hoped that the people of Vicksburg would see it my way. But then in defeat, you realize that they did not. Whatever the reasons for being defeated, it's still an experience that very few people have in their life.

No matter the future course I took in my own life, I knew two things: first, that I would never run for elected office again, and second, that nothing I could do would ever end the corruption of those in political office in Vicksburg and Warren County. I had tried my hardest to bring honesty, integrity, and professionalism to law enforcement in Vicksburg- and for that I was threatened, assaulted, and ostracized to the point of terror for that effort.

No amount of consolation from my family, friends, and supporters could change the fact that everything I had believed in and wanted was now defeated. It was an ironic case of evil overcoming good.

Looking back on my run for public office in 2002, there are many things that I would have changed and done differently in my campaign, but I still believed in making the fight to end the political corruption. That will never change. As I stated over and over in my election campaign, I believe that the citizens of Vicksburg and Warren County deserve a law enforcement officer who is impartial, incorruptible, and beyond reproach.

Unfortunately, they don't have that today and until they wake up and see the damage that the corrupt politicians and law enforcement officers are doing, Vicksburg and Warren County will remain one of the most corrupt, dishonest, and mismanaged areas of the country.

# CHAPTER THIRTY

Shortly after my election defeat, I was contacted by a deputy sheriff on the Warren County Sheriff's Office. He had been impressed with my candidacy and was himself concerned with what he believed to be a serious illegal conspiracy of corruption within the Sheriff's Office. This deputy asked to remain anonymous and never to be identified. I have honored his wishes and even now remain silent as to his true identity.

I had recently read Bob Woodward's book, *All The President's Men,* and was fascinated by the silent informant in his book that became so famously known as "Deep Throat". Setting myself up with my own private informer, into the halls of local power, was an opportunity to good too pass up. I just had no idea the direction that this new partnership should take.

I began referring to my new friend as "Deep Six"- a reference to his deep background and the six-pointed badge that he wore as a deputy sheriff. Deep Six was, and still is, an honest, fair, and professional law enforcement officer. He truly believes in the concept of not only protecting the citizens of this county, but also serving them as well.

Over the course of his career in law enforcement, Deep Six had witnessed numerous incidents of corruption and down-right unethical behavior by his comrades in the department. According to him there existed a conspiracy among the higher levels of administration in the Sheriff's Office that included everything from drug use and protection of drug dealers, to gun smuggling, operation of prostitution rings, and trading badges and law officer commissions in return for monetary kickbacks.

This history of corruption and unethical behavior is a long and convoluted one stretching for decades across the century. The former Sheriff of Warren County, Paul Barrett, who was elected in 1968 and served in office for thirty years, was convicted in the late 1990's of several different federal crimes, including perjury and obstruction of justice.

Sheriff Barrett's case began with a plotline one might read out of a Tom Clancy novel. In partnership with J.C. Herbert Bryant, Jr., a millionaire playboy and law enforcement "groupie", who had connections with the Nixon, Reagan, and Bush Administrations, Iran-Contra, the British Royal Family, and had created his own private police force organization run by Lt. Colonel Oliver North- ARGUS (Armed Response Group US), he used Sheriff Barrett to subsidize his love of law enforcement with fake, forged law enforcement credentials, badges and firearms. .

Elected sheriff partly with finances and support from the Bryant family, which reached way back into the recesses of "old southern money", Paul Barrett had been a retainer of the Bryant family, working for years on their antebellum plantation in Warren County, Mississippi.

Eager to return their patronage, Sheriff Barrett quickly became enmeshed in a conspiracy by Herb Bryant that would reach into the very top echelons of the federal government.

After securing, through admittedly nefarious means, a commission as a Special Deputy U.S. Marshal in the late 1980's (in part with Sheriff Barrett's assistance in forging a fake deputy's commission), Herb Bryant was appointed director over the U.S. Marshal's Foundation, an organization that was plagued by mismanagement, fraud, and misappropriated funds. Rather than getting the organization out of further trouble, Bryant only managed to deepen the financial crisis and bring attention to himself and those around him.

A government investigation was launched into the fiasco in 1992, facilitating Bryant's resignation as a Special Deputy U.S. Marshal and also as the Executive Director of the U.S. Marshal's Foundation.

Even though Herb Bryant had been stripped of his U.S. Marshal's commission and had been completely disassociated with that federal law enforcement agency, he still paraded around Washington, D.C. and Northern Virginia in a blacked-out Chevy Suburban registered to the Warren County, Mississippi Sheriff's Office, replete with undercover blue lights and siren.

On an aside note, this Chevrolet Suburban that would play such a major role in his and Sheriff Barrett's downfall had been given to Bryant by my grandfather and Atwood Chevrolet.

Bryant also still carried the forged Warren County Sheriff's commission certification and gold badge that he had been provided by Sheriff Barrett, along with a wide assortment of firearms.

The beginning of the end for Herb Bryant and Sheriff Barrett occurred on September 2nd, 1992 when Bryant illegally parked his suburban near the Mayflower Hotel in downtown Washington, D.C. before going inside a local restaurant for lunch. It was their bad luck that on that day, the Arab-Israeli peace talks were underway and a large portion of the Israeli delegation, was housed in the hotel.

A vigilant Israeli security officer noticed the illegally parked Suburban and upon closer inspection noticed a small armory of weapons in the back seat. Soon, an entire mesh of local, federal and foreign law enforcement agencies were involved in determining and locating the owner of the vehicle. Into this group stepped Herb Bryant who at first claimed to still be a U.S. Marshal.

When his U.S. Marshal's credentials didn't check out, he then claimed to be a deputy sheriff on the Warren County Sheriff's Office in Vicksburg, Mississippi, flashed his forged credentials and badge, and stated he was entitled to possess and carry the weapons that were in the vehicle- a story that Sheriff Barrett was only more than happy to confirm, unwittingly injecting himself into a maelstrom of controversy that would eventually bring about his downfall.

Later called to testify in the Bryant case, Sheriff Barrett perjured himself with several false statements in an apparent conspiracy to protect his friend and patron. Eventually convicted in federal court himself, Sheriff Barrett was forced to serve an eighteen-month prison sentence.

Removed from office amidst the scandal of his convictions, with investigators only on the verge of unraveling the true conspiracy behind his partnerships with Herb Bryant, ARGUS, the U.S. Marshal's Service, and other high ranking members of the federal government, Sheriff Barrett has chosen to remain silent on what, if any involvement the current members of the Warren County Sheriff's Office may have had in the corruption investigation.

However, what is apparent is that with the departure of Sheriff Barrett from the halls of power in Warren County, stepped, whom most said, was Sheriff Barrett's hand-picked successor, Martin Pace. Sheriff Pace's connections to Paul Barrett, Herb Bryant, and other nefarious characters would later precipitate my downfall when I began to further investigate the strange story of these rogue lawmen.

# CHAPTER THIRTY-ONE

From our first conversations, Deep Six held dark suspicions about Martin Pace's past involvement with Sheriff Barrett and their connections with Herb Bryant. Many rumors had been passed around town, talking of the dealing and importation of large amounts of illegal drugs- all sanctioned and protected by the Sheriff's Office and its top members in administration. Whether these rumors were based in fact, or were just rambling innuendos will never be known.

Apart from any involvement with Sheriff Barrett and Herb Bryant, Vicksburg and Warren County had a long and troublesome history as a cesspool of government corruption.

In a ten-year span, from 2000 to 2010, Vicksburg saw the arrest and/or convictions of several different politicians and law enforcement officers for a wide assortment of crimes.

The incident that precipitated my run for constable was

when the former incumbent, J.L. Mitchell, was arrested and convicted of extortion. At the same time, the county court judge of Warren County, Gerald Hoseman, was arrested and charged with the attempted murder of his mistress. Judge Hoseman was eventually allowed to bargain and plead guilty to a lesser offense, but the physical and psychological damage he did to his victim was irreparable.

The Vicksburg Police Department had their fair share of problems as well. A veteran patrolman, Dan King, was arrested and convicted of accepting stolen property which later proved to be the end of a large and intricate thievery ring. Another patrolman, Bart Henriques, was arrested and convicted for possession of child pornography. Anthony Lane, another Vicksburg Police officer, assigned to work in the public school system, was charged and admitted to having sex with an under-aged student at the school where he worked.

Even the Chief of Police of the Vicksburg Police Department had to deal with accusations that he was sexually harassing women who worked for him. The son of Michael Mayfield, an alderman on the Vicksburg City Council, was charged with a vicious rape of a young girl, but according to sources in the courthouse, the victim was pressured into not pursuing charges.

In more recent times, a detective on the Warren County Sheriff's Department, London Williams, described as a "rising star" in the law enforcement community was arrested, confessed, and charged with incest and the sexual battery of his own daughter.

The malfeasance doesn't stop there. Through Deep Six's insight and information I was able to uncover allegations that a detective on the Sheriff's Office, Mike Traxler, had been caught by his wife having extramarital sex in his patrol car with Georgia Lynn, an investigator with the district attorney's office. In a fit of rage, Traxler's wife used her car as a battering ram and severely damaged his patrol car. Years later allegations would surface of Traxler becoming engaged in violent domestic abuse against his wife.

Georgia Lynn would later go on to be involved in a DUI accident in which two city police officers would be fired for attempting to cover-up her intoxication. Georgia Lynn was eventually convicted by a jury of DUI, but was able to remain on as an investigator with the district attorney's office until Gil Martin's defeat in 2007.

Deep Six and I would spend hours on the phone discussing the different problems, ethical and corruption issues that plagued Vicksburg and Warren County. Since my defeat in the November election I had kept a low profile and remained out of the public eye.

The Vicksburg Post newspaper printed articles and kept tabs on the status of my Jones County arrest, but in private talks with the district attorney down there, I was assured that a very reasonable plea offer would be made, if not having the charge dismissed out right. No one seemed to care that my indictment was politically motivated and served no purpose except to assist the Warren County Sheriff's Office in defeating my election bid.

Deep Six not only sympathized with my plight, but was also determined to help me achieve what he was unable to do. Exposing the corruption and unethical behavior was not just a priority of mine, but as I came to learn, was also a priority of several members of the Sheriff's Office.

Not everyone on the Warren County Sheriff's Office or Vicksburg Police Department is a power-hungry, greedy, dirty cop. Many are hard-working, honest professionals who sincerely care about the people of this county. Unfortunately, they have been supplanted by those in power who will and have used whatever dubious means necessary to achieve that power.

While most of these honest cops choose to conduct their business outside the influences of those less integrity-minded, they nonetheless are unwilling to step forward and risk their job, safety and that of their family's safety to blow the whistle on the illegal and unethical conduct taking place within their department.

However, there are those few, who for whatever reasons, have chosen through their own methods, to exact responsibility for what they know to be a conspiracy of illegal conduct. Deep Six and I never spoke at length about why he was using me to try to bring exposure to the illegal activities in the Sheriff's Office, but whatever his reasons, he was deeply concerned about them.

Through our many conversations, it was finally decided to disperse our information through a website which I would build and administer. After much thought it was decided to call this website, appropriately, www.CorruptGov.com

Over the course of the Christmas holidays in 2002, I slowly compiled every rumor, every innuendo, every allegation and every complaint that I could possibly discover and published them onto the CorruptGov.com website. I also included a medium for viewers to respond and contribute their own information to the website in regards to personal incidences of corruption and illegal behavior they witnessed.

Deep Six was able to contribute a large majority of the information, but even he didn't have the full details on a lot of stories. However, once the website was operational, the influx of information that flowed through it was an eye-opening experience. While unable to attribute truth to everything that was posted, much of what was on the website could be used to confirm and corroborate much of what we had already suspected.

Citizens from all over Mississippi responded with horror stories of their own, recounting how they had been treated by sheriff's deputies and city police officers. Much of what was posted was only a "soundboard" to an otherwise voiceless group of people who were upset over an unfair traffic ticket, or someone merely upset for having gotten caught in the wrong place, at the wrong time. But some of the information that was posted absolutely confirmed to us and many others that there was a conspiracy of corruption and illegal behavior that permeated the Warren County Sheriff's Office.

One of the unfortunate consequences of having compiled and published this negative information was the unwelcome attention that I drew from not only the local law enforcement agencies, but also from the state and federal agencies who had begun receiving daily complaints regarding the information that was posted on my website about the Sheriffs and Police Departments.

Citizens were reading the postings, considering the evidence themselves, and then demanding that an outside investigation be launched. Those demands fell on deaf ears, as of yet, no outside investigative agency has taken any serious interests in investigating any criminal wrong-doing. As Deep Six said, the corruption has continued for so long, unabated, and unhindered; and with so much money flowing through this town, and so many pockets being lined with the efforts, that no one is willing to take a stand. Plainly said, everyone has their hand in the cookie jar and no one wants to be the one to get caught.

As good intentioned as Deep Six and others were, they had the advantage of remaining anonymous, whilst I did not. It is no doubt that, in retrospect, I was probably unfairly used by certain well-meaning individuals who had just as much "beef" with the Sheriff's and Police Department as I did, but who were only allowing me to be the crash-test dummy in their personal efforts to settle old scores with the departments.

Time and maturity have proven my efforts to be wrong and misguided- noble as they were. Publishing a compilation of criminal allegations and complaints of unethical conduct about elected officials and law enforcement officers on a public website served no legitimate purpose at the time, but only further alienated me from a group of powerful individuals who were at that moment crafting my doom.

As things heated up around town regarding my website, Deep Six became concerned for my safety. While remaining optimistic that no physical damage would be done to me, Deep Six was concerned with some of the chatter he was hearing around the Sheriff's Office. Apparently, several deputies had been discussing planting illegal drugs in my vehicle in order to facilitate an arrest and further cause me legal problems and public embarrassment.

Once the Christmas and New Year's holidays were over, I seriously considered moving out of town or even out of state. It didn't take much prompting from Deep Six that my safety and possibly my freedom were in jeopardy. It was a shame that I could be forced away from my hometown so easily, but I was honestly ready for a change and I began looking for the first opportunity that presented itself.

# CHAPTER THIRTY-TWO

It became clear after my election defeat that I no longer had a future within the borders of Warren County and Vicksburg. Had I remained in Vicksburg and not sought asylum elsewhere, there is no doubt that my downfall would have occurred more quickly and probably more thoroughly than it did.

Having published an expose' website that immediately generated more hate and wrath from the political community only solidified my belief that I should seek my fortunes elsewhere.

A close friend of mine suggested I come to Orlando and visit over the New Year's holiday. He had moved from Vicksburg to Orlando several years before and loved it down there. He understood not only my physical need to remove myself from the political scenes of Vicksburg, but also my emotional need to experience a more open and permissive society.

I had never let my sexuality drive me to make decisions based on my attraction to other men. I was not one of those gay men who desperately desired to get out of Mississippi and move to a larger city just to be around more and better gay guys. Not having a large selection of quality gay men to choose from never affected my desire to want to live elsewhere. My main motivation for wanting to get away from Vicksburg was because of the chaos and political heat that was against me after my election and website being published. Orlando only had the benefit of having a large gay community, which for me, was only another advantage of living there.

After spending several days in central Florida over the New Year's holiday, I returned to Mississippi long enough to pack all my clothes and personal belongings, say goodbye to my family, close out my bank account and drive back to Orlando. Not once did I look back or regret leaving. As far as I was concerned, I couldn't be happier getting away from Vicksburg and Warren County.

For the first time in my life I was utterly on my own. My friend was kind enough to allow me to sleep on his couch and stay in his apartment until I could get my feet under me, but doing so was harder that I had expected and my money wasn't going to last long.

I finally applied for a security guard position at a local company that was a contractor for the Department of Defense. I had never applied or interviewed for a job before, but I figured the best thing to do was dress nicely and use appropriate manners. Apparently they were impressed and hired me a few days later.

Soon after starting my first job, I found an apartment that I could share with a roommate and moved off of my friend's couch and into my first place. My roommate was a pilot with a commercial airline and was gone, off and on, about two weeks out of the month. The situation worked great for me because that meant I had the apartment to myself the majority of the time.

Within a month of having moved to Orlando, I had my first job, my first place, and was quickly becoming accustomed to being on my own. My roommate suggested that I also consider flight school since I had some extra time on my hands after work and on my days off.

It wasn't long before I had applied and been accepted to Air Orlando Flight Academy. The curriculum moved at an easy pace and between work and my free time, I managed to earn my private pilot's license within three months.

At the first of the summer I decided to make a return trip to Vicksburg to visit family and retrieve some more of my property. It would be the first trip home since my departure in January and I was a little tense on what awaited me there. I was hoping that I would be able to get in and get out without anyone noticing me.

My roommate was interested in going with me, and before long we had hatched a plan to fly a small plane back to Vicksburg ourselves rather than fly commercial or drive. I'd only had my pilot's license a short time, but I felt confident in making the four-hour flight.

Waiting at the Vicksburg airport when we flew in were Meme, my mom, and both my grandparents. They were so excited to not only see me, but also see me flying the plane, that it made me the proudest I had been in a very long time. Coming down off the election defeat and dealing with the chaos involving the Sheriff's Office had drained my energy and depressed my mood to such a point that I had been unhappy for several months. Making this return trip though, in some way, bolstered my feelings and for the first time since the election, I actually felt happy and confident in my future.

We didn't stay long in Vicksburg and I was almost saddened to be leaving again, but I knew Orlando was a better place for me and I couldn't wait to get back. I had made many new friends, but one important one will always be dear to me.

Bill Kitchens and I met at the Orlando Executive Airport one day and immediately became close friends. Even though Bill was older, he was also fairly new to the gay scene. He had a partner that he was completely committed to, but Bill, like me, was not into the bars, clubs and party crowd.

Bill was a engineer and had designed roller coasters and theme park rides for most of his career. His latest creation had been an indoor skydiving facility appropriately named SkyVenture. Small SkyVenture parks now appear in almost every major city across the world thanks to Bill Kitchen's ingenuity.

I went to Key West for the first time that summer and it was a wonderful experience. For the first time in my life I was experiencing a real culture outside of Mississippi and the knowledge I gained from my travels have stayed with me through all these years.

As Labor Day weekend approached in 2003, I had the opportunity to either vacation in Washington, D.C. or go back to Southern Decadence in New Orleans. At first I was partial to going to New Orleans, but at the last minute decided to fly to D.C. instead. That last minute decision would have profound consequences.

When I was in D.C., I met a Marine who was stationed at Bolling Air Force on the outskirts of the city. For confidentiality, I have changed the identity of this Marine from his real name to Tucker Williams.

Tucker was one of the Marines assigned to the HMX-1 Presidential Helicopter Squadron. Although their most visible role was saluting the President, Vice-President and Secretary of Defense as they boarded and departed their helicopters, the Marines of that unit played a much more valuable and less known role as well.

Because Tucker was a veteran of both the wars in Afghanistan and Iraq, and had been recently wounded during his tour while earning a Silver Star, the Marine Corps meritoriously decorated and promoted him to one of the most prestigious units in the Corps. Saluting the leaders of our country was a plush assignment that Tucker cherished. If there was a picture-perfect Marine, Tucker fit the bill.

Even though he was gay and had totally accepted the fact, Tucker was still not open or expressive of it. His main concern was his career in the military. Because of this paranoia, Tucker was at times difficult to deal with. But after meeting him, I immediately obtained an attachment to him that I have to this day.

My entire vacation in D.C. was spent with Tucker. We hit it off soon after meeting and became not only sexual partners, but close friends as well. Before leaving D.C. we discussed the possibility of dating and maneuvering through a long distance relationship. Because both of us had busy schedules and would not normally be able to see each other much even if we both lived in D.C., we decided that a long distance relationship might be possible.

My heart was all into it because I knew very shortly after meeting Tucker that I would come to love him. I had not been in any type of serious relationship since Kevin Southern and I broke up, and I was beginning to desire something more than a life spent alone. As hard as it was probably going to be to remain together, I was committed to making it work.

Leaving D.C. after meeting Tucker was one of the hardest things I had had to do up until that point in my life. I had felt an immediate attachment to Tucker that I had not felt since Kevin. Regardless of the long distance, I was determined to try to make our relationship work.

Once I returned to Orlando, when my life didn't revolve around work, it centered on Tucker. For the next few months I was either flying regularly to D.C. or he was flying to Orlando. Once I even traveled to Waco, Texas to spend two nights with him while he was traveling with President Bush to the Crawford Ranch.

Doing a long distance relationship wasn't that bad except for the amount of money we were spending on plane tickets. Shortly before Christmas I seriously considered moving permanently to D.C. but the only thing that stopped me was Tucker's uncertainty of where he might be transferred when his service obligation was up in the HMX-1 Squadron. The possibilities ranged from anywhere in the continental United States, to across the world.

For the holiday season of 2003, I put Tucker's and my relationship on hold long enough to return to Vicksburg and visit with my family. Meme had remained at the house alone during the previous year and my absence had begun to show. The property and surrounding pastures were in ill-repair, the house needed work, and other minor issues, which left unattended by the man-of-the-house, tended to become serious over time and were demanding my attention.

It was on this Christmas visit that Meme confided to me that things were not going well and that she desperately wanted me to return home and help take care of her and the property. Having to make a choice of whether to remain in Orlando where I was happy, contented, and doing well, or return to Vicksburg at the request of my grandmother, whom I loved very much and who obviously needed me, was not a choice I was willing to make easily.

Returning to Vicksburg meant giving up my friends and lifestyle that I had come to accept and enjoy in Orlando, and returning to a place that had only a short year before been hostile and aggressive to me. Devotion to my grandmother and a sense of responsibility for her welfare finally sealed my decision to return home. It wasn't an easy choice to make, but it was one that I felt compelled to follow. After all, Meme had practically raised me- the least I could do was follow her wishes.

# CHAPTER THIRTY-THREE

The first six months of 2004 proved to be the most demanding, stressful, and disturbing period of my life that I had ever dealt with. In retrospect, moving back to Vicksburg was the worst mistake I ever made. Had I remained in Orlando, as my initial conscience warned me, my life probably would not have taken the course it did.

It didn't take long, being back in Vicksburg, to become embroiled in more trouble, both personally and legally. Over the Christmas holidays Meme had deeded over a portion of her land and property to me as a gift. It had always been her wish that I inherit part of our property and farm and I woke up one morning and found, to my not-so-much surprise, that I was then the new owner of forty acres.

My excitement quickly turned to irritation when my Aunt June, who had been further deteriorating into mental decline, discovered what Meme had done and became violent with envy and rage. Even though Aunt June had been given a piece of her own land years before, she still expected to one day seize control of everything that belonged to Meme and claim it as her rightful prize.

Meme and Aunt June's relationship had disintegrated over the years to the point that neither would speak, even though they had to pass each other every day when coming and going from the property. Aunt June's expectation that Meme was going to give her any more land or leave anything to her in the will, was a deluded fantasy.

The problem that now presented itself when Meme transferred ownership of the back forty acres of the property, to me, was that in order to access my property, I had to cross a short section of Aunt June's land. Unfortunately, it was the only way to access my property and since there was not any sort of easement agreement in place, and Aunt June refused to grant one, I was effectively locked out of accessing my own land.

Up until this point in my life, I had been able to avoid any open hostilities with members of my family. I had always accepted Aunt June's difficulties, her mental illness, and drug and alcohol abuse without allowing it to directly affect me in a negative manner. But now, because of her irate jealousy and ineffectual ability to compromise or communicate, a petty dispute over land developed into an all-out war within the Atwood family.

My grandfather Atwood, who himself was no stranger to court battles and family squabbles relating to a bastard child he had helped conceive with an African-American woman, now fully enmeshed himself into this raging battle between my aunt and me.

By the first of February, 2004, battle lines had been drawn and the family feud that eventually wrecked the Atwood family was well underway. As ridiculous as it was, and would become, surveyors were called to lay out very defined property lines differentiating who owned what and where. Once the lines were drawn, clear boundaries were placed with warnings not to trespass lest dire consequences would be exacted from the offender; lawsuits were filed in the court system challenging the legitimacy of deeds and easement agreements; and local law enforcement was called upon to enforce the will and desires of an Atwood clan which now targeted me as their enemy.

Sheriff Martin Pace and his deputies were only too happy to comply with my grandfather and Aunt June's wishes. According to Deep Six, my grandfather called the Sheriff shortly after the family feud began and gave him "carte blanche" authority to target me without any further interference or protection from the family.

Dealing with the monstrosity of drama that emanated from my family on an almost daily basis put a severe strain on my relationship with others, especially Tucker in Washington, D.C. Because I was no longer working, I was dependent on Meme for money, and although we had never hurt for funds before, using that money to travel regularly to see my boyfriend was not something I felt comfortable doing.

Tucker's and my relationship was one of the first casualties of quitting my job and moving back to Vicksburg. We never fought, but the strain of a long distance relationship and being unable to see each other on a regular basis took its toll. We remained friends but soon came to the mutual agreement to break things off and see other people.

I was frustrated, depressed, and angry at the course of events that had taken place in such a short time of my return from Orlando. I tried to seek solace in different activities but that led to problems as well. During one attempt, I had invited several friends over to my house to enjoy a bonfire and party. Unaware of the events surrounding the controversy involving the land dispute, several of my friends crossed the boundary line and went across Aunt June's property.

Always watching with a pair of binoculars, Aunt June seized upon this terrible transgression, called the Sheriff and had four of my friends arrested and incarcerated for trespassing on her property.

At the beginning of this family squabble over the land and property boundaries, criminal law sometimes was blurred with civil, and my grandfather and Aunt June attempted to use the criminal courts to enforce unenforceable civil statutes. To aid in their endeavor, Sheriff Pace assigned one of his right-hand men, Detective Todd Dykes, to assist them. Todd Dykes soon became the personal envoy and chief enforcer for the Atwood family. No one tried to hide the fact that a new Chevy truck, direct from Atwood Chevrolet, sat in Todd Dykes' driveway.

Two weeks after my Aunt June had my four friends arrested and locked up for accidentally trespassing on her property, someone came out to our land and using a small caliber gun, proceeded to shoot bullet holes in every building and piece of farm equipment that was out there. According to later estimates, the damages were immense, requiring tens of thousands of dollars to fix.

Remarkably, neither Todd Dykes, nor any other investigator questioned Meme or myself in regards to my whereabouts, location, or even whether we had heard or seen anything ourselves at the time the shootings took place. As far as we could tell, no one was doing any sort of proper investigation.

Several days later, Deep Six called and informed me that a warrant was being issued for my arrest and that the justice court judge who signed the warrant had also set an exorbitant amount of bond, at the personal request of the Atwood family, in an apparent attempt to keep me from being able to raise the money and bond out.

Wanting to avoid being arrested at gunpoint by a trigger happy team of deputy sheriffs who already hated my guts, I immediately left the city and stayed overnight with a friend, while I planned a strategy and worked on raising the money needed to bond myself out.

Unable to locate me through deception, and disappointed in being unable to properly arrest me with a SWAT team, Detective Todd Dykes then proceeded to attempt to get me to turn myself in voluntarily at the sheriff's office the following day. Already having every intention of turning myself in, once I had my bond money in hand, I agreed to Todd Dykes' request.

From Detective Dykes I learned that my Aunt June had

filed an affidavit alleging that she actually saw me use a rifle to shoot her tractor, barn and other farm equipment. Based on the word of a woman who had had numerous mental health issues and a history of drug and alcohol abuse, the Sheriff's Department proceeded with a warrant.

Judge Joe Crevitt, a close family friend of the Atwood's; father to a detective on the Sheriff's Office whom I had heavily criticized and accused of corruption in my election campaign; and another one of Vicksburg's politicians at the beck and call of my grandfather, was only too happy to oblige their request for a monstrous bond.

I was charged with one count of malicious mischief and my bond was set at forty thousand dollars. On a level of seriousness, malicious mischief ranks with traffic tickets and jaywalking, but apparently I was already convicted of some wrongdoing and was being punished with an outrageous bond.

So for the second time in my life, I was arrested, fingerprinted, and booked into jail. Thankfully, I didn't have to wait long and after about thirty minutes of formalities, I posted my bond and was released.

Never was I asked for my version of events, or where I was when the crime was committed, or even if I had any explanations. I chose to remain silent and not volunteer any information myself. However, Meme was another story. From the moment she learned of the warrant for damaging Aunt June's equipment, she protested loudly and firmly to anyone who could hear that she was with me during the time that the crime was committed, and that it couldn't have been me that did it.

Whenever Meme would try to tell Todd Dykes of the impossibilities of me being able to commit that crime without her knowing about it, she was ignored and laughed at. The Sheriff's Office and everyone involved had made up their minds as to my guilt, and nothing that anyone could say differently would change their opinion. They had concocted a political barbeque and I was the pig on the stick.

# CHAPTER THIRTY-FOUR

My arrest on petty and trivial malicious mischief charges was not based on any evidence, but was instead relied entirely upon by the word of my Aunt June. Regardless of the trivial notions of the charge, it was still a felony and if convicted, I could face prison time. The thought of doing time in prison crossed my mind during the Jones County fiasco, but since that charge had been dismissed, albeit without first being bled for all the political damage that it could possibly do to me, I never seriously considered myself capable of committing any crime that would cost me my freedom.

When I began to recognize the lengths that those in power would avail themselves to in order to craft my demise, along with the rampant internal attacks by my own family, it gave me pause and time to consider whether my actions were rather for some noble cause, or only a detriment that would eventually lead to my downfall.

When I was young and immature, I acted young and immature. Rather than take counsel of my actions, and without honest guidance to lead me on a better path, I responded to my unfair arrest and the harassment by the Sheriff's Office with higher rhetoric and more abrasive action. I expounded the CorruptGov.com website to include not only the allegations of illegal and unethical behavior by politicians and law enforcement officers in Vicksburg and Warren County, but I also began systematically building a list of what I considered to be the top ten most corrupt and dirty individuals.

With pictures of the government offenders, short biographies, and a list of their transgressions, my website quickly came to look more like the FBI's Ten Most Wanted. Unbeknownst to me, the Sheriff's Office was circulating its own list and my name was at the top.

I tried to stay out of Vicksburg as much as possible, but with the obligations to my grandmother, lack of extra money, and a desire to avoid imposing on too many people, I was forced to remain a practical prisoner to my own creation. I was only twenty years old. I still felt that there was a huge future before me, but being caught in a bad environment, with no discernible way out, was a depressing situation.

Shortly after my malicious mischief arrest, I had begun dating a guy who lived in Vicksburg, only a few miles down the road from my house. Zach Booth was sixteen years old and went to school at St. Aloysius. My step dad and mom knew his family, as they were well known in the local community.

At the time, the disparity in ages vaguely concerned me, but I was assured that any relationship we might have would be perfectly legal under the laws of Mississippi. Sixteen is the age of consent and since I was only a couple years older, I didn't foresee or expect any problems. Zach Booth was very mature, (one could almost say a prodigy), and was farther advanced in accepting his sexuality and dealing with it than I was.

What did present a problem was the fact that neither Zach, nor myself, were out about being gay. Since neither of us was ready to disclose that fact to our families and friends, we chose to hide our relationship and remain discreet in our actions. Gay relationships are normally difficult enough navigating the social norms and customs of even a more permissible society. Having an openly gay relationship in Vicksburg was next to impossible.

Zach and I spent time together on the weekends and occasionally went out to dinner, but we did not share the same closeness as Kevin Southern and I had. Even when Tucker and I were in Washington, D.C. we felt comfortable enough in public to allow our guards down, but having any type of meaningful, openly gay relationship in Vicksburg was not something that I felt ready to tackle. Zach felt the same way and we kept our private lives private.

Phone texting was only becoming popular in early 2004 and in addition to long, in-depth instant message conversations on AOL and through email, Zach and I texted each other every day, sometimes all day. I was still emotionally attached to Tucker, but with the realization that the distance was an obstacle that couldn't be overcome, I tried my best to devote my energy and focus on Zach.

In early summer, as the weather turned warmer, I spent more time away from Vicksburg, Zach, and my family. By traveling as much as possible, I was able to briefly grasp a feeling of freedom. I had purposely been neglecting my website, and thankfully had not had any more altercations with my family or the Sheriff's Office. All that changed when Deep Six called early one morning in June.

Deep Six and I had tossed around the probability that certain members of the Warren County Sheriff's Office were being sanctioned to deal and distribute illegal drugs and were offering protection rackets to underworld criminals. Deep Six told me numerous times, that implications were made by the Sheriff and other upper level members of the administration, such as Billy Joe Heggins, that certain individuals in the community were to be allowed to operate freely, without interference from law enforcement.

This was done ostensibly as an arrangement with

undercover narcotics officers, headed by Detective Mike Traxler and Billy Joe Heggins, to avoid any intrusion into an ongoing investigation. While being a legitimate concern on the surface, this was the perfect cover needed to illegally deal and distribute drugs using protected dealers.

Without direct evidence or any substantiation of illegal activity, there was nothing that could be done. However, on the morning referenced above, Deep Six was excited about the possibility of finally discovering the truth. Prodding me to start investigating the details behind the Herb Bryant and Paul Barrett criminal trials, Deep Six was confident that the truth to the corruption and the evidence we needed to finally pressure for a legitimate investigation would be found in the details behind those two trials.

I was at first dubious as to how a millionaire playboy and the former Sheriff could play a role in the current corruption and ethical problems at the Sheriff's Office, but after that day I began digging deeper and doing more research.

Deep Six pointed out to me that had any additional illegal activity been going on, other than what Paul Barrett and Herb Bryant were convicted of, that it was conceivable that Martin Pace and his other deputies only continued their schemes after he took over as Sheriff in 1997. After all, Martin Pace had been Paul Barrett's right-hand man for many years and would have had access to Paul Barrett's most intimate business dealings.

I eventually discovered that the relationship Paul Barrett shared with Herb Bryant was more complex and intricate than ever imagined. Herb Bryant and his family had connections to the British Royal Family, U.S. Senators, Congressmen, the Presidents and even Oliver North. The Bryant family was involved in funding and equipping their own private army called (ARGUS); running multi-million dollar international corporations; and were even owners of a seventeen thousand acre game reserve in Vicksburg, known as Tara Wildlife, among many other things only available to the rich and powerful.

Conspiracy theorists accuse the Bryant family, ARGUS, and their associates of everything from drug dealing, intelligence gathering on U.S. citizens, funding Nicaraguan Contras, and playing deadly politics with their enemies.

According to court documents, it is not speculation to say that Herb Bryant was connected to the upper levels of government and benefited from those connections by being placed in plush political appointments throughout different presidential administrations. It is also safe to say that Bryant passed his lucky patronage on down to his friend, Sheriff Paul Barrett.

Whether Bryant abused those positions for personal gain is open to debate. However his actions did draw Sheriff Barrett into a government investigation and prosecution that covered a wide gambit of illegal actions, including the possibility that Sheriff Barrett was dealing drugs for Oliver North and the CIA out of Tara Wildlife facilities, and that subsequent to Paul Barrett's conviction and removal from office, Martin Pace and several of his deputies stepped in and continued their operations, albeit on a smaller scale.

If this were true, it would account for the federal government's lack of interest in investigating any criminal wrong-doing. Regardless of Herb Bryant's legal troubles and felony convictions in the early 1990's, the Bryant family and their associates still wield an enormous amount of influence and clout in Washington, D.C.

Frankly, Deep Six believed that it was exactly that scenario of the Bryant's influence that was prohibiting an honest and thorough investigation by the federal government into the obvious illegal and unethical activity ongoing in the Warren County Sheriff's Office.

In fact, since Martin Pace took over as Sheriff, he has been given the same "red carpet" treatment by federal law enforcement in the same way that Herb Bryant arranged for Paul Barrett to receive preferential treatment and glamorous awards from the same federal law enforcement agencies in the 1980's and 1990's.

Speculation or not, Deep Six did have solid points in making his argument for a larger illegal conspiracy. Not only that, he directed my attention to the fact that my grandfather, Emmett Atwood, had a lot closer connections to the Bryant family and Sheriff Barrett than most people would be comfortable with themselves, including the new revelation that my grandfather had undetermined "business" in Central and South America during the time of the ongoing operation that became known as Iran-Contra.

Grasping this complex information and deciphering what was fact, speculation, rumor and innuendo was something that I was unprepared to deal with. Deep Six was insistent that regardless of whether I believed such an intricate conspiracy, I had an obligation to at least publish what I knew and let the evidence, or lack thereof, speak for itself.

After compiling numerous investigative reports from the Washington Post, FBI, U.S. Attorney's Office and numerous other sources utilizing FOIA requests and other means, I firmly believed that a scheme existed between the Bryant family, Oliver North, Sheriff Barrett and other Reagan Administration officials to export illegal drugs from Central America and distribute them on the streets of America in an attempt to further fund the Contra Rebels in Nicaragua.

This conspiracy was part of the Iran-Contra Affair that almost brought down the Reagan presidency and led to the convictions of numerous government officials. That Sheriff Barrett, Martin Pace and the Warren County Sheriff's Office played a part in that national crime was unbelievable. But as I searched and discovered more evidence, the truth became startling clear.

The Iran–Contra Scandal was a political scandal in the United States that came to light in November 1986. During the Reagan administration, senior Reagan officials secretly facilitated the sale of arms to Iran, the subject of an arms embargo. Some U.S. officials also hoped that the arms sales would secure the release of hostages and allow U.S. intelligence agencies to fund the Nicaraguan Contras. Under the Boland Amendment, further funding of the Contras by the Reagan administration had been prohibited by Congress.

The scandal began as an operation to free American hostages being held by terrorist groups with Iranian ties. It was planned that Israel would ship weapons to Iran, and then the U.S. would resupply Israel and receive the Israeli payment. The Iranian recipients promised to do everything in their power to achieve the release of six U.S. hostages, who were being held by the Lebanese Shia Islamist group Hezbollah, who in turn were connected to the Army of the Guardians of the Islamic Revolution.

The plan deteriorated into an arms-for-hostages scheme, in which members of the executive branch sold weapons to Iran in exchange for the release of the American hostages. Large modifications to the plan were devised by Lieutenant Colonel Oliver North of the National Security Council in late 1985, in which a portion of the proceeds from the weapon sales was diverted to fund the Contra Rebels in Nicaragua.

One of the reasons the Boland Amendment was passed, outlawing support for the Contras, was because of the overwhelming evidence that the Contras had been actively importing drugs into the United States to generate funding for their rebellion against the legitimately elected government of Nicaragua.

Support for the Contras was at one time funded and operative thru the CIA. When the Boland Amendments were passed by Congress forbidding funding for the Contras, the operation went "private" with much of the new funding coming from private organizations and corporations owned and operated by former intelligence and high ranking military personnel.

Lt. Colonel Oliver North secretly organized many of these organizations and individuals to support his illegal schemes to fund the Contra Rebels. One of the organizations that he used was ARGUS (Armed Response Group US), owned by Herbert and Magalen Bryant.

Part of ARGUS's inventory was a surplus military aircraft that had been purchased ostensibly to be used to carry company personnel, but it instead was used in an effort to fly weapons and armaments into Contra strongholds in Honduras, El Salvador and

Nicaragua and fly cocaine and other illegal drugs back into the United States.

The CIA and Oliver North used private airplanes owned by companies like ARGUS during the Iran-Contra Affair to do business and transport weapons and drugs. It was one of these "private" airplanes doing CIA bidding that was shot down over Nicaragua while illegally carrying supplies to the Contras that started the unraveling of the Iran-Contra affair.

Rumors of this illegal drug running became so rampant that numerous U.S. senators, including John Kerry, launched official inquires and hearings into these allegations. The "Kerry Committee" published its Congressional Report in 1988 called: *"Drugs, Law Enforcement, and Foreign Policy"*. It stated unequivocally that administration officials involved in Iran-Contra were also involved in drug trafficking. Oliver North's own personal papers reflected his knowledge and complicity in this illegal drug importation.

According to government documents and numerous sources, the private airplane owned by Herbert Bryant and ARGUS made numerous trips out of Nicaragua and Ilopando Air Base in El Salvador to Vicksburg, Mississippi during the time this drug importation scheme was being operated. In addition, this same aircraft, along with numerous others, made identical trips to Mena, Arkansas, Los Angeles, and several other airstrips, all of which have been identified as drop off points for the cocaine and illegal drugs being smuggled out of Central America.

What was more surprising, was that this aircraft was being flown directly from Central America and off-loaded at a private airstrip in northern Warren County on land owned by the Bryant family and famously referred to as Tara Wildlife.

Tara Wildlife is a twenty thousand acre wildlife reserve that has been owned by the Bryant family for many decades. Before Paul Barrett was sheriff, he was employed by the Bryant family as their personal overseer and game warden at Tara.

Later, when Paul Barrett and Herbert Bryant were being prosecuted in federal court by Eric Holder, who at the time was a U.S. Attorney, but is now the Attorney General of the United

States, it was revealed that the airstrip at Tara Wildlife was specifically constructed at the request of Oliver North so that the ARGUS military aircraft could make flights there instead of having to land at a public airport in the Vicksburg area.

Through investigations done by the federal government and the Washington Post, it was theorized that when Oliver North and the other Reagan Administration officials began looking for ways to import illegal drugs into the United States to help fund the Contra Rebels, they sought out other corrupt government officials to aid in their endeavor.

Herbert Bryant, eager to assist in such a complex, international scheme, involved his friend Sheriff Paul Barrett. Because of Sheriff Barrett's connections to the drug underworld of Mississippi, and his apparent immunity from oversight, it was the perfect scheme to import drugs from Central America; off-load them at a private airstrip in the backwoods, rural area of Warren County; use a corrupt and unethical sheriff and his deputies to distribute and sell them; and then divert and launder the money back through private companies like ARGUS to secretly fund and equip the Contra Rebels to fight a war that the Reagan Administration had been outlawed from waging.

If the special prosecutor, Lawrence Walsh, who investigated and prosecuted the Reagan officials behind Iran-Contra, and Eric Holder, the now current Attorney General of the United States, believed that Oliver North and others were importing drugs into the country to help illegally fund the Contra Rebels, and using small town sheriffs like Paul Barrett to distribute and sell those drugs, then I considered it to be evidence enough to believe it also.

The question that now posed itself was what, if any, part Martin Pace and the other deputies at the Warren County Sheriff's Office played in these illegal schemes.

According to Deep Six, and backed up from the investigative reports of the federal government and Washington Post, Martin Pace's role was larger and more complicit. At the time these drugs were being imported into Vicksburg through Tara Wildlife, Martin Pace was Sheriff Barrett's right-hand man and Chief of Narcotics.

Deep Six and others firmly believed that Martin Pace and other deputies at the Sheriff's Office were actively assisting Paul Barrett to distribute and sell the illegal drugs by operating a covert ring of underworld criminals.

Several of these "criminals" that were being sanctioned by the Sheriff's Office to sell and distribute these drugs have gone on to give statements alleging the illegal conduct referenced above.

Although unaware of the intricacies and depth of their schemes, Deep Six assured me that the conspiracy of which I had uncovered and was about to publish on my website was completely and totally true and that with the departure of Paul Barrett from the Sheriff's Office, Martin Pace replaced him as his hand-picked successor and co-conspirator.

On June 28th, 2004, I published to the front page of my website a detailed, intricate, and complicated compilation of every piece of evidence, rumor, and innuendo I could locate on Herbert Bryant, the Bryant family, ARGUS, Paul Barrett, Martin Pace, the Warren County Sheriff's Office, illegal drug dealing, Iran-Contra and whatever other information I could find that would portray the Sheriff's Office in a negative light. It was the last posting I ever made to my website.

# PART THREE

# CHAPTER THIRTY-FIVE

Two days after publishing what was admittedly one of the most slanted conspiracy-story contrivances ever to have emanated from my young mind, Deep Six called me later that night in a panic. Posting that story on my website had sent shock waves through the Sheriff's Office and they were gearing up for retaliation.

Already aware that the Sheriff's Office was working to end my short career in journalism by having me arrested on false charges, Deep Six and I were nonetheless surprised when the Sheriff's Office, working with federal investigators, moved with unusual speed two days after my last posting on my website. Deep Six had been informed that the following morning, the Sheriff's Office, along with the FBI, ATF, and Mississippi Highway Patrol would be leading some type of raid on my house.

Unsure whether it was merely to execute a search warrant

or to arrest me on further criminal charges, the only thing that Deep Six could do was to suggest I "clean house" of anything I didn't want to fall into the hands of law enforcement. Since I wasn't doing anything illegal, and was confident that I didn't have anything to hide, I merely shrugged off his suggestion.

Deep Six was further concerned about his identity being discovered. We had taken steps the year before to ensure that all possible care was exercised in preventing his exposure, and even though I faced an unknown fate, I assured Deep Six that I would never reveal his identity. The only thing left to do was sit and wait.

The following morning, Thursday, July 1st, 2004 began like any other. I had not slept much the previous night and by nine o'clock when nothing had happened, I decided to leave and drive into town to meet with my attorney, Thomas Setser.

On the way into Vicksburg, I passed by one of the local churches. The parking lot was filled with police cars, blacked-out suburbans, and other law enforcement vehicles. As I passed, Todd Dykes recognized my truck and waved for me to stop. I pulled off the road and waited for someone to come give me directions on how to proceed. I was told that the FBI had some paperwork for me and that I should return to my home.

Once I returned to the house, an armada of law enforcement descended upon our property like a swarm of locusts. I was handed a piece of paper by a rude and arrogant man who identified himself as a Special Agent with the FBI. He told me I was under criminal investigation, but didn't say what for, and they were executing a search warrant on my house and property, but again, he didn't say why.

Meme and I were basically frozen out of our own residence while a myriad group of tough and dour-looking men and women searched every inch and foot of our home. By reading the search warrant, I was able to ascertain that I was a person of interest in an investigation by the FBI and Mississippi Joint Terrorism Task Force.

The word "terrorism" struck me as odd. Why would a terrorism task force be investigating me? Then I remembered vague references to the USA Patriot Act and the new found authority that had been given to law enforcement. The seriousness of the situation aside, I found it amusing that such an accumulation of money, time and manpower was being spent on someone as small and insignificant as me. Surely the federal government could have exercised better caution and restraint in their manner and operations.

After spending nearly ten hours at our home, the FBI and Mississippi Joint Terrorism Task Force were finally preparing to leave. With them they confiscated everything from my personal computers, to random paperwork, tools, clothes, my truck and jet-ski, and even used water bottles. I never discovered how empty water bottles, hammers, and screwdrivers could pertain to a federal terrorism investigation, but they felt justified in taking them.

When their search was over, I was no more aware of what they were investigating than I was before the fiasco began. What I was aware of was a feeling of violation, abuse, and injustice. I was certain this latest harassment, although on a much larger level, was only the result of my open political war with the Sheriff's Office. However, when they left, I still was no closer to finding out their true intentions. I was told to wait and that they would be in contact with me in the future.

The following day, I met with my stepdad and Thomas Setser. They were just as lost as I was on the intentions of the FBI. I was thoroughly interrogated by Tom, who was just beginning private practice, but had been an officer in the Navy JAG Corps for many years and was aware of the tactics of the federal government. No matter how hard Tom pushed and prodded, nothing I had done would seem to stir the ilk and attention of the FBI. I just honestly could not think of anything illegal I had done to justify their attention.

I returned home that afternoon confident that I had done nothing wrong and that this search warrant was only a maximum effort to intimidate and harass me. As shallow as my thinking was, I never seriously prepared myself with the thought that I would be arrested and incarcerated. But my lack of preparation only hardened the shock of what was coming next.

Shortly after arriving home there was a hard knock on the door. As I went to see who it was I noticed men dressed in SWAT gear, with heavy weapons, surrounding my house. Realizing that my time had come to an end and that I was about to be arrested again, I took a deep breath and opened the door.

Immediately I was surrounded and held at gun point. I was placed in handcuffs, belly chains, and leg irons. I was dragged to a waiting FBI vehicle and whisked away. Unbeknownst to me, it would be the last time I saw my house for a very long time.

The FBI agents who arrested me and were now taking me to the jail in Madison County, where they held federal pretrial detainees, informed me that I was being arrested and charged with one count of communicating an interstate death threat, via the internet.

I assumed this would normally be the point where most people in my situation would have had a moment of clarity about how they came to be handcuffed, detained, and headed for jail, but in my situation, I was at a total and complete loss as to who I had allegedly threatened and why. The FBI agents weren't forthcoming with any answers either and I felt it best to remain silent and not speak.

After arriving at the Madison County Detention Center in Canton, Mississippi, I was placed in a concrete holding cell and left by myself for several hours before anyone came to process me. The Madison County Detention Center, known as MCDC, was unlike any jail I had ever been in, although I only had two short stints in previous jails to judge it by.

Immediately I sensed a certain pervasiveness of violence that permeated the place. MCDC had a well-deserved reputation as one of the worst jails in the state and its bad conditions were compounded by staff, who sometimes were too quick to use violence, and too slow to use common sense. As I sat in their concrete holding cell, I was terrified of what I faced.

After what seemed like eternity, one of the guards removed me from the holding cell and took me down to their central booking office. I was asked a dozen questions regarding my medical history and charges, fingerprinted, and had my picture taken. They printed out a hospital type arm band and placed it on my wrist. I was then given a booklet of jail rules and threatened with dire consequences if I didn't follow them.

After booking, I was taken to a shower room where I was forced to strip naked and expose my genitals and buttocks to the guard while he visually checked my orifices for illegal contraband. Since this was a new experience, I didn't know what to expect and was somewhat offended by his assumption that I would be carrying illegal drugs in my asshole.

Once I had been properly strip searched, I was given a delousing solution and told to bathe with it. The shower water was cold and had the guard not been standing beside me, watching my every move, I would have thrown the delousing solution in the toilet, wet my hair, and gotten out. But since he insisted that I actually bathe in the solution and water, I was forced to take my first and what was certainly not my last, cold shower.

Next I was given an orange jumpsuit, a pair of worn, dirty socks, and flip-flop shoes to put on. I then was issued a blanket and a thin, dirty mattress. After I had been properly outfitted according to jail standards, I was led down several long hallways and placed in a "pod" with twenty-three other men.

Before the guard closed the cell door and locked it, I asked him what I was supposed to do. His response was that I should just keep my mouth shut and not drop the soap. His attempt at jailhouse humor was not funny and not appreciated. I was being literally thrown to the wolves without any preparation or guidance and the lack of understanding and uncooperative help from the guards was rattling.

Once the door was locked, I had no choice but to turn and face my new roommates, who were just as anxious to meet me as I was them. The first question that I was asked by the other inmates was what I was locked up for and whether I was a state or federal inmate. I meekly explained that I was a federal inmate and that I had been arrested for supposedly threatening someone, but I honestly didn't know any further details.

Most of the inmates thought this was funny and absurd. The majority of them were incarcerated for mega-drug crimes, bank robbery, and other much more serious offenses than a mere "threat" charge.

Since no one had told me any details of my case and charge, I was unsure what would happen next. Thankfully, an older inmate took me aside and explained to me that since I had just recently been arrested that the next step was to take me downtown to the federal courthouse and have a bond hearing. Those were usually supposed to happen within forty-eight hours of being arrested, but as he explained that this was July 4th weekend, that it would probably be Tuesday before I actually went before a judge for bond.

The thought of having to spend three or four days in jail was devastating to me, but at the time I felt sure that once I got in front of a judge and he saw what a nonthreatening person I was, he would for sure grant me a reasonable bond and release me from custody. This was my mindset as I slowly counted down the days until my appearance in front of the federal magistrate.

# CHAPTER THIRTY-SIX

Because of the Independence Day celebrations, and a quirk in the court's office, I was not actually brought before the judge for my initial appearance and bond hearing until July 12$^{th}$. I had been forced to sit in MCDC jail for almost two weeks, without bond, and totally unaware of what my charge was pertaining to.

When I finally did make my appearance in court, I went before federal magistrate, James Sumner. Tom Setser was representing me and had given me vague assurances that the judge should grant me bond. He pointed out that I was not a danger to society and I was not a flight risk- the two criteria that have to be met in order for a judge to justify denying someone a constitutionally protected right to bond.

Before we could begin, however, the Assistant U.S. Attorney (AUSA) who was prosecuting my "crime", Harold

Brittain, made a motion to the court to require me to undergo a psychiatric evaluation to determine my competency to stand trial. Unsure what was happening, I only pressured Tom more to push for a bond. Recognizing what the government was trying to do, Tom agreed with my pleadings but Judge Sumner was unwilling to consider much more than the government's position.

Without hearing any evidence or testimony, Judge Sumner agreed with the government and ordered me to undergo psychiatric evaluations at a federal hospital. Everything happened so fast that I was unable to fully grasp what was taking place. For anyone who has been in the court system as a defendant, such scenes as I had just witnessed quickly leaves you with a feeling of being in a charade or "kangaroo" court.

I was immediately returned to the MCDC jail and told by one of the U.S. Marshals that I would eventually be transferred to a federal hospital as soon as a spot could be reserved for me on the "airlift". Still completely ignorant of what was happening and what the "airlift" was, I began to despair. I had believed and hoped so much that I would be granted bond and could leave the MCDC jail, that when that fantasy did not occur, it devastated me. For the first time in my life, I seriously considered suicide. I just could not face the possibility of having to do time in jail.

One of the only benefits of my day in court was that I had learned more details about my case. According to the AUSA, several months in the past, I had sent an email to an unnamed individual, threatening to kill him. By their account, I was supposed to have told this person, "That little house you have is gonna be burnt to the ground, and one night as you walk out to your vehicle, I'm gonna be waiting there with a knife and I'm gonna slice you from your belly to your throat."

When I heard the AUSA read that statement to the judge, I nearly came unglued from my seat. I knew beyond any shadow of possibility that I had never in my life said something as horrible as that to another person. At the initial hearing, the AUSA made vague representations to the court that the threat was found on my computer, but I knew that I had never sent anything like that to anyone.

Once I was returned to the MCDC jail, determining the source of that threat, if one even existed became an obsession. As the days ticked by waiting to be transferred to a federal psychiatric hospital, I contemplated every possible scenario of how a threat like that could have gotten on my computer. I even considered the possibility that one of my friends had used my computer and sent it, but I could never come up with any plausible excuse.

While I waited to be transferred, I had the opportunity to study my surroundings. The Madison County Detention Center was, and probably still is, one of the worst jails in the nation. I say that with the hindsight of a person who has now seen dozens and dozens of jails and prisons. By all accounts, MCDC is a facility where inmates are abused, neglected, ill-treated, and sometimes left to die rather than be treated for medical emergencies.

My first experiences there were horrible. The guards were arrogant, rude, and prone to violence without provocation. An inmate could be sprayed with pepper spray for only the smallest infraction or beat down by a posse of testosterone-driven guards. The food was deplorable and barely met the nutrition requirements under law.

Inmates were sometimes denied contact with their families and attorneys for long periods of time, or were threatened with more violence if they snitched to anyone about their treatment. There were inadequate research and law library facilities, and what was available was most often denied to the inmates who asked.

The Sheriff of Madison County, Toby Trowbridge, operated a group of guards within the jail called the "goon squad." Their purpose was to enforce discipline through violence and terror. I witnessed numerous inmates beaten and assaulted by this group for only the smallest violation of jail rules.

The guards at MCDC sometimes encouraged inmates to fight and would make bets and wagers on the outcome of the illegally sanctioned altercations. If an inmate drew the negative attention of certain guards, he would be denied phone privileges, hygiene items, writing paper, stamps, and any other wide assortment of "trinkets" that are necessary to live somewhat comfortably in jail life.

Unlike other prisons and jails, MCDC did not have any system in place to deal with legitimate inmate discipline problems. Their solutions, more often than not, was to allow individual guards or supervisors to personally handle problems inside the jail. These guards were effectively the judge, jury and executioner, with punishments ranging from minor to severe.

For especially difficult inmates, whether they were overly violent or just constant complainers, the guards at MCDC had a special treatment for them. The problem inmate would be stripped down completely naked and placed in a small concrete holding cell without any clothes, blankets, mattresses, hygiene or personal items. The guards would then turn the air conditioning on in the cell to the point where the inmate would nearly freeze.

Before being released from this arctic punishment, the inmate would be questioned as to whether he was going to file any more complaints on the guards or whether he was going to complain about the conditions and treatment he was receiving in the jail. During my incarceration at MCDC, I witnessed dozens of inmates whose spirits were broken using this kind of punishment.

For inmates who were sick and had legitimate health problems, the quality of care available to them was just as bad as the conditions in the jail. The medical staff are private contractors, hired at minimum bid to provide minimum care to inmates. Profits were the bottom line and inmate healthcare suffered. Sick inmates would lay in excrement and vomit until finally the other inmates would get tired of it and clean it up themselves.

Even though MCDC had recently expanded to include two newer pods, built specifically to house federal inmates in better conditions, those inmates were still being kept with state inmates in the older, worst part of the jail.

Attempts to file official complaints or rectify the inhumane treatment, were always met with more harassment and worse treatment. The conditions and treatment were so bad, that the federal public defender for the area, Dennis Joiner, urged for an official criminal investigation to be launched against the Sheriff and his correctional guards.

Sheriff Trowbridge ignored these complaints and continued to allow his correctional guards to operate the jail in the manner of a Soviet Gulag. All inmates deserved better and fair treatment, but it seemed to me that federal inmates there received the worst.

By contracting with the government to house federal pretrial detainees and charging the government over forty dollars per day for each federal inmate, Sheriff Trowbridge was not only able to increase the profits of the jail, but he was also able to house and incarcerate city, county, and state inmates for less than six dollars a day.

It didn't seem right that the Sheriff could submit claims to the federal government asserting that it costs forty dollars a day to care for a federal inmate, then deprive and deny that inmate of needed services, food, and medical care, while subsidizing the cities of Madison County, which are only charged six dollars a day for their inmates.

If the forty dollars were actually spent on federal inmates, rather than being used to subsidize city, county, and state inmates, then I truly believe some of the problems at the MCDC jail could be alleviated. If the Sheriff charged the same price for all inmates equally, then there would be plenty of money to provide inmates with better clothing, food, and medical care, while also allowing guards to be paid more and attend better training programs.

As I quietly endured these atrocities, I couldn't help but wonder how a person could handle being incarcerated in these conditions for long periods of time. I had only been at MCDC for less than a month and already I was ready to hang myself.

Some guys had been at the jail for over a year and were not even close to having their cases finished. I felt nothing but compassion for a lot of the inmates who were incarcerated with me. Even though some of them had committed serious crimes, I believe that many were decent people who only needed a better direction in life.

Some, I came to find out, were only truly in the wrong place at the wrong time and had been caught up in large federal investigations. Unwilling, or unable to snitch and testify against their codefendants, many were purposely left to rot in the MCDC jail in hopes that they would eventually break under the harsh conditions and agree to cooperate with the government.

Several inmates were so intent on getting away from the MCDC jail, that they quickly agreed to any, and everything the government charged them with, even if it meant a longer sentence than if they stayed and fought their cases. According to them, doing three years in federal prison was better than doing one year at the MCDC jail. This was a sentiment that was backed up by the federal public defenders and attorneys who represented these inmates.

I was quickly receiving valuable lessons on the criminal justice system that I had at one time truly believed to be a noble and righteous pillar of our country. I have always believed that we have prisons and jails for a deserving purpose. There are people out there who are dangerous, violent and cannot function in our society. They deserve to be in prison. However, there are also many out there who either didn't deserve to be prosecuted in the first place, or either were unfairly given exorbitant sentences for their crimes.

A defendant cannot help but feel like a criminal, no matter how innocent you might be. As you sit in court, waiting for your hearing or trial, there is nothing like a legal arena to ram home the enormity and reality of a situation that sometimes seems totally surreal. Even though you still try to cling to a hope of innocence, the amount of shame and embarrassment you feel is overwhelming. This is what courts and trials do to you. It cloaks you in shame.

As I waited to leave MCDC jail and go to a federal prison hospital for a court-ordered psychiatric exam, I couldn't help but become disgusted and repulsed by what I was seeing. The more I saw of our criminal justice system, the less faith I had in my ability to receive a fair trial in my quasi-terrorism threat case.

# CHAPTER THIRTY-SEVEN

I have since been told that when the government wants to thoroughly discredit a person or defendant, one of the first tactics they use is to question their sanity. I had been doing a lot of questioning myself over the stupidity of taking on an entire Sheriff's Office in a political battle of which I was sorely equipped to handle, but never was I ever in doubt about my competency to stand trial, participate in my defense, and appreciate the seriousness of my situation.

Doubting my psychiatric competency, and publicly calling attention to it in the newspapers, was only a tactic used by AUSA Harold Brittain, in what was an apparent ploy to sway public opinion against me. Many people in Vicksburg, who had been following my website, were outraged by my arrest, and truly believed, as I did, that it was a gambit to punish me for my outspoken criticism.

Several days after I was arrested, the FBI moved swiftly and had my website shut down. If I was truly being prosecuted for a legitimate violation of a U.S. law, and not as a punitive punishment for operating a website critical of the Sheriff's Office, then I am still at loss as to why the FBI felt compelled to have my website shut down so quickly. If my arrest wasn't politically motivated, and no one really cared about my website, as they now claim, then why did they move with such speed to terminate it?

Calling my mental stability into question was only a further maneuver to discredit me, my reputation, and anything I had previously written. Granted, I used bad judgment in some of the information I posted on my website, but regardless, it was still constitutionally protected speech. However unpopular it was to those who were on the website, and who now held the keys to my freedom, I still had a right to publish it.

After waiting for over a month in the MCDC jail, the U.S. Marshals finally came to transport me on Tuesday, August 10th, 2004. I was again shackled in handcuffs, belly chains, and leg irons and put in a large van. The marshals then drove me to the Memphis Airport.

When we arrived at the private terminal facility on the airport, there were several other marshal vans and also numerous large buses that belonged to the Federal Bureau of Prisons (BOP). We waited almost an hour before a plain white Boeing 737 aircraft pulled in. Immediately, all the buses and vans maneuvered into a circle shape around the plane with their doors facing inward towards the plane.

About a dozen heavily armed air marshals exited the plane and surrounded the group of buses and vans. I had watched the movie *U.S. Marshals* with Tommy Lee Jones, but seeing how the marshals actually operated was an intriguing experience. Thankful to finally be away from the horrors of the MCDC jail, my spirit was only slightly dampened by the unknown of what awaited me.

Once a secure perimeter had been established, the air marshals began unloading shackled prisoners off the plane. One by one they walked down the stairs to the hot tarmac and lined up under the wing of the aircraft. At the same time, marshals and BOP guards began unloading prisoners from the buses and vans and assembling them on another section of the tarmac.

I was one of the first to be unloaded and was quickly searched for contraband and made to answer numerous questions to confirm my identity. I was then placed in line and told to listen for my name to be called. Once all the prisoners were off the airplane, they were sorted and loaded on their appropriate buses or vans. Some were going to federal prisons in the area- others were going back to court and the county jails on the marshals' vans.

My group of prisoners was then loaded on the aircraft. As I boarded the plane, a second marshal searched me and confirmed my identity. I was told to walk down the aisle and follow the instructions of a third marshal who assigned me a seat in the rear of the plane.

When I sat down, the marshal handed me a paper sack and told me to buckle my seat belt. After fumbling for several minutes to get my seat belt fastened, I looked in my paper sack and discovered a bottle of water, an apple, and a bologna sandwich- the common food served on marshal transport planes.

Shortly thereafter we taxied away from the tarmac and took off into the skies. I had no idea where we were going and didn't ask, but several prisoners volunteered the information that we were headed to Oklahoma City where the BOP kept their inmate transport facility.

An hour after takeoff, I began to feel the plane decrease speed and drop in altitude. We landed a few minutes later at an airport that I had no clue the location or name of. But as the plane exited the runway and headed for some unknown destination on the airport, several inmates stated that we were at the Federal Transport Center (FTC) in Oklahoma City.

The 737 pulled up to a large multi-story building that I could tell housed inmates. A gangplank jutted from the building and was quickly attached to the main door of our aircraft. Once things were secure, the marshals removed us from our seats and ordered us to exit the plane and walk up the gangplank to a spot inside the building where our shackles would be removed.

After being released from our metal bondages, we were all placed in large concrete holding cells. We were eventually taken out, stripped searched, given new clothes, fresh linens, blankets and hygiene items. The medical staff asked us numerous questions and seemed legitimately concerned for our welfare.

Once we were processed, we were taken to our pods. The cells at the FTC were more like college dorm rooms. Even though they were only lockable from the outside, the doors had regular handles and the room themselves consisted of a regular metal frame bed, comfortable mattress, porcelain sinks and toilets, and a clear polished mirror. These were simple luxuries that we didn't have at MCDC.

By the time I actually got to my cell at the FTC, it was late at night and I was exhausted. Even though there were televisions, books, and a small outdoor area, all I was concerned with was getting some sleep.

Shortly after falling asleep, I was awoken by a BOP guard and told to pack my linens and be ready to leave in ten minutes. Unsure of what was happening, I asked the guard for clarification. He told me that I was catching another airlift in a few hours to another facility and I had to be processed out.

Doing the entire procedure in reverse from the night before, I turned in my linens and hygiene items, spoke with medical, was stripped searched and given new clothes, placed in a concrete holding cell, then shackled and placed in line to be loaded onto the aircraft.

The marshals called each inmate's name and loaded him on the plane. There were over a hundred inmates that morning and this took a while to do. As the marshal went down the list to the end, my name still had not been called. The marshal had called every name on his list except mine. I was beginning to worry. The unknown is a frightening thing to face and so far, everything that had happened was an unknown to me.

When the marshals realized that I was still waiting for my name to be called, they began searching for the same answer as me. No one seemed to know what was going on and why I hadn't been called. It took them a few minutes to sort things out, but they finally found out that a special plane had been requested for me and I was waiting for it to arrive.

About an hour later, a different set of marshals came to the holding cell and got me. One of the first questions that they asked was who I was. My name didn't satisfy them and they asked, again, exactly who I was, also explaining that a special Leer jet had been requested from Washington, D.C. to transport me and it was such an unusual request, the marshals figured I was some VIP prisoner.

Obviously not a deadly domestic terrorist, or a former illegitimate foreign head of state, and neither a convicted politician, the marshals and I both were in a quandary as to why I deserved my own Leer jet and preferential treatment for transport. They were however, able to answer one very important question that had been on my mind, and that was where I was going.

The flight from Oklahoma City to Fort Worth, Texas was a plush and pleasant one aboard my special Leer jet. Even though it was a short flight, it was my first time to ever fly in such a nice plane and I enjoyed it- minus the armed marshals and shackles.

There was a federal prison hospital in Fort Worth called the Federal Medical Center-Low. Its primary purpose was to house and care for low security, sick and terminally ill federal inmates. They also had psychiatrists there who performed competency evaluations for the court system on pretrial detainees.

The marshals took me from the Fort Worth airport and drove me to the front door of the prison. Once there I was met by two nice, polite BOP guards who processed me through the prison, stripped searched me, gave me new clothes, hygiene and bedding items, and served me my first real meal since getting arrested. I was assigned a two-man room in a pod of over one hundred fifty other inmates, told to behave myself, stay out of trouble, and mind my own business.

Upon arrival at the FMC, I noticed a world of change

from the life I had been enduring at MCDC. There was better food, cleaner cells, showers and bathrooms; the guards were more professional and polite; it was easy to get soap, razors, toilet paper and toothpaste to take care of yourself with; and the pervasive feeling was one of being more laid back and calm than the atmosphere at MCDC.

Although I had no idea how long I would have to stay at the FMC, I wasn't going to complain much because I knew that I would eventually have to return to Mississippi and the MCDC jail, and the thought was not something I was looking forward too. I determined to harden myself and do whatever was needed in order to deal with the problems of incarceration and fight my charges.

# CHAPTER THIRTY-EIGHT

On my second day, I was introduced to my BOP counselor and case manager. The counselor handled things such as cell assignments, phone accounts, and visiting lists. I was allowed to make phone calls anytime I wanted, but they were limited to fifteen minutes each. I called Meme, Mom, my grandparents, Tucker and Zach on a regular basis. Even though I was in Fort Worth, Meme and my mother insisted on coming to visit. My counselor handled the arrangements and getting them approved.

The case manager worked on things dealing with my charges and was a liaison with the courts. My first question to both my counselor and case manager, was how long I would be at the FMC before being transferred back to Mississippi. Both were unsure, but said that most inmates stay for ninety days. According to them, a lot depended on what my psychiatrist recommended.

I was in a catch-22 situation. On the one hand, I wanted to get back to Mississippi as soon as possible and fight my charges. I knew that I had not threatened anyone and that I could prove it in court. However, the sooner I returned to Mississippi the sooner I would be placed back in the MCDC jail, and that was not something I was looking forward to. At that time I totally appreciated the inmate's actions who pleaded guilty to anything and whatever, just to get out of MCDC and to a federal prison.

Several weeks after arriving at the FMC, I still had not seen any psychiatrists. My case manager explained to me that the psychiatrists were extremely busy, but that I would be seeing one soon. It was also around this time that Tom Setser and I finally received the discovery packet from the U.S. Attorney's Office detailing the evidence in my case.

First and foremost, the FBI, with all of their sophisticated computer forensic wizardry had not been able to locate any type of threat or anything even remotely threat-like on my computers. They had confiscated five different computers from my house and every computer they searched was clean and clear of any type of terrorist or threatening information.

Once I had received the discovery, I was finally able to determine how I had been arrested and charged with this crime. Now that I finally understood what had happened, I was able to explain to my family and attorney how these events had occurred. In order to do that, I had to go back to the summer of 2003.

When I was living in Orlando, and before I started dating Tucker, I used internet chat rooms to talk to other gay guys. During one of these chats, I met and became friends with a guy who said he was in the Air Force, stationed between Colorado and Maryland, was a computer programmer, and was twenty years old. According to him, his real name was Josh and his screen name on AOL was "CowboyJosh16".

Josh was fun to talk to and it seemed like we had a lot in common. Looking back, I understand now that "Josh" was only paralleling my own likes and interests in order to manipulate me into liking him. At the time though, we talked regularly and nothing in our conversations gave me pause to think that he was anything other than what he said he was.

As the summer progressed and I became more proficient in my pilot training, I would engage Josh on the subject of planes and flying. Josh also claimed to be a pilot, but as we talked more on the subject, I noticed that Josh didn't seem to be as fully aware of certain things that a real pilot would have been. This is when I began suspecting that Josh wasn't being totally truthful about things.

I soon thereafter confronted Josh with my suspicions and after at first denying them, Josh eventually admitted that he hadn't been as truthful about himself as he should have. Josh went on to tell me that in actuality he was an older man in his late forties, was not a pilot and was not in the air force. He went on to tell me that his real name was Allen, and that he had an obsession with talking to younger, cute gay guys. This was the excuse that Allen gave me for lying to me, sending me fake pictures, and pretending to be someone he wasn't.

Even though Allen apologized profusely and begged that I forgive him and still be his friend, I wanted nothing to do with him. I persistently blocked his every effort to contact and talk to me. Allen even sent me a long and detailed email confessing his "love" and attraction to me and at one point in his letter threatened to commit suicide if I didn't continue to talk to him.

During the course of two weeks, Allen either called or emailed me over three hundred times. In every instance I ignored him. When Allen finally realized that he was not going to get any sympathy or continued friendship from me, his tactics changed to harassment and threats.

Somehow, Allen was able to discover my real name and began threatening to "out" me to my family for being gay. When his threats didn't elicit a response, Allen began calling all of the Atwood's in Vicksburg. He distributed pictures of me, along with my phone number and lewd sexual messages across the internet. Because of Allen and the messages he posted, my phone rang constantly from people calling for everything from phone sex to hook-ups.

The final straw was when Allen printed off dozens of

pages of emails and instant message conversations between he and I and mailed them to Meme. It was at this point that I felt something needed to be done, but because of the sensitivity of the issue, and the fact that I wasn't out about being gay, I was reluctant to properly report the harassment to the police. Instead, I turned to Gil Martin, who was at the time, the district attorney of Warren County.

Gil and I had been friendly towards one another for several years and Gil had quietly given me advice and guidance in my election campaign. Most everyone knew that Gil Martin was gay, but it wasn't something that Gil discussed openly. However, I'm sure he caught on pretty quick to my sexuality when I chose to confide in him and seek his advice when I ran for constable. One of Gil Martin's unfortunate vices though, was his propensity to make inappropriate sexual remarks and to become too free with his sexual advances toward guys he liked. It was this behavior that made me uncomfortable around Gil and prevented our friendship from going any further than casual acquaintances.

With all this in mind, I was still hesitant to bring Allen's harassment to Gil's attention. In the first place, it was probably out of his jurisdiction since I was living in Orlando, and second, there was probably not much Gil or his office could do anyway. But I contacted him regardless and explained my situation.

The most Gil was willing to do was subpoena the account records of Allen's emails and perhaps determine who the real owner and user was. He also agreed to subpoena my phone records to show where Allen had been calling me nonstop. Because of Allen's past dishonesty, I was dubious whether his new moniker was even real or not, but Gil said it was worth a shot. At the most, I could press harassment charges in Orlando against the person, once we discovered who he was.

Several weeks later, one of Gil Martin's investigators, Gary Haygood, called and told me that they had received the subpoena back from AOL and that the email address, "CowboyJosh16@aol.com" belong to Allen Cousby Jaques of Ashburn, Virginia. Gary agreed to fax the information, along with my phone records, to my apartment in Orlando so that I could press charges on Allen Jaques if I chose to.

Since the harassment was still continuing, I developed a plan that I hoped would stop Allen Jaques from contacting me again. After doing a little research on the internet, I discovered that Allen Jaques was indeed a computer programmer and worked for a software company called Adelphia. I also was able to locate his address and home telephone number.

I waited until Allen Jaques started calling my phone again, but instead of ignoring it, I answered. In his cocky, arrogant voice, Allen Jaques asked me if I was finally willing to forgive him and be his friend. Without missing a beat, I explained to him that I knew who he was, where he lived and where he worked and that if he didn't stop harassing me, I would press charges on him. Obviously thinking I was lying, Allen Jaques called my bluff. Before I could finish saying his name and address though, Allen Jaques disconnected his phone.

That was the last contact I had with Allen Jaques. I never attempted to contact him again and certainly never threatened to burn his house down and cut him with a knife. As far as I was concerned, the situation was over after that night, and since Allen Jaques never contacted me again and the calls to my family stopped, I was perfectly content with forgetting the matter.

Unbeknownst to me, Allen Jaques, feeling outmaneuvered, defeated in a game he had started, and made to look like a fool, sought retaliation in any way he could. After the night of our last conversation, Allen Jaques went on a spree of paranoia, calling the local sheriff, state police, and FBI. Allen Jaques' statements to them ranged from the bizarre to the downright kooky. He claimed everything from being harassed and stalked, to assault and battery, and of course, being threatened. His paranoia knew no bounds.

After an initial investigation, those law enforcement agencies probably came to the same conclusion I did- that Allen Jaques was a nut case and pedophile. Whatever their opinion, his complaints were filed away in someone's drawer and weren't looked at for almost a year.

It is still my opinion, along with many of those familiar with my case, that the FBI, at the behest of the Warren County Sheriff's Office, began to seek out any possible criminal charge they could contrive to punish me. Allen Jaques presented an easy opportunity.

# CHAPTER THIRTY-NINE

As I was working with Tom Setser and my stepdad to plan my defense, I still had not seen one of the prison psychiatrists. I had been at the FMC for over a month and was beginning to wonder whether I was truly there for a legitimate evaluation or had just been purposely sent there to be forgotten.

I spent most of my days reading books or watching television. Several of the inmates taught me how to play spades and gin rummy. We were allowed to go outside to a recreation yard once a day, and even though I didn't play basketball, I still enjoyed being outside in the warm sunshine.

Since I had been arrested, Zach and I had begun to lose touch, but Tucker stepped into his place and was a rock of support for me. I tried to call him at least three or four times a week, but after I had been at the FMC for a month, Tucker quit answering his phone. When I called, it wouldn't even ring- it just went straight to voice mail. After a week of this I began to seriously worry.

Finally, after two weeks of not answering my calls, Tucker finally picked up. What he told me not only devastated our friendship, but sent me on a guilt trip from which I've yet to recover.

When the FBI seized my computers, they were not only looking for information to use to convict me, they were also looking for any information in which to hurt my friends and family. After locating and reading all the emails and instant message conversations being Tucker and I, the FBI decided to turn them over to the Marine Corps and push for Tucker to be discharged from the military for being gay.

The two weeks that Tucker wasn't answering his phone was because the Marine Corps had stripped his security clearance and confined him to base while they determined how best to handle the situation. Tucker was a Marine who saluted and worked with President Bush every day. It was an unpardonable sin to be gay and remain in such a prominent and prestigious position.

Tucker's discharge and banishment from the Marine Corps was swift and wrathful. Never mind that he was a decorated war veteran of both Iraq and Afghanistan, and had earned the Silver Star for heroism under fire. Merely the fact that Tucker was gay and had had the bad luck of getting caught up in my criminal case, cost him his service to our country.

Tucker and I never seriously tried to continue our friendship after that day. The guilt was hard on me, and the seriousness of what he had lost at my expense weighed on his mind. The unfairness of it was infuriating. It was one thing to target me for my actions; it was totally different for the FBI to play dirty and target Tucker, only because of his association with me. It only made me more angry and more determined to fight them any way I could.

Even though the FBI had been unable to find any evidence on my computer that indicated I had threatened Allen Jaques, their forensic experts located several images somewhere in the deep recesses of my hard drive that were pictures of Allen Jaques' house. Their theory of thought was that even if they couldn't find any evidence of a threat on my computers, pictures of Allen Jaques' house proved I was stalking him and meant him harm.

It was pointed out to the AUSA Harold Brittain that I was charged with threatening to kill Allen Jaques, not stalking or harassment, and without evidence of a actual threat, they didn't have a case. The only problem was that I had no idea how pictures of Allen Jaques' house came to be located on my computer's hard drive.

Even though I had sworn and promised everyone who would listen, that I never threatened to kill Allen Jaques, prior to obtaining the discovery, no one really believed me. But once the proof was there, or lack thereof, I think people began to see what this really was. Without finding any evidence of an actual crime, the FBI and AUSA's case was practically over. Now their tactics moved to keeping me locked up as long as possible before having my charges dismissed.

Having pictures of Allen Jaques' house on my computer presented several issues that we were going to have to explain. My position was that I had never been to Ashburn, Virginia and taken pictures of his house. Other than that, I had no explanation for how they came to be on my computer.

On a whim, I decided to talk to another inmate who was a computer whiz and professed to know anything and everything about computers. After explaining the details of my case and the problem of the pictures on my computer, this inmate offered a very simple explanation and all of a sudden, it became very clear.

If Allen Jaques knew that the FBI was eventually coming to seize my computers and arrest me, using his skills as a computer programmer, he could have easily encoded pictures of his own house into a "Trojan horse" type email, sent it to me, and when I unknowingly opened it, had the pictures attach themselves to my hard drive. According to this computer expert-turned-federal-prisoner, it was a simple enough operation for even a novice computer programmer.

It was also brought to my attention during one of our defense planning sessions, that the Bryant family, whom I had criticized so negatively on my website for their connections to the Sheriff's Office, was from the same county and area in Virginia that Allen Jaques was from. Coincidence or not, the circumstantial evidence was building.

If what I was told was true, then it was becoming essential for us to have Allen Jaques' computers subpoenaed and seized for the exculpatory evidence they might contain. Explaining this to Tom and my stepdad was difficult. They didn't understand or accept the importance of this but we came to the agreement that Tom would file for a subpoena to have Allen Jaques' computers seized, even though we would have to pay our own computer expert to examine them. That took time, and in the meantime I was going to have to sit and wait.

Finally, after six weeks at the FMC, I was called to meet with the psychiatrist. But whatever expectations I had for this first meeting were quickly dashed when the psychiatrist merely introduced himself and ordered me to get ready to take a battery of tests to gauge my mental and emotional status. No discussion, no talks on my background, nothing. I was just placed behind a desk and given a bunch of multiple choice questions to answer.

As my afternoon was being spent answering some of the dumbest questions I'd ever been given in my life, I wondered whether this was to be literally taken serious, or if I was just a crude circus performer in a carefully orchestrated dog and pony show.

When I finished my tests, I turned them over to the psychiatrist's secretary and went back to my pod. I wasn't told when I would see the doctor again or when I was leaving. I just had to wait.

The presidential election was heating up and I tried to follow it as closely as possible while I was at FMC. I had at one time been a Bush supporter, and when the 9/11 attacks occurred, I firmly supported his efforts to capture and punish the terrorists. When Bush invaded Iraq in early 2003, I supported his plan because I believed, like many Americans, that Saddam Hussein possessed weapons of mass destruction and posed a threat to the free world.

Realizing a short time later that Hussein was not as big of a threat as Bush made him seem, and that there were no weapons of mass destruction, made me reconsider my support for the president. When it was learned that Bush and other members of his administration had fabricated evidence to support their invasion of Iraq, I became disgusted and withdrew my support.

As the November election approached, I couldn't help but like and support John Kerry and the platform for which he stood. I felt that my duty to vote should not be diminished by my current circumstances, and since I had not technically been convicted of a crime, I wrote to the Circuit Clerk of Warren County and requested an absentee ballot be mailed to me at the FMC. When it arrived, I dutifully voted for John Kerry and sent it back.

When I had been at the FMC for a little over two months, the prison psychiatrist finally called me into his office for a detailed chat. He apologized for making me wait so long, but dutifully shrugged off this annoyance with excuses of having a heavy case load. I politely refrained from reminding him that his failure to quickly and efficiently handle mental competency cases such as mine, wrongfully deprived me of my freedom and my right to a speedy trial.

We only spoke for about fifteen minutes and only covered the bare essentials of my life, family, and criminal case. The psychiatrist told me my earlier administered tests looked fine and that it was his opinion I was suffering from no mental disease or defect that would prohibit me from understanding and participating in a criminal trial. He closed the file, shook my hand and informed me that I would be going back to Mississippi as soon as a spot could be reserved for me on the airlift.

Two weeks later, George Bush was reelected and I was on my way back to Mississippi. Instead of rolling out the private Leer jet to transport me, the BOP put me on one of their transport buses and drove me and several other inmates from the FMC back to the transfer center in Oklahoma City. I spent the next few days in Oklahoma before being placed back on the same 737 aircraft and flown to the Memphis airport.

The same scenario played out as the first time I was transported there and the same marshals drove me back to the MCDC jail. I arrived back for processing in the concrete holding cell on the afternoon of November 8th, 2004. Depressed, unhappy, and not looking forward to having to deal with the deplorable conditions of the jail, I couldn't be but somewhat excited to finally be home and able to properly defend my criminal charge. I was ready for it to be dismissed, or either take it to trial and prove my innocence.

While I was being transported back to Mississippi, we had received a mirror image copy of Allen Jaques' computer hard drive that had been seized. When we turned it over to our computer expert, he immediately located evidence that proved Allen Jaques had not only fabricated a fake threat and sent it to the cops claiming it had come from me, but the computer expert also found where Allen Jaques had taken pictures of his own house, secretly encoded them in an email, and sent them to me. When I unknowingly opened that email, those pictures attached themselves automatically to my hard drive and remained there until they were conveniently found by the FBI.

In subsequent searches of Allen Jaques' computer, hundreds of images and pictures of child pornography were found on his hard drive. I had long suspected Allen Jaques to be a pedophile but now with the proof, I felt it was only a matter of time before the tables were turned and I was freed, and Allen Jaques was behind bars.

Not only was possession of child pornography a serious crime, but so was fabricating fake evidence, lying to federal investigators, and filing false police reports- all of which Allen Jaques had eagerly done. We felt that it was only a matter of time before the federal judge would have to dismiss the threat charge and set me free.

Once back, I immediately began pushing Tom to either file a motion for dismissal or a motion to grant me bond. We felt that with the new evidence, a judge would be forced by sheer conscience to grant our motion and dismiss the charge, or allow me out on bail pending a trial.

The U.S. Attorney's Office, no matter how sham their case, was determined to keep me locked up as long as possible. When informed of the evidence we had located on Allen Jaques' computer, the AUSA only responded that they would forward the information to the proper authorities in Virginia, but that their only concern was prosecuting me.

Determined to push forward with a motion to dismiss or have me granted bond, we continued to be confident that my case was almost over. When I finally appeared before the magistrate judge, several weeks after returning from Texas, Tom and I were shocked to discover that the FBI and AUSA were charging me with a new, much more serious crime. As the new charge was being read to me, I glanced over my shoulder and noticed Detective Todd Dykes in the federal courtroom. A Cheshire grin spread across his face, and as he winked, I fully understood that they had finally gotten me.

# CHAPTER FORTY

The federal government of the United States of America, having been made fools once in my case, was determined not to let it happen again. They brought the full weight of their resources and manpower down on my head.

As their terrorist threat charge fell apart, they immediately began looking for something new, something more powerful to charge me with. They settled on a computer sex offense and officially charged and indicted me with one count of using a computer in interstate commerce to entice a minor, under the age of eighteen, into engaging in sexual activity.

As serious, big and important as that criminal offense sounded, it basically came down to the fact that I was twenty years old and Zach Booth was sixteen, and even though we were not violating state law, because we had personal conversations about sex on the computer, according to the federal government,

I'd violated the law and faced a mandatory minimum of five years in prison.

The actual act of me having sex with Zach Booth was not in violation of any law. Having *conversations* with Zach about sex, through the computer, even though technically that sex was legal, *was* a violation of federal law as interpreted by the FBI and AUSA Harold Brittain.

There was no doubt that the federal statute prohibited an adult from having conversations of a sexual nature with a minor, especially if there was some type or enticement or inducement offered by the adult to lure the minor into sexual activity.

The difference that set my specific case and circumstances apart was first off, neither Zach, or myself, had ever had any computer conversations across state lines. This was a crucial criteria of the statute in order for the federal government to claim jurisdiction. Our computer conversations were only technically a few miles apart.

Secondly, Zach Booth and I were in a completely consensual relationship. There was never any enticement or inducement on my part to coerce Zach into anything he didn't want to do. A later, in-depth analysis of the copies of our conversations through email and instant messages would show exactly that. Zach was always the one to push for something more in our relationship than what I was able to give.

These were two very specific criterion that had to be met before I could be convicted of this criminal charge. Our argument became that since we never crossed state lines, the federal government lacked jurisdiction to prosecute the case, and second, even if the feds had legal jurisdiction, there was never any enticement or inducement on my part. Zach Booth was a perfectly willing and consensual partner in our relationship.

The news of this latest development in my case devastated me. Tom made a meager argument to the judge asking for bond, but the request was denied. I was returned to custody at the MCDC jail where I was to wait several more months for a trial. As expected, the conditions at the jail were just as bad as before, and the thought of spending the holidays in that hell hole was driving me crazy.

Shortly after I was charged with this new offense, more problems arose in my case. My attorney, Tom Setser, went to church and was friends with Zach Booth and his family. Even though we learned that the Booth family was refusing to cooperate with the FBI and AUSA, they were nonetheless shocked with discovering the revelation about Zach being gay.

Under the circumstances, Tom felt uncomfortable defending me against this new charge and asked to be allowed to withdraw as my counsel. This then forced me to start searching for a new attorney.

Since I was incarcerated and was severely limited in what I could do, I was dependent on Meme, my Mom, and stepdad to locate and hire a new lawyer. Because of the aggressiveness in which the FBI and AUSA were pursuing this new charge, I felt like a strong, outspoken, assertive attorney was needed. My stepdad suggested several that I should contact and I eventually settled on hiring Cynthia Hewes Speetjens.

Cynthia had a background as a prosecutor in the state courts and had only recently began practice in the private sector. She had a reputation for tenacity and devotion to her clients. She was currently defending against the only federal capital murder death penalty case in the state of Mississippi and would go on to successfully save her client from being executed. By all accounts, Cynthia was the attorney we thought I needed.

After paying Cynthia fifteen thousand dollars, she began work on my case. I was very upfront with her from the beginning and assured her that I wanted this case to go to trial and that I did not want to plead guilty. We shook hands with the understanding that she was supposed to handle my case with the ultimate objective of securing a not-guilty verdict by a jury.

At first she was confident that we could obtain a dismissal by arguing the federal government lacked proper jurisdiction. Failing that, she felt strongly that I had a good chance of being found not guilty by a jury. We also discussed the possibility of appealing the magistrate's decision denying me bond. Cynthia felt that we might have better luck with the district court judge, David Bramlette. She left the MCDC jail before Christmas, assuring me that she would work hard on my case and do everything possible to get me out on bond. Having paid her fifteen thousand dollars, I was hoping she would.

As days turned into weeks, and weeks turned into months, nothing of tangible value had been done on my case. Cynthia wasn't answering my phone calls or returning my letters. Her secretary kept assuring me she would write back and come visit me at the jail, but nothing ever happened. It was a frustrating and maddening situation.

As the middle of February passed and I still had not had any contact with Cynthia since before Christmas, I was determined to produce some response. I wrote Cynthia a very detailed letter complaining of the lack of communication between us; the lack of any obvious progress on my case; the lack of filing an appeal for another bond hearing; and her inability to return the phone calls of my mother, stepdad and Meme. I plainly stated that if I didn't hear from her within a week, I would fire her, request my fifteen thousand dollars back, and hire another attorney.

Several days after mailing the letter, the jail guards called me to the front for an attorney visit. Cynthia had finally shown up. Apologizing profusely, Cynthia tried to explain how busy she had been and how many cases she had been swamped with. She repeatedly pointed out that she had recently beaten the federal government by preventing them from sending one of her clients to death row. It was little consolation when I later discovered that her client received a life sentence without the possibility of parole. Under the same circumstances, I would have preferred death.

After the apologies and pleasantries were dispensed with, Cynthia informed me that she hadn't filed an appeal for another bond hearing because in her opinion, it would be denied. She believed that Judge Bramlette would not grant me bond anyway and didn't want to waste the time to try.

More infuriating was the fact that not only had she not tried to secure me a bond, but now, going against everything we had initially agreed to, she was pressuring me to plead guilty to this crime. She argued, that in return for my guilty plea, the AUSA would agree to only recommend five years in prison. According to her, it was only with her superb negotiating skills and connections with the AUSA that she was able to strike this wonderful deal.

Cynthia didn't know that the AUSA had offered the same "deal" to Tom and my stepdad when I was initially charged with this crime. The only difference was that I had paid Cynthia fifteen thousand dollars to arrange for a plea deal that I was already going to get before I hired her.

Our conversation that day quickly broke down to arguing and confrontation. Cynthia kept telling me that there was no way I could have this charge dismissed, nor would I be able to convince a jury to find me not guilty.

Judge Bramlette was such a conservative judge that he would never agree to dismiss a sex charge like mine based on a minor technicality such as the government not having proper jurisdiction. It was also made very clear to me that any potential jury members would be more than likely conservative Republicans who would not be very sympathetic to a homosexual defendant charged with a homosexual crime.

Up until that day I had never considered pleading guilty and I wasn't about to start. It became apparent that even if Cynthia took my charge to trial, and tried to defend me, her heart and energy would not be fully in the case. Without having an aggressive advocate in my corner to fight for my rights, I knew I would not stand a chance in court. When Cynthia became unwilling to do that, I knew I would have to fire her.

Fortunately, Cynthia agreed to return a large portion of the money I had paid her and withdraw as my lawyer. Having gone through two attorneys in my case, without any luck from either of them, the next step was to locate someone different. I was becoming extremely frustrated and depressed at my situation and was on the verge of giving up.

After discussing everything with my family, we decided to allow my stepdad and his brother, Frank Campbell, to defend my case. Jerry and Frank had both been involved in the details of my charges from the very beginning. Both were seasoned attorneys who had spent many years in the court room.

Frank was a former elected district attorney of Warren County and Jerry had experience serving as county prosecutor and judge. They both felt that I deserved better representation and quickly signed on to help me. Within several days of becoming my new attorneys, Jerry and Frank were able to file an appeal for a bond hearing and set up a court date before Judge David Bramlette.

As the March 15th, 2005 court date approached, I was excited about the possibility of being finally released on bond. My trial had been scheduled to start on April 1st, and we felt it was imperative that I be released on bond to help assist in preparing for my defense.

# CHAPTER FORTY-ONE

In order to help overcome the AUSA's argument that I was a danger to society and a flight risk, we arranged to have sixteen different friends and family members come to court and testify on my behalf. The group ranged from close friends, professional acquaintances, and all my family still loyal to me and willing to support with the help I needed.

On the day of the bond hearing, the federal marshals transported me from the MCDC jail to downtown Jackson. Since this would be the first time appearing before Judge Bramlette, I was more nervous than usual. Jerry and Frank had assured me that the judge *should* let me out on bond, but I also knew the reputation of Judge Bramlette to be one of conservative politics, partiality to the prosecution, and harsh sentences to the defendants. Expecting him to allow me released on bond was a gamble.

The AUSA's argument was that because of the "severity" and seriousness of my charge, I posed a danger as a sexual predator upon the community. If a person believed the prosecutor, I had perpetrated a vicious sexual assault on Zach Booth and the aftermath to him was unrecoverable.

Since this was only a bond hearing and not a criminal trial, any evidence that we would normally try to offer to refute the AUSA's claims would not be allowed. We had tried to subpoena Zach Booth to court and allow him to testify on my behalf, in order to set the record straight and offer evidence that I was not guilty of enticement, but the prosecutor blocked those efforts.

Even though the prosecutor had made me out to be a violent and dangerous criminal, we still felt we could overcome that negativity by the sheer number of witnesses that we placed on the stand to testify on my behalf.

When it was our turn to present our side, every witness testified that I was a good, decent person and that they had never witnessed or heard of me doing anything harmful to myself or others. They also testified that they would take on the personal responsibility of ensuring that I stayed out of trouble and appeared for court if I was released on bond. Regardless of whether Judge Bramlette released me on bond that day, I was proud that I had so many friends and family still willing to stand up for me.

When the five-hour hearing was over, the judge took a moment to consider the testimony and then prepared to issue his ruling. Before doing so, he gave a long, detailed statement justifying his decision. Judge Bramlette basically said that he felt I was guilty of the crime and that I had no chance to overcome that assumption in a jury trial.

He further felt that this type of "serious" offense was deplorable and that I deserved a lengthy prison term. In somewhat coded language, Judge Bramlette made it clear that if I was to proceed with a trial, waste the court's time, and be found guilty, he would thoroughly punish me for my actions. He finished his diatribe by denying me bond and ordering me returned to custody at the MCDC jail.

As I returned to the jail, crestfallen and shaken at the judge's decision, I was nonetheless ready for what I thought was going to be my trial on April 1st. Shortly after returning to the jail, Jerry came for a visit. He had been as shaken by the judge's attitude as I had been and was now convinced that the judge would sabotage my trial.

For the first time since being arrested, Jerry was advocating that I plead guilty, accept the five years and move on. He was convinced that Judge Bramlette would improperly influence a jury, and then once convicted, sentence me to some astronomical amount of time.

Jerry pointed out that the Supreme Court of the United States had recently ruled the federal sentencing guidelines unconstitutional and that technically Judge Bramlette could sentence me to the maximum amount of time under law- which was thirty years. After hearing the judge's diatribe, I became convinced that if convicted I would face a lot more than five years in jail.

As much as I believed in my innocence, and as much as I believed that I should have taken my case to trial, it was becoming obvious that it would be an effort in futility. Judge Bramlette did not like me as a defendant, didn't like me because I was gay, and wasn't going to allow me to walk free. He could easily have influenced the jury against me, or made rulings that would have basically hindered our defense and prevented us from introducing any evidence that was beneficial to me. It was not a chance that I wanted to take.

After verifying with the AUSA the five-year plea deal, both Jerry and Frank recommended that I accept the agreement, take the five years, and move on with my life. Even though accepting the deal would mean more time in prison and the requirement that I register as a convicted sex offender upon release, the alternative was not any better.

Cynthia Speetjens had been right when she told me that it would be impossible to find a fair jury in Mississippi that wouldn't be predisposed to having some type of biases against a gay defendant. Add the additional influences that Judge Bramlette was sure to exert on the jury members and it was a scenario for a lynching, except instead of being black, I was gay, and there was nothing we could do to stop it.

The more I thought about it, the more scared I became. Everyone who had testified at the bond hearing had heard Judge Bramlette's diatribe and was also convinced that I could not receive a fair trial. In a few short minutes, they all became convinced that I should plead guilty and accept the five years rather than risk taking it to trial. The alternative was more than I or anyone else was willing to face.

On April 1$^{st}$, 2005, I was taken back to the federal courthouse and appeared before Judge Bramlette. As unwilling as I was to do so, I forced myself to plead guilty to a crime that I knew that I had not committed and that I was being politically pressured to accept responsibility for.

When the entire weight of the federal government is brought to bear on top of your head, a person will not think or act correctly. This was one of those times. Even though I knew I had not committed this crime, I also knew that I could never receive a fair trial in front of Judge Bramlette or a jury. Had I proceeded with one anyway, I would most likely have been convicted and then sentenced to a very likely thirty years in prison.

Pleading guilty was, in hindsight, the worst mistake I've ever made in my life. At the time I didn't understand the avenues of appeal that would have been available to me had I been convicted. My immediate concern was getting out of jail. I was unwilling to risk getting that thirty years in prison. So like a fool, I accepted the plea agreement, admitted my "guilt" and was sentenced to sixty-three months in federal prison.

Rather than give me an even five years, Judge Bramlette I'm assuming, was disappointed at missing his chance to send a homosexual to prison for thirty years, felt justified in tacking an additional three months to my five year agreement, because even though the Supreme Court had ruled the federal sentencing guidelines unconstitutional, Judge Bramlette still abided by them when convenient.

After being sentenced, I was returned to the MCDC jail to await transfer to the Federal Bureau of Prisons. My stay at the jail had not been uneventful. As my initial assessment of the jail and its staff had been correct, I'd had to endure torment, harassment, and deplorable conditions. One thing was clear; no one received special treatment at the MCDC jail- every inmate was treated equally bad.

Some of the guards at the jail were better than others. Some guards only used their position and authority for personal greed and aggrandizement. Some staff members there, such as Major Chuck McNeil, Lieutenant Perry, TJ Alexander, Benjamin Blaine, Officer Hitchcock and several others could probably be criminally prosecuted and held liable for some of the treatment they subjected inmates too.

Two weeks after sentencing though, the U.S. Marshals transported me from the MCDC jail and took me to the Grenada County Jail in Grenada, Mississippi. The GCJ was a temporary holding facility the Marshals utilized to hold federal inmates who had been sentenced and were awaiting classification and transport to the BOP.

While the MCDC jail was a terror for any inmate who was incarcerated there, the GCJ was just the opposite. It's hard to sit and write that a jail is actually a nice place, but the conditions under which I had to live in the MCDC jail made the GCJ look like a small piece of heaven. That's how bad things were at the MCDC.

At the GCJ, the food was better quality and they fed you more of it. The guards didn't scream and threaten you, and they certainly didn't assault you with tasers, fists, or pepper spray for no reason. Inmates could obtain more hygiene items, better bedding and blankets, and could also purchase food items out of a commissary once a week. Even though many of the inmates said the BOP's prisons were better, Grenada still felt like a piece of heaven to me.

# CHAPTER FORTY-TWO

I remained at the Grenada County Jail for several months waiting to be classified by the BOP. Judge Bramlette had recommended that I be sent to the federal prison in Yazoo City, Mississippi, but it was not certain that that's where the BOP would send me.

When August rolled around, the Marshal's finally arrived to pick me up and transport me to the BOP. Once I was shackled and loaded onto the bus, they informed me, much to my surprise, that I would be going to the medium security prison which had recently opened in Yazoo City, Mississippi.

Although I had requested to go to Yazoo City, I was shocked to discover that they were sending me to the medium security custody level. I had heard horror stories from other inmates about the violence levels in the medium and maximum security prisons and I was not looking forward to going to one. I had expected to at least be sent to a low security prison since I was a first-time offender and had not committed a violent crime.

As the Marshal's van pulled away from Grenada and headed towards the airlift in Memphis, I sat in stunned silence at the latest turn of events. It seemed to me that nothing I ever did could catch me a lucky break. I had made up my mind that things were going from bad to worse.

Once we arrived in Memphis the same scenario played out as it had months before when I was being transported to Fort Worth. Except this time I wasn't placed on the airplane. The Marshals only removed me from their van and transferred me over to a BOP bus that was headed to Yazoo City.

As I looked around the bus, I noticed that I was surrounded by hardcore criminals. Almost all of them had gory, violent and fierce-looking tattoos. Many had deadly glints in their eyes that screamed violence. Even though we were all currently shackled, I still couldn't feel but a slight tension in the air. I was genuinely frightened and I was not looking forward to being placed with these obviously dangerous and violent criminals.

While we were making the three-hour bus ride south, towards the prison, I was able to start a conversation with the inmate in the seat next to mine. He had been doing time most of his life and wore the well recognizable scars and tattoos to prove it. Recognizing that I was fresh meat, my new friend took it upon himself to explain some of the things that I had to look forward too. Assuring me that a medium security prison was not all *that* violent, and that I would be okay as long as I minded my own business, and wasn't a snitch or child molester, my friend said I had a lot to look forward to.

When we arrived at the prison in Yazoo City, we were unloaded from the bus, marched through the front doors and taken to an area of the prison called "Receiving and Discharge". This was the area where new inmates were processed in. Our shackles were removed and one-by-one we were stripped searched, given new clothes, blankets, bedrolls, hygiene items, made to fill out paperwork, consult a nurse, given a bed assignment and turned loose to fend for ourselves on the prison compound.

As I walked through the exit doors and onto my first real prison compound, I was struck by the immensity of it all. There were three main housing units, each four stories tall and divided into four individual pods. Each pod held about one hundred and fifty inmates.

There were three television rooms in each pod, each belonging to a different race; one TV room for blacks, one for whites, and one for Mexicans. A few additional televisions were scattered around the day-room and were considered "neutral". Even on my first day, I was quickly learning that everything was broken down by race in prison.

For the most part, whites only celled and roomed with other whites. The same went for the blacks and Mexicans. There were special areas of the chow hall reserved for the individual races and all of the inmates respected those boundaries. The guards, recognizing the importance of these arrangements, left the inmates to police themselves and rarely interfered.

What wasn't made obvious to me was quickly pointed out by some of the inmates who had been doing time for most of their lives. They recognized me as a young, naïve inmate in need of direction. As the first day turned into the first week, and later into the first month, I quickly grasped the rules and unwritten inmate codes that a prison operates by.

The medium security prison at Yazoo City had just opened several weeks prior to my arrival and there were only several hundred inmates on the compound. The BOP, however, was bringing in fresh busloads almost daily. Shortly after my arrival, Hurricane Katrina ravaged New Orleans and the Mississippi coast. When Hurricane Rita swamped Texas, it destroyed a large portion of the federal prison in Beaumont.

Unable to place the inmates elsewhere, the BOP transferred over eight hundred prisoners from Beaumont to Yazoo City in less than a week. Beaumont had the well-deserved moniker "Bloody Beaumont" for its vicious gang riots, high violence level, and murder rate. Upon hearing the news that the Beaumont inmates were going to be transferred to Yazoo, most of the prisoners began complaining of the inevitable trouble that would ensue.

Since this was my first real prison to be assigned, I had no other experience from which to judge it. Even though fights and violence escalated once the Beaumont crew arrived, I mainly was able to avoid any trouble.

I obtained a job working in the prison library as a law clerk, helping other inmates research their cases and prepare for their appeals. In my free time, I walked the track or played handball on the yard.

There was a prison commissary where I could shop once a week to buy food and hygiene items. My mother, Meme, family and friends visited every weekend and I began a long correspondence with many people who had supported me but were unable to visit.

I made several close friends with some of the other inmates. One that became especially close to me was a guy named Sonny Breckenridge. Sonny had at one time, been the chief deputy of the Marengo County Sheriff's Office in Demopolis, Alabama but had been caught up in a federal investigation and was now serving a life sentence for an assortment of different drug crimes.

Whether Sonny was actually guilty of his crimes has been a matter of public and judicial speculation for over a decade. From what I've read and what I know about his case, I sincerely believe that Sonny was not guilty. At the least, he never should have been given a life sentence for what he was convicted of, even if he was actually guilty.

Sonny and I walked literally hundreds of laps around the track talking and discussing our different cases. I became a thorough believer in his innocence and would later advocate for a presidential pardon for Sonny. If there was ever a more unjust conviction than mine, Sonny Breckenridge's would be at the top.

After being at Yazoo for several months, I began to adjust and soon got into a good routine. In early December, my stepdad informed me that the district attorney of Warren County, Gil Martin, whom I had considered a friend, was pushing for a conviction on the malicious mischief charge I had been arrested on shortly before my federal incarceration.

Up until this time, I had practically forgotten about it; but unlike me, my Aunt June and grandfather, Emmett Atwood, had not. They were pushing Gil Martin to prosecute the case and make me spend more time in prison. The depravity disgusted me, especially when I had at one time considered Gil Martin a friend whom I could trust and confide in. This latest sell-out to the Atwood's was only a recent reminder that money talks, and bullshit walks in Vicksburg.

Because of the friendship I had shared with Gil Martin in the past, I felt it was inappropriate for his office to prosecute the malicious mischief charge. Even though it didn't seem important, the fact that Georgia Lynn was a family relative of Zach Booth's, also made me feel that it was necessary for Gil Martin and his entire office to recuse themselves and a special prosecutor be appointed to prosecute the case.

Jerry took my request to Gil Martin but was quickly told that there would be no recusal. Gil simply refused to remove himself from the case regardless of the monstrous appearance of impropriety. Under the circumstances, and knowing full well the history of corruption and malfeasance of those in political office in Vicksburg, I shouldn't have been surprised.

Up until then I had remained silent to the fact that Gil Martin had at one time made sexual advances on me and had sent me inappropriate emails alluding to sexual acts between him and another guy that he wanted to make me part of. Feeling their exposure would not serve any legitimate purpose I chose to remain silent. However, when it became apparent that Gil Martin and his office was trying to steamroll me into pleading guilty or going to trial on a charge that was instigated at the behest of my Aunt June and grandfather, I felt that my silence was no longer a virtue.

Composing a motion for recusal, and laying out all the facts as to why Gil Martin and his office should be removed from the case, including the information that Gil had made sexual advances towards me, I requested that the circuit judge who had been assigned my case, Isadore Patrick, issue a ruling and remove Gil Martin from prosecuting the charge. I also asked that Judge Patrick appoint Tom Setser to be my attorney.

Shortly after sending in the motion for recusal, I was informed by my stepdad, that not only had my motion stirred the courthouse into a frenzy, but that Judge Patrick was going to grant it and request the Attorney General to appoint a special prosecutor.

Even though no one had any idea when a trial might actually be held on the charge, I felt like a small victory had been achieved in getting Gil Martin and his office removed from prosecuting me. Whether they would have actually used nefarious means to have me convicted is open to debate, but merely the appearance of impropriety should have been enough for him to willingly recuse himself and maintain some dignity for his office.

I started the New Year, 2006, feeling confident and ready to take on anything that the court system in Vicksburg or prison life in Yazoo City might have to throw my way.

# CHAPTER FORTY-THREE

I had for the most part chosen to keep my sexuality to myself while I was incarcerated. Being out about being gay in prison could potentially invite unwanted sexual advances from other inmates. I chose to forego this problem by not revealing much information about myself.

When other inmates asked me what I was in prison for, I explained to them that I was arrested for sending threatening messages to another person through email. Since I did not "look" like a criminal, compared to the other inmates in the prison, most of the guys believed me. Most considered my charge a "white collar" crime and didn't pay me anymore attention.

Shortly after the New Year, I witnessed my first small scale prison riot. A black inmate had been assaulted by a group of Mexican gang members and in retaliation, a larger group of black inmates exacted revenge on some other Mexicans. The violence quickly escalated as quid pro quo assaults occurred back and forth across the compound.

Having been warned of the oncoming violence, most of the white inmates chose to remain in their cells and avoid the chaos. The guards responded by locking down the prison and restoring order to the compound. All the inmates, minus the ones who had participated in the riot, were returned to and locked in their cells. The inmates who had been in the fights were taken to a special part of the prison called the Special Housing Unit (SHU).

The SHU was a solitary confinement type place where inmates were confined in two man cells of approximately ten feet by eight feet. There were two bunk beds, a sink, toilet and shower in the cell for the inmate's use. By policy, inmates were supposed to be allowed out to a small dog-cage-like recreation area once a day for one hour, but in practice, many of the guards refused to grant even this small privilege.

An inmate was allowed two books per week and very few other personal items. Food was brought to the inmate's door and pushed through a small opening. SHU confinement was meant as punishment and whether or not the boredom and seclusion produced insanity was disregarded by prison staff. SHU was only meant for the most incorrigible of inmates, but it was also used for protective custody inmates who could not be safely placed on the regular prison compound for fear of violence from other inmates.

Because of a lack of an effective system within the BOP for dealing with inmates who had been government witnesses, or who had child molestation charges, they were forced to wait out their time confined to SHU in solitary confinement for years at a time in some instances. When these inmates were eventually released, the boredom and seclusion had caused irreparable damage in some cases.

Whenever an inmate violated the rules, they could also be sent to SHU for short periods of time- sometimes for as little as a couple weeks; sometimes a couple of months. In some prisons the staff and guards tried to minimize the amount of time that an inmate was forced to endure in seclusion, others used the SHU for petty torment against inmates who had only marginally violated the rules. I knew that I never wanted to be placed in SHU, but I was told that it was only a matter of time before I was placed there for some infraction.

We remained on lock-down in our cells for over a week due to the intensity and simmering feuds over the riot. When we were finally released off lock-down, thankfully no further violence occurred and our lives returned to our normal routines soon after that.

In March of 2006, I was called to the Lieutenant's Office to meet with the Special Investigative Service (SIS). The guards who were assigned to work as SIS Agents investigated crimes that occurred within the prison. They most often handled situations where illegal drugs were found on an inmate or in an inmate's cell.

Even though I had never been involved in any drug dealings, I quickly learned that in most cases, heroin and marijuana were more easily obtained in prison than they were on the streets. SIS investigated those cases, among other things. When an inmate was called to meet with the SIS, it usually meant trouble.

Scared and nervous that I had done something wrong or was being fingered for something I didn't do, I prepared to meet with the SIS with a sense of dread. I had done my best to behave myself and follow the rules at Yazoo City, but I had seen numerous other inmates get caught up in trouble that they neither instigated, nor were a part of.

When I finally met the SIS Lieutenant, he merely informed me that I had a family relative who would be beginning work at the federal prison soon and that because of the connection, I could no longer remain at Yazoo City. I would have to be transferred to another facility.

If the latest turn of events was as unwelcome as it sounded, it was also confusing as hell. To my knowledge, I had no clue of any relative who had been trying to get hired at the federal prison and since the SIS Lieutenant refused to tell me who it was, I was at a total loss- neither Meme, my mother, nor my grandparents had any clue either.

Even while we couldn't discover who this family relative was, the news that I would be transferred to another prison was mortifying to me. I had fully adjusted to being at Yazoo and was somewhat happy there. I had made a few friends and felt as comfortable as was possible inside a prison. I was not looking forward to being moved at all.

Several weeks later Meme informed me that she had located this long lost relative who was now causing me so much strife. A distant fourth or fifth cousin, who had married into the Atwood family on a totally separate side than my immediate family, had been hired at the Yazoo City prison and by some unknown knowledge claimed me as a relative currently incarcerated at the prison.

I had never even heard of this relative, even though I had always kept detailed listings of everyone in my family tree. But regardless of the lack of closeness in kinship, the BOP considered this a potential danger and ordered my transfer away from Yazoo. Using their logic and measurements of family kinship, there were probably a good many guards there that could have claimed me as an outlaw cousin, too.

The other closest federal prisons near to Vicksburg would have been the mediums at Memphis and Forrest City, Arkansas. There were also prisons in Pollock, Louisiana and Talladega, Alabama within semi-close driving distance. Even though I wasn't being given a choice in the matter, I asked that they transfer me somewhere close to home.

Most people have the presumption that once a inmate is sent to a federal prison, that is where he will remain for the duration of his sentence. Except in rare cases, this is not accurate. The BOP and U.S. Marshal's Service spend over two hundred million dollars ($200,000,000) a year transporting inmates between county jails and federal prisons.

It became my experience that the BOP would transport an average inmate two or three times during that inmate's stint in the federal prison system. Some inmates, such as myself, would be transferred multiple times. In almost all cases, these transfers were the result of either a lowering or raising, of an inmate's custody level, or an inmate's inability to remain on a specific compound because of a danger that is posed to him by the other inmates. Some transfers though, were a waste of time, energy and most importantly, taxpayer's dollars. I believed my transfer from Yazoo City was a waste of money.

The BOP also runs a secret and unofficial program designed to punish inmates who are consistent discipline problems or who file multiple and frivolous lawsuits against the prisons. This program is called "diesel therapy". It consists of putting shackled inmates on a Greyhound-type prison bus and literally driving around for weeks and months at a time without any particular destination.

Inmates are housed overnight in county jails or prisons. Their involuntary travels could take them anywhere from the east to west coast, Florida to Washington. They remain unable to communicate with their family or attorneys. It is a system designed to break inmates from bad behavior. Even though the lawsuits filed by many of the inmates receiving diesel therapy might seem trivial, to the inmates themselves they are not. But this is a method used by the government to prevent lawsuits of that nature.

Even though the conditions in the federal prisons were a thousand times better than what I had endured in the Madison County Jail, many of the inmates had the lucky exception to not having been placed in a jail like the MCDC. I could understand how they could view the conditions in the feds as unsatisfactory; however, unless they had served time in a hellhole like MCDC, than they could never grasp what a true torment prison could be.

As I waited on my transfer I could only imagine what awaited me at my next facility. Several inmates had told me that Yazoo City was a "bad" prison. They complained because there were no microwaves to cook with, the cell layout was wrong, the guards were too strict, the food atrocious, and the warden a piece of shit. I, however, found everything to still be better than what I had come from and therefore didn't complain.

The warden at Yazoo City was a woman named Constance Reese. Her greatest claim to fame was not protecting a former border patrol agent, who had been convicted of shooting an illegal drug smuggler and then lying about it to investigators, from being severely beaten and almost killed by inmates at the prison.

Ignacio Ramos and his partner had been convicted in federal court and sentenced to more than a decade in prison. Ramos arrived at the medium security prison at Yazoo City and was allowed by the warden to enter the regular prison compound instead of going to protective custody, even though the warden knew of specific threats to his life from other inmates.

As a result, a huge national outcry occurred demanding the resignation of Warden Reese and other administration officials at Yazoo City. Bill O'Reilly on his Fox News Show demanded the removal of Warden Reese after evidence surfaced that not only was Ignacio Ramos not protected, but after being viciously assaulted he was denied medical treatment for several days. Bill O'Reilly also produced a prison official who claimed that Warden Reese had lost control of the prison and that the inmates were in figurative control.

Although Bill O'Reilly may have been using some hyperbole in his criticism of Warden Reese and the BOP officials, I came to discover throughout my five years in the prison system that the BOP does in some ways cater to certain segments of the inmate population in order to maintain control of the prison. I'll cover some of those instances in later chapters.

However, during my time at Yazoo City, I saw very few instances of what was described by Bill O'Reilly on Fox News. Granted, I understand that prison conditions changed considerably after I was gone, but while I was there, things were fairly calm and orderly.

On May 15th, 2006, my transfer was approved and I was moved to the medium security prison in Memphis, Tennessee.

# CHAPTER FORTY-FOUR

What Yazoo City was, Memphis FCI was not. Upon arriving I could tell that this was a different type place. I had left Yazoo City early on the morning of May 15$^{th}$, 2006 and was driven along with a dozen more inmates to the airport again in Memphis. Upon arriving I was immediately taken off the Yazoo bus and placed on the Memphis bus. After all the inmates had been transferred around from the plane and buses, we left and headed toward the prison.

After being processed through the receiving and discharge part of the prison, I was given a bed roll and assigned to a prison unit. Instead of only having one cell mate though, I had two. The bunk beds inside the cells were stacked three high. There were also, much to my surprise, a porcelain toilet and sink much like we have in our homes. This was a big improvement over the cold, hard stainless steel toilets and sinks I'd had in the county jails and at Yazoo.

At the time, Memphis had a very small Mexican inmate population- there were probably fewer than forty Hispanics on the entire compound. The demographics were instead broken down mostly by the blacks and whites. There were also very few gang members there except Vice Lords and Gangster Disciples. Immediately I could tell that this was a much more laid back prison than Yazoo. There just was not a lot of tension between the inmates.

Memphis had a better commissary and a wider selection of food and hygiene items for the inmates to choose from. There were also several microwaves and a ice machine in the units. I was able to order small pizza kits, pasta, and numerous other things off the commissary once a week. With the wider selection of things to order and cook, I stopped going to the prison chow hall except for lunch. I just preferred to cook my own meals in my unit.

Softball season had just started at the prison and I was invited to join my unit's team and play against other unit's teams in the afternoon. I had not played baseball in several years and had never played softball, but I was a quick learner and became very good at it.

Memphis also had pool tables, a leather and paint shop, and work-out equipment. The BOP had stopped allowing weights and upper body work-out equipment in the newer prisons, but since Memphis had had the weights prior to that rule, they were allowed to keep them. One of the favorite things for inmates to do is work out their bodies, and from the looks of many inmates at Memphis, they weren't slacking.

There was a larger group of gay inmates on the compound at Memphis than I had seen at Yazoo and although I wasn't ready to come out of the closet, I did notice that no one ever bothered them. They were able to live comfortably on the compound with little or no harassment from other inmates.

A person has to understand that there are two types of gay men on a prison compound. The first, and most common, are the transvestites. These are gay men who purposefully look, act and carry themselves as women. They are called different names in prison such as punks, T-girls, trannies, and prison bitches. I refer to them as trannies.

Most trannies are able to obtain make-up from some of the female guards. Others use candy products like Skittles to produce make-up. These trannies usually wear their prison issue clothing altered and tight on their bodies to project a more feminine appearance. In addition to wearing make-up, they also grow their nails out and wear their hair long. They enjoy looking and acting like women and they sometimes assume that role permanently.

The other type of gay men in prison are what I would classify myself as- normal, straight-acting, and like most of the other inmates. Some of these straight-acting gay guys were out about being gay, others were not, and chose to remain in the closet.

Contrary to popular belief and stereotypes, rape and sexual assault is not common within the BOP. Perhaps in the past it has been, but the BOP has an official zero tolerance policy for sexual assault and it is strictly enforced.

The best way I can explain it is like this: there are so many openly gay inmates who will freely and openly have sex with other inmates, that there is no point in raping someone. Sex is very easy to get in prison. If you do commit a sexual assault, the penalty is extremely stiff and usually results in you being confined to solitary confinement for several years and having an additional ten or twenty years added to your sentence. It's just not worth it.

What one will see on occasion is a "press game". A press game is where one inmate uses intimidation and scare tactics to get another inmate to have sex. This most often occurs when an extremely effeminate inmate first comes into prison and is scared, naïve and unsure of their self-confidence. Feeling afraid, they are subjected to other inmates offering them protection in return for sex. Sometimes they will succumb to this press game and agree to submit themselves to another inmate, although this is not very common.

Unfortunately, homophobia is more prevalent in prison than a person might realize. Even though most of the gays were left alone and tolerated, there were certain instances where they were not. Many inmates would not want to be a cell mate with a gay guy because of the innuendos and jokes that they have to endure from other inmates accusing them of having sex with their cell mate. Some don't care. It just depends on the person.

After I finally came out about being gay, I had numerous inmates approach and offer me sex, however, they were extremely discreet about it and wanted it to remain a total secret. It became my experience that sexuality in prison is very fluid. I ran across very few guys who would not consent to participate in some type of sexual act with another guy. Granted, the extent of their involvement usually just meant getting a quick blow job, but others would go further than that, provided of course that there was not any chance of getting caught.

Just about in all cases, guys in prison would consent to doing something sexual with another guy as long as they felt no one would ever find out. It was almost comical the cloak and dagger games that these inmates would play back and forth. On the one hand they had the burning desire for some type of sexual contact, but on the other, the paranoid fear of being caught and ridiculed by the other inmates. It's like the old adage about the scooter- everyone wants to have fun riding it, but no one wants to get caught driving one. Prison sex was almost the same way.

The psychology of heterosexual men also played a part in prison sex, too. Because the majority of men in prison are heterosexual and have not had any desire to sleep with other men prior to coming to prison, their attractions don't range much past the gay guys in prison who look and act like women- the trannies. Because these guys are technically straight, they feel it is more acceptable to have sex with something that looks and acts like a woman, since that is normally what they would be attracted to.

Straight-acting, masculine gay guys, like myself were sometimes turned down and ignored in prison because we didn't look and act like women. These straight guys only wanted something feminine and girly because that's what they were normally drawn to. It made for interesting observation, especially to someone like me who was grappling with coming to terms still with my own sexuality.

There were times when some inmates would question whether I was gay or not. I always claimed to be straight and never volunteered my sexuality, but I was beginning to feel like that needed to change.

After being at Memphis for a month, I met and became friends with another inmate named Phillip Kerr. Although I didn't know for sure that he was gay, I had my suspicions. Phillip was from Mobile, Alabama and had been convicted of kidnapping, carjacking, and numerous gun crimes when he was seventeen years old. Feeling zero compassion for his young age and circumstances, a federal judge had sentenced him to twenty-five years in prison.

Phillip had been sent to one of the most violent maximum security prisons to start his time, but slowly worked his way down to a medium. He was twenty-seven when we first met and had been at Memphis for several years. He carried the scars of someone who had fought his way through many battles, but deep inside I could tell that Phillip was a good person.

We quickly became good friends and soon began spending all our free time together. Phillip lived in one of the better units on the compound and only had one cell mate who was usually never there. Even though it was against the rules, I was able to sneak over to Phillip's cell and hang out there with him. The more we were together, the more I suspected that Phillip was gay.

Finally building the nerve to tell him, and hoping it wouldn't ruin our friendship, I took a chance and revealed to Phillip that I was gay. Much to my surprise, Phillip told me that he already knew and that while he didn't consider himself gay, he occasionally messed around with other guys himself. He went on to explain that he still felt attractions to girls and wanted to marry and have kids when he got out of prison, but that he could also have fun having sex with guys.

Phillip and I began a very close and very intense relationship that day in June, 2006. I had not had sex in over two years, since before I was arrested, and I had never been very close to anyone while I was locked up in prison. Even though our circumstances and surroundings prevented us from doing many things that I would have liked to have done, we were able to continue having a regular and wonderful sex life.

When we weren't able to spend time by ourselves in his cell, we exercised together, played handball and softball, cooked for each other, and hung out as much as possible. For the first time since getting arrested, I was beginning to be able to accept my circumstances and achieve some level of happiness that I was depending on to get me through the next few years of my incarceration.

The summer of 2006 went by quicker than any other time I had so far done. If it's possible for someone to understand, it was like living in a fairy tale within prison. My family was still coming to visit as much as possible, although it wasn't every weekend, and we were even able to get my mom on Phillip's visiting list so that he was able to come out and meet my family and spend some time outside of the prison environment.

It was the happiest time that I ever did during my five years of incarceration. Again, it's hard for a person to understand who hasn't been in my shoes, but when you are incarcerated, you crave some type of close connection to another person. I had that close connection with Phillip and I fell very much in love with him.

In hindsight it was wrong and foolish to do. I knew that nothing could ever come of our relationship outside of the prison walls, but I was living in the moment, and at that time I felt that nothing could come between us. As the summer wore on though, storm clouds hung on the horizon, and our fairy tale relationship, for which I cared so much about, was about to be tested.

# CHAPTER FORTY-FIVE

Shortly before Labor Day weekend, a new inmate appeared on the compound. His name was Darwyn Horey and he was a very high-up leader of the Vice Lord's prison gang. Although I never knew exactly what rank he held, several people later told me that he was one of top five leaders in the entire organization.

Normally I would not be concerned with who-is-who of the prison gangs, but this guy was trouble. I could tell from looking at him that he meant no good and I was determined to avoid him. Unfortunately, Darwyn Horey was one of the few overt sexual predators I ran across in prison and he decided to target me.

At first, he would only make crude sexual comments about making me his prison bitch. Other times he would purposefully single me out and make statements to the effect that he was going to rape me.

Since Phillip and I had begun our relationship, we had eased our secrecy and many people had begun to discover that we were both gay and in some sort of relationship together. For the most part, no one treated me any differently. It wasn't really discussed and very few people asked me about it, but when they did, I told them the truth.

That was the first time I began to accept the fact that I was gay and not be ashamed about it. However, it drew heat on me and opened me up to sexual advances from other inmates, even though they knew Phillip and I were together. This openness drew the attention of Darwyn Horey and it was the first consequence of my decision to be open about being gay in prison.

When my denials of his sexual advances were not sufficient to thwart his behavior, I got myself into a situation that I was unprepared to deal with. On the first hand, I could not go to the guards with my problem. The guard's solution would have been to lock both of us in the SHU- him for punishment, and me for protective custody. The other Vice Lords would not have allowed me to remain on the compound if I was the one responsible for getting their shot-caller thrown in the SHU.

If I were to physically fight with this predator, I would probably not only lose, but I would still have to go to the SHU and be transferred to another prison. I was in a dire predicament and there was no easy solution. Phillip tried to intervene and protect me, but Darwyn Horey was set on one thing, and that was fucking me in the ass- something that I would never allow to happen.

I was finally given an ultimatum. Darwyn Horey had involved the rest of his Vice Lord gang members to get them to pressure Phillip and me to leave the compound and check into protective custody. Darwyn Horey had decided that since he couldn't pressure me into having sex with him, and since he was not willing to risk an actual rape charge, that he would just scare Phillip and I into leaving the compound like cowards.

Faced with an ultimate decision, and not willing to put up with any more bullshit from Darwyn Horey, and realizing there was no way to avoid having to leave the compound, Phillip and I decided to exact revenge and punish Darwyn Horey.

We basically had three choices. We could either stay on the compound and wake up one morning with three or four Vice Lord gang members beating the shit out of us in our cells; we could go to the guards and ask to be placed in protective custody, which meant staying in the SHU for several months until we could get transferred to another prison; or we could execute a surprise attack on Darwyn Horey and beat the shit out of him. Either way, it was apparent that Phillip and I were going to have to leave the Memphis prison. The manner in which we did so was up to us.

Getting our asses beat was not a very desirable alternative. Checking into protective custody was a weak and cowardly move and something that would follow an inmate's reputation around no matter what prison he went to. Beating the shit out of Darwyn Horey before leaving the compound would insure we had the respect of the other inmates. A man's reputation is very important in prison and although I had wanted to avoid any type of trouble, Darwyn Horey had made me so furious, that I was ready to exact a vicious punishment on him.

Every day Darwyn Horey played pool in the pool hall on the recreation yard. Most of the time, none of his other gang members were around. Phillip and I decided that this would be the best time to jump him. Phillip had had to fight and claw his way through the prison system before. He never had any second thoughts about picking up a prison shank and stabbing another inmate.

Even though I was willing to do anything that Phillip wanted me to, he would not allow me to carry a shank to stab Darwyn Horey. Stabbing another inmate could sometimes result in getting extra time added to your sentence and that's not something Phillip wanted to risk for me. Instead, I got a padlock, hooked it onto a belt so that I could swing it, and put it in my pocket. Phillip carried a ice pick shank that had been constructed out of steel and duct tape. As he made clear, he had nothing to lose.

We caught Darwyn Horey in the pool hall just as we

expected. Thankfully, few other inmates were around. Before he realized we were there, Phillip had grabbed a pool stick and knocked the shit out of him in the head. Darwyn Horey went down and never got up again. When we got finished, Darwyn Horey had been stabbed, beat severely, and was laying in a puddle of blood.

We discarded our weapons and immediately went to the Lieutenant's Office and turned ourselves in. Unbeknownst to what he was doing, Phillip took full credit for the assault and told the guards that I had nothing to do with it. Before I could protest, Phillip told me to shut up and not say anything.

As the guards escorted us towards the SHU, I watched as they wheeled Darwyn Horey into the infirmary. The guards knew that Darwyn Horey was a sexual predator and they knew that sooner or later he would get hurt because of it. Even though they were required to properly investigate the assault, I truly felt like they did so in a manner to minimize the consequences to Phillip and me.

Once we were in the SHU part of the prison, the guards separated Phillip and me and placed us in different cells. This was an extremely disturbing turn of events because I had assumed that we would be able to stay together. I had never been separated from Phillip more than overnight during the past three months and I was very upset to be stuck in a ten foot by eight foot cell, twenty-four hours a day and unable to see or talk to him. The guards merely informed me that I would have to seek approval from the SHU Lieutenant to get placed in the same cell with Phillip.

Once placed in the SHU, my life became mundane and boring. Meme and my mom regularly sent books through the mail, and I had a radio to listen to, but doing time in solitary confinement is tough. I was told that I would be confined there for several months while I waited on the SIS agents to finish their investigation and get me transferred to another prison.

Because Phillip and I had assaulted a high-up leader of the Vice Lord's gang, we would have to be sent to a prison that didn't have any members on the compound or else we would be in danger. Unfortunately, the majority of prisons that do not have Vice Lords on the compound are on the east coast and I was not looking forward to getting transferred so far away from home.

What was more irritating was the fact that the SHU Lieutenant had been blowing smoke up my ass for over a month about getting Phillip and me moved into the same cell together. The guards knew that he and I were gay and they were reluctant to put us together because of their personal prejudices against homosexuals. They willingly allowed inmates to choose cellmates and pick who to live with in the SHU, but they would not accommodate us.

I was becoming frustrated and aggravated at the circumstances I was in. After a two-month-long investigation, the SIS agents had decided not to charge Phillip or me with the assault on Darwyn Horey. They instead were transferring us to different prisons without further punishment, but wouldn't tell us where we were going. I had not seen Phillip or been able to talk to him since the day we came to the SHU. I missed him and I was tired of the SHU Lieutenant and guards giving me the run-around.

Shortly before Thanksgiving, I had finally had enough. There are several things which an inmate can do to aggravate the guards in SHU. One of them is flood their cells by overflowing the toilet. This usually forces the guards to shut everything down and clean up the mess. It's petty behavior, but one of the few weapons available to an inmate confined in SHU.

Feeling that I was being played and lied to by the guards, I decided to act out in any way possible and cause so much chaos that they would either get tired of it and give-in to letting Phillip and me cell together or hurry up and transfer me to another prison.

I began by sealing my door frame with toilet tissue. I next tore dozens of magazines into small strips of paper. When I was ready, I jammed my toilet and let it overflow. Once the toilet was stuck, it overflowed with hundreds of gallons of water. I let it overflow for almost an hour and since the door frame had been sealed, the water just backed up and built inside my cell. After that hour, I had water up to my knees.

When I thought that the cell was sufficiently flooded, I pulled out the seal and watched as all that water and torn up magazines flooded into the hallway and down the range towards the guard's offices and computer equipment. The strips of paper clogged the drains in the hallway and the water had nowhere to go except towards the guards.

The guards quickly responded but there wasn't much they could do. I was already locked in a cell twenty-four hours a day. I had little or no privileges and I was separated from Phillip. When the guards got to my cell, I made it clear that from then on I was going to act as big of a fool and idiot as I could until they put Phillip and me together in the same cell.

I had also decided to start a hunger strike if flooding the cell didn't produce the right results. This was the first time in my life that I had acted in such a way toward other human beings, but I felt that all my dignity had been stripped from me and I had nothing to lose. I missed Phillip and I was determined to do whatever I had to in order to be with him again. The thought of not seeing him again had really depressed me.

The guards turned off my water and I was unable to take a shower or flush the toilet for several days, but I had started a hunger strike and I was going to stay on it until they let me see Phillip.

On the eighth day of my hunger strike the assistant warden at Memphis came to see me. Apparently no one had told him *why* I was acting a fool, causing chaos and on a hunger strike. When I told him that I only wanted to be celled with Phillip or be able to at least see him, the assistant warden was willing to work with me.

After flooding the cell multiple times, beating on the door nonstop, breaking out the windows, popping the sprinklers, going on a hunger strike and otherwise acting like a total heathen, I was finally getting somewhere. Although the assistant warden would not allow Phillip and me to cell together, he did order the SHU Lieutenant to allow us to be taken out of our cells every day and placed in a recreation cage together.

The recreation areas were more like small dog cages that an inmate barely had enough room to lay down and do push-ups in, but every day Phillip and I went out and sat down and talked. It was better than not being able to see each other at all, and although I would have preferred to be able to lay in bed with him and cuddle at night, getting to see and talk to him every day was good enough for the circumstances we were under.

We continued to do this every day as we waited for our transfers to process through the system. Right after Christmas I was told by my case manager that I was being transferred to the federal prison in Ray Brook, New York. Phillip was going to be transferred to the federal prison in Big Sandy, Kentucky.

I knew that they would probably send me far away, but I had no idea that they would send me to upstate New York, to a small federal prison that no one had ever heard of. Facing the prospect of leaving Phillip and getting shipped thousands of miles away from my family made for a horrible New Year holiday, but as I waited, I was comforted by the fact that I had finished another year of prison and only had two more to go.

# CHAPTER FORTY-SIX

On January 4th, 2007, the guards woke me early in the morning. I was taken from my SHU cell and walked to the receiving and discharge area of the prison. Unfortunately, Phillip was not being transferred at the same time as me so I didn't get to see him before I left.

Once at R&D, I was stripped searched, put in new prison clothes, shackled and loaded onto another transport bus. The guards then drove me and another dozen inmates to the airport. We were put on the airplane by the U.S. Marshals and off we went. Sometime later, we landed at the Atlanta airport in Georgia.

When the guards took us off the airplane at the airport, they loaded us on more transport buses and drove us a short distance to the maximum security United States Penitentiary. USP Atlanta was one of the oldest federal prisons still in existence and had had such famous inmate guests there as Al Capone. It was known for being a violent, dangerous, filthy, disgusting place and unfortunately, inmates were housed there sometimes while being transported to different prisons on the east coast.

Knowing that I was being sent to Ray Brook in upstate New York, I didn't expect to stay more than a few days at Atlanta USP before catching another flight or bus somewhere else.

It took several hours for the guards to get us processed, but once we were finished we were allowed to go to our cells to sleep. The inmates who were being transported through the prison were kept separate from the inmates who were actually doing time at the prison. The area where they kept us, was for the most part, locked down. We were allowed out of our cells for a few hours a day to shower, watch television, make phone calls home and grab some books or magazines off the book cart.

Regardless of the violence and chaos that raged on the compound of the regular part of the prison, the transport area was fairly calm and laid back. Most inmates just wanted to sleep and relax while waiting for their turn to catch the next bus or flight out of there.

After four nights at Atlanta USP, I was finally called out early one morning and put back on the U.S. Marshal's airplane. The next stop for me was the airport at Harrisburg, Pennsylvania. Several other inmates and I were met there by a bus from the maximum security prison at Lewisburg, Pennsylvania.

Even though it was below freezing and snow was beginning to fall, we were left outside, under the wing of the aircraft for almost thirty minutes before all the inmates had been shuffled between and around the buses and airplane. It was a scene that was very similar to what always occurred at the Memphis airport when I was transferred through there.

Snot freezing on my face, shivering uncontrollably, and shackled down more tightly than normal, I trudged onto the Lewisburg bus hoping for better tidings. I had heard good things about Ray Brook prison and I was anxious to get through Lewisburg as quick as possibly.

# INTO HELL I RODE

It was a three hour drive from the Harrisburg airport to Lewisburg USP and by the time we got there, all of the inmates were tired, hungry and ready to sleep. After we had pulled into the prison compound and the doors of the bus opened, my name was the first to be called to exit. Soon we were all processed and sent to a dormitory-type barracks. Instead of individual two-man cells, it was all open area with bunk beds down the middle. There was no privacy and little personal space. As I picked a bunk and made my bed, I was thankful for not having to stay there long.

My stay at Lewisburg was fairly quiet. There was one television that had to be shared by over a hundred inmates, but everyone was fairly reasonable in splitting up the time between the whites, blacks, and Mexicans. There wasn't a phone and no way to write letters, but I assumed I would be at Ray Brook soon enough and be able to contact my family.

On the morning of January 11th, 2007, after three nights, I left Lewisburg USP on another transport bus and began the long ride to upstate New York. It was an eight-hour ride and it was late afternoon by the time we arrived at the prison. We had traveled through some of the most beautiful parts of the country that I had ever seen. The snow was thick on the ground and most of the lakes were frozen over, but I had never seen that part of the United States before and it thoroughly impressed me.

Ray Brook prison impressed me as well. It had been built in the late 1970's and before it became a prison, it was used to house many of the Olympic athletes in the 1980 Winter Olympics. It was very uniquely built and situated on the side of a mountain. The snow covered everything in sight but the surrounding views were magnificent.

I had heard nothing but good things about Ray Brook and as I entered the prison I didn't feel quite so bad about being so far away from home. It took the guards most of the evening to get us processed and it was late at night before we were turned loose onto the compound. I was assigned to Delaware Unit and as I entered my new home I was quickly welcomed by several inmates and assisted in finding my new cell.

My new cellmate was a bank robber from South Carolina

who was doing a twenty-five year sentence. He had been locked up since the early nineties and was nearing his release date when we first met. His name was Wilton Julian and he would soon become one of my best friends and by far the best cellmate I ever had during my five years of incarceration.

Once Wilton and I discovered our mutual love of history and southern culture, we quickly became inseparable. Within the first few days of arriving at Ray Brook, Wilton had shown me the ropes and explained how everything worked.

Ray Brook consisted of mostly inmates from the New England states and New York City. Most of the white inmates were from Boston and compared to inmates from which I had been doing time with in the South, were totally different. There were no Aryan white supremacists, and for the most part were not any gangs there, period. The Hell's Angels were the only white gang at the prison and they seemed to remain to themselves and purposefully did not maintain a big presence on the compound.

There were a large number of Mexicans at Ray Brook, but the vast majority were poor immigrants who had had the misfortune of getting caught in the United States one too many times. Even though some had been involved in the drug trade, many were not criminals at all. It surprised me the number of Mexican inmates there who had been given four or five years, simply for entering the country illegally.

As far as the blacks were concerned, there were few gang members there. Mostly, the black inmates grouped together by geographic location. New York City blacks in one group, Washington, D.C. blacks in another. I quickly learned that gang activity was not tolerated at Ray Brook like it was at other prisons.

The warden was a woman named Deborah Schult. She had been a prison psychologist most of her career and Ray Brook was the first prison where she would be a full warden. I had never heard of her before, but from what I could tell, she was doing a very good job of operating the prison.

My case manager was Michelle Picerno. Out of all the staff members and case managers that I had come in contact with during my incarceration, Mrs. Picerno and my unit staff at Ray Brook were a par above excellence. There was not a lot that Mrs. Picerno could do for me, but when I needed attorney phone calls, or just needed someone to talk to about my case, she was always willing to listen.

Another case manager, Julie Bedore, worked on my case some and was astounded at the reasons for my prosecution. Even though Mrs. Bedore and Mrs. Picerno never understood the reasons for why I was in prison, they had a job to complete, but they never treated me like a sub-human. Except in rare cases from individual guards, I was always treated with respect and dignity at Ray Brook.

Wilton introduced me to most of the inmates in our unit and several from other units as well. There were very, very few guys from the southern states at Ray Brook, but even though I was thousands of miles from home, many of the inmates there welcomed me like I was a home-boy.

About a week after I'd arrived there, I was in the lunch room and was approached by the shot-caller for the Hell's Angels. Mark Christian was the stereotypical biker. Muscular, ponytail and tattoos all over his body, he was an imposing figure. When he called me by name and asked for me to get up and go speak with him, I was terribly frightened. I had no clue what had prompted him to want to talk with me, but I had no choice but to go with him. What was worse was that everyone in the chow hall was watching us.

Mark pulled me over to a corner and after introducing himself and telling me who he was, asked if I had stabbed a Vice Lord when I was at Memphis. Unprepared for having had the news travel so fast, and unable to feign a lie, I admitted that yes, I had stabbed a Vice Lord in a fight. I didn't feel it proper or necessary to go into the exact details of who did the stabbing and who used the lock and belt, but felt that whatever Mark was going do next wasn't based on the exact details either.

Much to my surprise though, Mark explained that I had stabbed a personal enemy of the Hell's Angels and that the Vice Lords and Hell's Angels had been enemies on the streets, and in prison, for years. Mark went on to explain that Darwyn Horey had a "hit" out on him from the Angels and that I had accomplished more than they'd been able to do in years.

Shaking my hand, and having a good laugh at the obvious relief on my face, Mark went on to tell me that even though Ray Brook was a laid back compound, if I had any problems, that I was to let him know and he would handle it for me. Mark went on to spread the word that I was not to be messed with and that I was under the protection of the Angels for the rest of my stay at Ray Brook.

Before accepting his generous offer, I felt it was important to first inform him that I was gay. I had made up my mind not to remain in the closet about being gay any longer, and I felt it was something I should make clear to Mark and the other Hell's Angels before they took on the responsibility of looking out for me.

Surprised at first, Mark sat in disbelief for a moment and then told me that it didn't matter. Gay or not, they respected me for what I had done in Memphis and for how I was upfront and honest with people at Ray Brook. I soon came to learn that guys from the east coast don't care as much about another inmate's sexuality as the inmates from the South had. It was a favor from Mark and his Angel's that I greatly appreciated.

# CHAPTER FORTY-SEVEN

I quickly adjusted to life at my new prison and time began to pass quickly. I had never been in such cold weather before and living in an environment that far north took some adjustments. On many days the wind chill was twenty below zero and the snow would fall so hard and fast that you could barely see in front of you. It was not uncommon to have snow drifts over ten feet high.

The prison had an indoor hockey team that played in the gym every Sunday afternoon. Even though I had never played hockey before, and didn't know a thing about it, I was invited to join. We didn't have pads or any protection, but we played rough anyway. It wasn't long before the guards began to question me about the bruises and cuts, but the recreation staff always vouched that I had received them playing hockey.

Even though I was out about being gay, it didn't prevent

me from participating in the same sports as the other inmates. I was treated fairly and given every chance to play and participate. Besides hockey, we also played softball, handball, racquetball and tennis. The recreation area had movies that could be checked-out and watched, weights and work-out equipment, and numerous other things to stay busy.

While at Ray Brook I didn't have to work at a prison job, but instead spent my time on the recreation yard, in the library reading books or watching television. I slept every day until around ten, had a shower, went to each lunch and then spent the rest of the afternoons and evenings doing as I wanted. There were few fights, few problems and less trouble.

The commissary was wonderful and many times I never went to the chow hall. I stayed in the unit and cooked lunch and dinner for Wilton and me. As I began to approach the point in my sentence where I had eighteen months left before release, Mrs. Picerno and Mrs. Bedore began setting me up in pre-release classes. Even though I knew how to balance a checkbook, manage money and deal with the chores of life, I was still required to attend and complete the classes mandated by the BOP prior to release.

During the summer of 2007, I was surprised to discover that the temperature never rose above eighty degrees. Ray Brook did not have air conditioning in it like the other prisons, but it wasn't needed. We could partially open the windows in our cells and it was cool enough at night to lay under the covers on our bunks.

One time, Wilton and I decided to make some homemade ice cream with ingredients we had been able to steal from the prison's kitchen. We put our cream in clean, empty peanut butter jars, tightened the lids and placed them all in a large five gallon bucket. We then added lots of ice and salt, placed the lid on top, wrapped blankets around the bucket for insulation and spun it around for an hour. The cream froze perfectly and provided us with some delicious refreshments.

Meme and my mother came to visit in the early summer too. They flew to Albany, New York, rented a car and came to spend the weekend. They visited me Friday, Saturday and Sunday before going back to Mississippi that following Monday. I had not seen them in over six months- the last time was shortly before I left Memphis, and it was a bittersweet reunion. It was very hard seeing them go on Sunday afternoon when the visit was over, but I was brightened by the knowledge that my Mamaw and Papaw would be coming a few weeks later for a visit as well.

Later in the summer, my Uncle Randy, Aunt Ludie, and my cousins Scott and John Wesley, vacationed in the Adirondack Mountains and came to visit me, too. It was the first time they had ever been inside a prison and I was a little hesitant about letting them come see me, but they are good Christian people and wanted to see me regardless of the surroundings.

It was around this time that the United States Congress began to consider a bill in the House of Representatives that would increase the good time for federal prisoners from fifteen percent to thirty percent and bring back a system of parole allowing inmates an opportunity to release earlier for good behavior.

The process currently in place forces an inmate to do eighty-five percent of their sentence before being able to be released. Inmates lose their good-time for serious violations of the rules, however, in most cases, inmates only have a few months to lose and it is not a very effective incentive to encourage good behavior.

Many liberals, few conservatives, several private inmate organizations and the BOP's correctional guard's union, all support an increase in good-time. It has several advantages. First, more good-time encourages better inmate behavior. If an inmate has more to lose, he is less likely to get himself into trouble.

Second, by releasing inmates early who have maintained good behavior in prison, the BOP is able to free up space for the prisoners who deserve to be in prison and whom can't function appropriately on the streets. While I fully believe that there are many inmates who do not deserve to be in prison, I just as strongly believe that there are people who deserve to be in prison and never released.

The good-time system that is in place now leaves little room to differentiate between those reformed inmates and those who will never be contributable members of society. My dear friend, Sonny Breckenridge, will never have a chance at parole or early release under the current laws. A life sentence for him is literally a life sentence. Even though he never hurt anyone, or was caught with any drugs, Sonny was given a life sentence because two convicted drug dealers, who had turned prosecution's witnesses in return for lesser sentences, testified that they had seen Sonny with hundreds of kilos of marijuana and cocaine.

It is an unfair system, but thankfully there are people in Congress who recognize this injustice and are working to repair it. Unfortunately, these congressmen and senators are never able to get the legislation passed that would bring relief to inmates in the BOP. The summer of 2007 was the closest that I have seen the congress come to passing effective legislation, but it was fought and defeated by certain conservative Republicans, who would rather see inmates rot in jail, than be given the opportunity to lead positive lives in the free world.

Senator Joe Biden, who is now our vice president, was able to pass the Second Chance Act in 2007, which helped facilitate an easier transfer from prison to civilian life for inmates, but it shouldn't have stopped there. Comprehensive criminal justice reform is required, across the board, from the courts to the prisons, in order to ensure that defendants are treated justly and have every opportunity for a fair trial, and that those who are convicted are given reasonable sentences and every opportunity to reform themselves and improve their lives while they are incarcerated. That is not happening today.

While at Ray Brook, I became active in supporting numerous organizations such as Families Against Mandatory Minimums (FAMM), The Justice Project, and Citizens United for the Rehabilitation of Errants (CURE). I believe that our justice system is flawed and that it must be reformed to protect the liberty and rights of millions of people. There is no easy path, but allowing inmates more good-time is a wonderful start.

As I look back, my stay at Ray Brook is more easily compared to an extended summer camp than it would be prison. I don't want to leave the reader with the impression that it was easy, it was most certainly not. Any prison is a difficult and depressing environment to live in, but compared to Madison County, Yazoo City, and Memphis, it was a lot better. This mostly had to do with the efficiency and manner in which the warden and staff operated the prison, but it also had a lot to do with the inmates who were there.

Ray Brook was a good prison as far as prisons go. It wasn't a "Club Fed" like many federal prisons used to be, but it was a lot better than most. All of the inmates realized this and strove to maintain good behavior because the alternative was to get sent somewhere else that was most likely worse. I had fun at Ray Brook and I made the most of what it had to offer, but I was still depressed that I was so far from home and unable to see my family on a regular basis.

The BOP attempted to place inmates in prisons as close to the inmate's home as possible, especially when that inmate was nearing his release. Around the first of November, Mrs. Picerno offered to have me transferred to another prison that was closer to Mississippi. It was felt that I should be closer to home since I was about a year from my release date.

The next closest prison to Vicksburg was Forrest City, Arkansas. I knew Forrest City was a gang prison and that the violence level there was high, but I also craved being closer to my family and having them visit me more often. Although Ray Brook was by far a better place, I felt the trouble that inevitably waited at Forrest City would be offset by being able to see my family more.

I agreed with Mrs. Picerno and had her petition the warden and BOP for a transfer to Forrest City. Shortly after Christmas my transfer was approved and I was placed on the list to await transport. On January 11th, 2008, exactly a year to the day after arriving at Ray Brook, I left on the transport bus headed back to Lewisburg USP. Unfortunately, because of snow and bad weather, I was forced to wait with dozens of other inmates at

Lewisburg USP for over a month. When I finally did leave, I was so sick of Lewisburg, I welcomed anything negative Forrest City had to throw my way.

From Lewisburg I was put on the U.S. Marshal's airplane at Harrisburg, Pennsylvania and flown directly to the Federal Transfer Center at Oklahoma City. After four nights at the transfer center, I was put on another transport bus and driven across Oklahoma and Arkansas to the medium security prison at Forrest City. I arrived there determined to do the last year of my sentence the best way I could.

# CHAPTER FORTY-EIGHT

The Forrest City prison was built exactly like the prison in Yazoo City. It was similar in more ways than one. The Aryan Circle, Aryan Nation, and Aryan Brotherhood ran the compound for the whites, and there were a lot of them.

The Mexican Mafia, Aztecas and Texas Syndicate composed the Hispanic gangs, while the Gangsta Disciples, Bloods and Crips were operated by the blacks. There was a large number of non-gang members who practically only ran together because of geographic locations. This included the inmates who were mostly from St. Louis and Dallas.

Almost everyone at Forrest City was part of some gang. About the only ones who weren't gang affiliated were the gay inmates, and there were more on the Forrest City compound than at any other prison I had been to.

The BOP used the prison to house inmates who had

historically been incorrigible and unable to behave themselves. The warden at Forrest City was T.C. Outlaw. We never learned what his initials stood for, but instead just called him "Takes Cock Outlaw". He was the worst warden I had ever experienced during my five years in prison.

Warden Outlaw cared nothing about the inmates, nothing about his staff, and was inefficient in his operations and the manner in which he conducted the business of the prison. Many of the guards had lost confidence in his ability and openly advocated his removal. More lawsuits and complaints were filed on Warden Outlaw than any other federal warden to my knowledge.

It was a sore disappointment to go from having a caring and effective warden like Dr. Schult, to having a reject loser like T.C. Outlaw. My first few days at Forrest City were a rude awakening to what I was normally used too. I soon regretted having made the choice to transfer, regardless of the ability to receive more visits.

Soon after my arrival I received my first visit from my family. It was at this visit that another inmate got caught trying to accept illegal drugs from his visitor. Marijuana and heroin are easier to obtain in prison than they are on the streets. Drugs are usually brought into the prison by two means: either a corrupt guard is working with an inmate and sneaking them in, or an inmate is bringing them in through the visiting room.

Some inmates who do this will secrete small packages of drugs in their rectum. When an inmate leaves the visiting room, he is stripped searched, but the guards never check any of the inmate's inner cavities. It is an effective method of introducing drugs into the prison if the inmate is sharp and knows how to avoid the suspicions of the guards.

Sometimes though, inmates get caught, and it was at my first visit that one of them did. There had been ongoing problems at Forrest City with inmates trying to bring illegal drugs into the institution and apparently this was the final straw. Warden Outlaw immediately terminated all future visits between the inmates and their families and ordered privileges restricted throughout the prison.

With tensions already on edge, the gang members began organizing and plotting a riot. Before the prison staff knew what was happening, more than half the prisoners were actively engaged in destroying parts of the prison and rioting uncontrollably. For my own part, I took it upon myself to join the melee.

What wasn't bolted down was used to break out windows and glass. What would burn was lighted afire. For a very brief time the inmates controlled a large portion of the prison. Although I was taking part, I also realized that we were placing ourselves in a very dangerous position. Without the protection of the officers, it could very easily turn into an opportunity for one sect of inmates to exact revenge on another group for some past petty differences.

Before the riot reached its crescendo, I made a hasty exit and returned to my cell and closed the door. I watched, as soon after, the guards made a return to the compound in their riot gear, with tear gas canisters and rubber bullet guns. Unable to fight back against such weaponry, and choking on the tear gas, all the rioting inmates surrendered and submitted to the commands of the guards.

I was thankful that I had not been gassed and shot with rubber pellets, as many of the other inmates had, but I was also excited to know that I had participated in my first, and what would be my last, prison riot.

After the guards restored order, we were locked in our cells for almost a month while portions of the prison were repaired and the instigators of the riot were confined to SHU before being transferred to a higher security prison. When we were finally released off lock-down, none of the inmates had the willpower to cause further trouble, but fortunately, the warden had returned our visits to us, albeit with some otherwise necessary restrictions.

Other changes were apparent, too. It seemed that Warden Outlaw was more agreeable to the different inmate grievances that they had so long been asking for. The food in the chow hall improved, more items were added to the commissary, and the staff members seemed to work harder to improve the overall conditions of the prison.

One unfortunate outcome of the riot was that it emboldened the different gangs to turn to violence or extortion to seek solutions to their problems. Wishing to avoid a second riot, Warden Outlaw and the administration accommodated the gangs as much as possible. While this tactic might have seemed necessary under the circumstances, in the long run it engendered more problems between the staff and inmates.

I kept a calendar and I regularly counted down the days till my release. I tried as hard as I could to tune out the different problems that plagued all the inmates at Forrest City, but there were times that it became difficult. I did not have the friends and recreational outlets that I did at Ray Brook, and since Phillip in Memphis, I had no desire to become involved in another relationship.

Someone from my family usually came to visit every other weekend, but it was still not as much as I wanted. Meme began suffering more health problems and got into financial trouble my last year of incarceration. We had had to hire an attorney to handle the land and property case with my Aunt June and for three long years it had been working its way through the court system without any resolution.

Aunt June was fighting us tooth and nail over an easement allowing us access to the back forty acres of our property that Meme had placed in my name Christmas of 2003. When Meme had signed that deed over to me, it had ignited a firestorm of jealousy and hate in our family and ultimately lead to Aunt June filing the malicious mischief charge against me shortly before I was arrested by the FBI.

The attorney's fees had mounted and with no end in sight, Meme was struggling to survive. Aunt June had wanted the forty acres for herself and she was determined to either get it, or prevent me and anyone else from ever having it. Recognizing the inevitable outcome, Aunt June was determined to stall and procrastinate on a settlement for as long as possible. Meanwhile,

Meme was forced to continue paying for an attorney that was neither capable, nor willing, to settle or litigate the case in an efficient and quick manner.

I finally interjected myself into the case personally and demanded some type of action. Threatening to fire the attorney, sue him for ineffective assistance of counsel and hire someone else, finally elicited the motivation that he had been lacking for three years.

By the end of the summer, we were able to forcibly obtain an easement across Aunt June's property in order to access the land that I owned. Even though I was still in prison, I was finally able to say that I had beat Aunt June and my grandfather. I quickly had the attorney compose a letter stating my intent to develop my forty acres into a low income trailer park and mail it to my Aunt June and grandfather. Needless to say, it produced the right result.

Shortly thereafter, Aunt June offered to give a large tract of land in the front of the property that she owned, in trade for the back forty acres that I owned. Making the switch was productive for both parties. First off, it united everyone's ownership of different pieces of property into one sect each. Aunt June added the forty acres that bordered her property, and Meme and I added the front acreage to our property that we owned.

Instead of having chessboard type pieces of land, all of the property was now divided into two large sections- one owned by Aunt June and the other owned by Meme and me. Since we had decided to sell the land and house as soon as I was released and move away from there, this ended up being a good deal because it increased the value of our property and made it more accessible.

Negotiating by force and not out of goodwill only engendered more animosity between Aunt June and I. She had always expected to receive all of the land and property from Meme and was furious when she finally learned that that was not to be the case. It only made her more determined to have me prosecuted and forced to do more time in prison.

Over the past few years, I had occasionally tried to force

the Warren County courts to bring me to trial on the malicious mischief case, but they always denied my requests for a speedy trial. Under state law, a defendant is exempted from a right to a speedy trial if he is incarcerated in another jurisdiction. Rather than pay the costs to have me transported from whatever prison I was incarcerated in at the time, the Warren County court merely kept continuing my case.

Shortly before my release I again petitioned the courts for a trial, but it was denied and instead moved to some indeterminate date in the future. I had received a discovery of the evidence that the prosecutors were going to use against me and even they admitted it was meager. I honestly believed that they purposefully denied me a speedy trial while I was incarcerated to avoid the expenses of transporting me and paying for a trial that they did not feel sure of winning.

After Gil Martin had recused himself from prosecuting my case, the Attorney General of the State of Mississippi had appointed a special prosecutor. That prosecutor took one look at the case and decided not to prosecute because of lack of evidence. When he took his decision to my Aunt June and grandfather, they raised so much hell and threatened so many repercussions, that the special prosecutor was forced to continue the case.

I knew that I would eventually have my day in court, I just didn't know when it would be and it was apparent that nothing I could do was ever going to force them to try me before I was released. It was just something I would have to face after I got out of prison.

# CHAPTER FORTY-NINE

As my January 23$^{rd}$, 2009, release date approached, my days became boring, long and mundane. I literally did nothing but sit in my cell and read books, write letters and plan for my future. There were so many uncertainties about what I faced, it was impossible for me to plan anything beyond the first few days of getting out.

I knew I was going back to Vicksburg, I knew I was going to have a house to live in, and I knew that my family was going to be there to support me in any way they could. Meme and I were determined to sell our house and what property we had left and move away from Aunt June and the chaos and turmoil that raged with her, but I was unsure what the next step would be.

I was confused and frightened after almost five years of being inside a correctional institution. For the most part, I always had someone telling me where to go to the bathroom, where to shower, when and where to eat, how to dress, what to do and what not to do. There were always rules to follow and immediate consequences for not adhering to them.

Living in an environment where violence lurked behind every corner made me paranoid and skittish. I constantly had to mind every spoken word, lest I offend someone and be forced to resort to fighting. I had made it through prison fairly unscathed. There were times that I was forced to fight, but thankfully it was usually with an evenly matched opponent and I won.

I had not been stabbed or beat down with a lock on a belt. I had watched untold horrors occur to other inmates for only minor transgressions against other prisoners. Even though the conditions in the federal prisons are sometimes better than in state correctional systems, the violence level can be just as high, if not worse. Murders were not an uncommon thing, and I had seen more than I cared too and I gained many valuable lessons during my incarceration.

I learned that weakness in the face of terror is only an invitation for more aggression. I was forced to learn to stand up for myself and face the possibility of getting hurt, rather than let other inmates take advantage of me. Prisons possess the power to dehumanize good people and turn them into something that is neither positive for themselves or for society after they are released.

Correctional institutions have basically become human warehouses with no incentives for inmates other than to merely survive. There is a problem when this country spends more money to prosecute and imprison its citizens than teach them education in the schools and colleges. We cannot incarcerate ourselves out of all our problems.

In the face of an obvious losing battle with the "war on drugs", we get more laws that ratchet up arrests, punishments and incarceration. We are deceived by the notion that the law will save us from harm. Lady Justice's blindfold does not ensure that everyone will be treated fairly.

We are trying young juveniles as adults in criminal cases and prosecutors are justifying it because these children are supposedly becoming more mature at younger ages and are having to make more important decisions in their lives. But these same prosecutors are very quick to treat them as minors when it suits them to do so. I think of my case in this instance and how Zach Booth was used and manipulated as a minor to persecute me.

As was in my case, few voices will be raised for an unpopular defendant and a politically unacceptable verdict. Our courts have basically become de facto legislatures, creating rules and laws without the consent of the people. The criminal justice system is a sporting event in which the defendant has a sporting chance to evade punishment. Our personal freedoms would be protected if we could voluntarily resolve the problems of society rather than allowing the heavy hand of government to do it for us.

I came to realize that the vast majority of people in prison are incarcerated for drug crimes that otherwise could have been prevented. Poverty and desperation have led many of them to earn money through illegal means. Others have become addicted to drugs and are unable to find effective help. Incarcerating these people, while denying them the ability to solve their economic and social problems, is not the solution.

Thomas Jefferson wrote: "There is a debt of service due from every man to his country, proportioned to the bounties which nature and fortune have measured to him". If everyone who didn't suffer from drug addiction, or financial woes, would contribute something to building this society into a functioning and caring environment, exactly as Jefferson intended us, then desperate people would turn less to illegal behavior and more to self-improvement.

I saw a divine spark in so many different inmates who only needed a second chance. They didn't want a handout; they wanted a hand-up in the world and an opportunity to improve their selves. Unfortunately, because of money shortages and cut-backs, our prison systems are unable to give them that. Instead, they have become warehouses for society's undesirables and crime schools for the criminals.

Most inmates leave prison with nothing more than a few

dollars and a bus ticket home. We expect these people to leave the best crime schools in the country, where they received little or no legitimate training, education or rehabilitation, and become productive, law-abiding citizens. Inevitably, former convicts return home with absolutely nothing to discourage further criminal behavior.

During my five years in prison, I had the opportunity to learn how to counterfeit money, cook methamphetamine, rob banks, forge checks, make moonshine, and venture into numerous other illegal activities. I never had the chance to take college classes, or anything else that would significantly improve and better my life upon release.

Some inmates do not have much to look forward to upon their release. My friend from Ray Brook, Wilton Julian, didn't have anything whatsoever when he was released. No car, no family, no home, and no money. He barely managed to scrape by and sometimes commented how much easier things were in prison. This is the future that many inmates face.

Rather than struggle with finding legitimate employment in an economy that is not friendly to former convicts, many return to drug dealing and other illegal behavior. Our prisons are not preparing inmates for release and their failure to do so is contributing to the criminal recidivism rate. Trying to fix this problem now is going to be expensive; fixing this problem later on is going to be exorbitant.

Thankfully, I knew I had my family and a great support group of friends to help me when I got out. This is not something many inmates have and it's something that I felt privileged for. As the final holidays of my incarceration passed, I began planning the details of my release day.

My mother and Meme wanted a big party with the whole family. I wanted something special too, but within reason. Throughout the entire time of being imprisoned, my mother and I had joked back and forth about having a limousine bring all of the family to pick me up. It was never seriously considered until shortly before January 23$^{rd}$, when it became a logistical problem of getting all of the family to the prison together on my release day. Then it became apparent that a limo would be necessary, rather than taking several individual cars.

The only big thing I wanted to do on the day I was released was eat barbeque in Memphis and spend the weekend there. I left the other details to be worked out by Meme and my mother. They eventually would rent a stretched Hummer limo, and the idea of getting picked up from prison in it was my perfect idea of a final "fuck you" to the prison system.

At eight o'clock in the morning, on January 23$^{rd}$, 2009, the guards pulled me from my cell and took me to the receiving and discharge part of the prison. I was not shackled or treated like a high security inmate. The guards were nonchalant about whatever it was I was doing. My mother had sent in a very nice suit of clothes for me to wear, and for the first time in five years, I put on civilian clothes.

I was asked to sign a few forms, told to report to my probation officer in Jackson, Mississippi within seventy-two hours of being released, given the remaining money I had on my commissary account and walked to the front of the prison. I sat down in the visitor's waiting room and waited on my family.

When the guards saw the huge stretched limo pull into the prison parking lot, they came and got me and walked me through the double sliding doors. I took my first breath of freedom as I headed towards the limo. Before I could get there, the doors swung open and everyone poured out to see me. Through tears, hugs, and laughter, I began the journey to recovery and triumph, and ended the voyage that had taken me through hell, but through which I had survived and persevered.

# EPILOGUE

Shortly after being released from prison, Meme and I sold the house and remaining property we owned and moved to a new house in the northern part of Warren County, but the legal wrangling over land, houses, and property would continue for years.

My battles with the Warren County Sheriff's Office continued to the point of rhetorical stalemate. As this book is going to print, Vicksburg and Warren County are still plagued by judicial and law enforcement corruption. Martin Pace is still the sheriff and still allows his deputies to run rampant. Deep Six is still with the Sheriff's Office and occasionally shoots me information of which I can neither act upon, nor have the desire to publicize.

Gil Martin was defeated for the district attorney's post in

his reelection bid in 2007 by my stepdad's former law partner, Ricky Smith. Many people contributed Gil's defeat to the publication of my expose of his sexual advances towards me. Ricky Smith had tried and failed in 2003 to defeat Gil Martin, and it is my firm belief that he was only able to overcome Gil Martin's support in the community by using the knowledge that Gil was not only gay, but had made those sexual overtures towards me.

The justice court judge, Joe Crevitt, who had been so willing to allow my aunt and grandfather to unethically manipulate him into purposefully trying to keep me in jail, by setting an extortionate amount of bond when I was arrested for the malicious mischief charge, had died. Judge Eddy Woods stepped into his place as the personal executioner and go-to judge for the Atwood family and their legal shenanigans.

Deputies Jay Ghrigsby and Lionel Johnson are no longer employed at the Sheriff's Office and to my knowledge are not involved in law enforcement anymore. Georgia Lynn was fired by the new, incoming district attorney and now is employed at the Humane Society.

Zach Booth was treated as an outcast by his parents after they discovered he was gay. He was forced to seek reparative therapy counseling by his ultra-religious parents, in an effort to change him straight. When that failed, his relationship with his parents deteriorated to the point of open rebellion. He finally left his home and moved to Hattiesburg, Mississippi.

Zach is completely and totally open about being gay, but still heavily resents the FBI outing him. In what was seriously an obvious lack of good judgment on his part, Zach would later be investigated by the same FBI for also having sex with an underage minor, although at the time of this printing he has not been prosecuted.

Zach's right-wing conservative parents, who were so ashamed to have an openly gay son, would themselves bring scandal and embarrassment to their family when it was discovered Zach's mother was having affairs with other men, assaulting her husband, and needing substance abuse counseling for alcoholism. The hypocrisy and double standards of life never cease to amaze me.

Shortly before my release, my friend, Dane Davenport, who was a state trooper, was arrested and charged with child molestation after his wife claimed to have discovered he was gay and had been fondling his stepkids. I firmly believe Dane was innocent and that his wife was only motivated by keeping their vastly acquired sums of money during their divorce, however, that didn't stop the same prosecutors who had been appointed to prosecute my malicious mischief charge, and who were also prosecuting Dane, from offering to dismiss my charge if I agreed to lie and testify against Dane in court.

I had known Dane since I was fourteen or fifteen years old, but he had never been anything but a positive role model in my life. To lie under oath and help convict a man that I knew to be innocent went against everything that I believed in.

After four different trials, two hung juries and two not guilty verdicts, Dane was able to remain out of prison and prove that in some cases, the justice system works and the wrongly accused can achieve vindication in this tainted criminal justice system.

For my failure to lie and fabricate evidence to help the Attorney General's Office prosecute Dane, I was finally brought to trial for the malicious mischief charges in September, 2009.

After a two-day trial in which my Aunt June was caught lying under oath and laughed at by several jury members for the absurdity of her testimony, the judge was forced to declare a mistrial. After four hours of deliberation, my jury was unable to reach a verdict. The final vote was ten to two. Ten voted not guilty, and two voted for conviction.

I later discovered that one of the two conviction-minded jurors had been illegally influenced by Georgia Lynn during the trial and the second jury member had a personal prejudice against gays that led her to vote guilty. The Attorney General's Office, having recognized the impossibility of obtaining a conviction, was then forced to dismiss the case against me.

My Aunt June and grandfather, Emmett Atwood, are still

desperately pushing the legal system and using their money and influence to harass me in whatever way they can. In one unfortunate embarrassing confrontation, my grandfather stated to me that he would use whatever money, influence and power he had to pay off any and every judge that he could to have me sent back to prison. From the conduct of Judge Eddy Woods, when I've been in his court, I would say that my grandfather means to carry out that promise and that Judge Woods is more than happy to accept his bribes and endeavors to reincarcerate me.

Further proof, was the clear and convincing evidence that my grandfather bribed and paid off Judge Marie Wilson in Greenville, Mississippi. In an unfortunate confrontation with Emmett one afternoon, he stated to me unequivocally that he had used his money and influence to manipulate Judge Wilson into ruling against me in the property battle that was on-going within the Atwood family at the time.

Judge Marie Wilson had been assigned to preside over the land and property dispute after the local chancery judge in Vicksburg recused herself because of a conflict of interest. This same "conflict of interest" that forced the first judge to recuse herself also became an issue with Judge Wilson, but because she had been paid off by my grandfather, she refused to remove herself from the case even after my attorney requested she do so for ethical reasons.

Judge Wilson was so hostile to me that she refused to allow me to present evidence or allow some of my witnesses to testify. She even illegally had evidence removed from her courtroom that was beneficial to me and refused to allow my attorney or me to present it in my case.

Numerous attorneys who have practiced in her court attribute to Judge Wilson the reputation as the craziest, most bizarre, unethical and ineffective chancery judge to ever sit on a judicial bench. Knowing the ease at which her influence and rulings can be purchased for the highest bid, I would tend to agree with these attorney's assessments.

Living on the outside can be just as tough as surviving in prison. Admittedly, I would much prefer to live outside the boundaries of Mississippi, but while on federal probation I'm prohibited from moving. I am forced to make the best out of an otherwise bad situation even though I know that the corruption and unethical conduct continues to grow and spread. But no matter how much I might despair, I never lose faith that there is hope for the future. As long as there is one person to stand up to tyranny and abuse, there will be a majority willing to do what is right.

# INTO HELL I RODE

"Some things you must always be unable to bear. Some things you must never stop refusing to bear. Injustice and Outrage. Dishonor and Shame. No matter how old you've got. Not for kudos and not for cash. Not for your picture in the paper, nor money in the bank. Just refuse to bear them."

William Faulkner- *Intruder In The Dust*